THE SACRED HEART
IN THE
LIFE OF THE CHURCH

THE SACRED HEART
IN THE
LIFE OF THE CHURCH

MARGARET WILLIAMS, R.S.C.J.

"The intimate bond which, according to Sacred Scripture, exists between the divine charity that must burn in the souls of the faithful and the Holy Ghost, clearly shows to all the real nature of Devotion to the Sacred Heart."—Haurietis Aquas

SHEED AND WARD · NEW YORK

CONTENTS

DEDICATION

With deep reverence and gratitude this book is dedicated to His Holiness, Pope Pius XII, through whom our times have drawn waters with joy from the Savior's Heart.

Manhattanville College of the Sacred Heart
Feast of the Sacred Heart, 1956

FOREWORD

In his masterful Encyclical on the Sacred Heart, *Haurietis Aquas*, Pope Pius XII cautions us "not to say that this devotion began when it was privately revealed by God or that it suddenly came into existence in the Church." For if we examine closely its nature, we shall find that "essentially this devotion is nothing else than worship of the human and divine love of the Incarnate Word and the love which the Heavenly Father and the Holy Ghost have for sinful men." Since this love was clearly revealed in the pages of the Gospel, the substance of devotion to the Sacred Heart goes back to the dawn of Christianity.

The special merit of the present volume is the evidence it gives to show that devotion to the Sacred Heart was never unknown in the history of the Church. Saints and theologians, mystics and the Sovereign Pontiffs are called upon to witness to this fact—at length and in their own words, in context and often from sources hitherto not available in English.

Though not directly intending to do so (since the present book was nearing completion when the Encyclical appeared) the author has actually traced the second of three ancestries of the cultus of the Sacred Heart recommended for prayerful study by the Holy Father. "The faithful must trace devotion to the Most Sacred Heart of Jesus back to the Sacred Scriptures, *tradition* and the liturgy if they wish to understand its real meaning."

The value of such a survey is not academic. It is at once probative and deeply penetrating. We need to be convinced that the love of God which surpasses all understanding was not only revealed in the New Testament and professed by the early Christians, but ever since has been the mainstay of those who profess the apostolic

Catholic faith. If it seems strange that so obvious a truth had to be revealed and specially entrusted to an infallible Church, we have only to reflect on the distorted notions of the deity prevalent among those who are strangers to divine revelation even in modern America. We also need to penetrate beneath the surface of that simple statement which declares that "God is love." Since the love in question is that of the Trinity and of God become man, it is beyond the capacity of unaided reason to understand. But, as the Vatican Council teaches us, the mysteries of faith are not nebulous realities unintelligible to the human mind. On the contrary, with God's grace we can attain "a most profitable understanding of mysteries, from analogy with truths that are naturally known as well as from the relation of mysteries with one another and with man's final end." Divine love which is the heart of devotion to the Sacred Heart is no exception to this rule of intelligibility. While remaining a supernatural mystery, it is capable of a deep and soul-satisfying comprehension which is a foretaste of the beatific vision, provided we make the inquest under the guidance of the Church's teaching and in the company of her saints as offered in the following pages. In proportion as we come to understand this love in its breadth and length and height and depth, Saint Paul assures us we shall be "strengthened with power through the Holy Spirit" and "filled unto all the fulness of God."

John A. Hardon, S.J.
West Baden College

CHAPTER I

A DIVINE THOUGHT

"My Work is Love."

The story of the growth of the Devotion to the Sacred Heart is an integral part of Church History, which is itself the story of the growth of the Mystical Body "unto the measure of the age of the fulness of Christ."[1] That story will here be told largely in the words of those whose lives have, in the past, made the Devotion to the Sacred Heart what it is today. This book is an anthology of the passages taken from the writings of the men and women best qualified to speak: lovers and thinkers and doers, apostolic scholars, saints of all walks of life, persons heart-conformed to Christ who have put into their own words "the purposes of His Heart to generation upon generation"[2] in the life of the Church. Excellent and exhaustive histories of "the great Devotion" have already been written, providing theological exposition along with a wealth of fact; in all of these works quotations from the documents in which the Devotion is best revealed are numerous. But by the very fact of the historical nature of such books, the quotations are necessarily brief. The present book offers passages of greater length, so that the significance of the references to the Sacred Heart may expand in a fuller context. The passages are set in a running commentary meant to place them in their proper order and perspective.

The closeness of the relation between the life of the Church and the Devotion to the Sacred Heart is indicated by our Holy Father Pope Pius XII in the Encyclical *Mystici Corporis,* where he gives as one of his reasons for writing it the fact that today "a more fervent devotion to the Sacred Heart of Jesus has brought many souls to a deeper consideration of the unsearchable riches of Christ which are preserved in the Church."[3] The history of the Devotion runs through the whole of the larger history of the Church, implicit and latent at

first, then explicit and all-pervading. Since it is rooted in the same
dogmatic foundations from which the Church springs, the Devotion
is seen to grow stronger with her growth, and to record the changes
in her expanding life. It remains consistent and true to its own
character throughout, yet at each step it reflects the special spirit
of the age, the *Zeitgeist* that draws harmony from conflict and contrast. The Church is, as Bossuet says, the Incarnation extended in
space and time. As such she is theandric, divine and human in
nature. "Incarnate, she assumes all the social and cultural forms of
the people she teaches; supratemporal and transcendental, she
is and never ceases to be herself in the civilizations she passes
through."[4] A greater understanding of the Devotion to the Sacred
Heart as an element of the time-spirit of each century, as well as an
integral element of the unchanging Christ-life that animates the
Church, will throw light upon our own times, and upon the chapter
of Church History that is being written today. Thus the value of the
documents here quoted lies largely in their continuity; their chronological sequence will reveal the interplay of cause and effect in suc-
cessive periods unfolding in a divine pattern. Each opens a vista
upon the life and times of its writer, and each shows the features of
Mother Church wearing the expression of a passing age as she turns
her face towards eternity.

To look back at the beginning of any movement from the vantage
point of our own times is to light the past from the present. There
are two ways of so looking back over the development of the Devotion to the Sacred Heart. One is analytic, accurately seeking the
meaning given to the terms employed in different ages, according to
the mentality and circumstances of those times, thus defining by
limitation.[5] According to this method, it has been claimed that Devotion to the Sacred Heart as such existed only implicitly before
the eleventh century; that it took distinct form only in the seventeenth, and did not become the cultus with which we are familiar
until the eighteenth.[6] The second way is the synthetic which, looking
to the spirit rather than to the letter, finds the Devotion in the varying
blends of its elements, tracing it back to the early ages of the Church
and even into Old Testament times. In this sense, Devotion to the
Sacred Heart has been at work since God first set his heart upon
man.[7] These methods are not contradictory but complementary.
The first is needed for an accurate understanding of the nature of

the Devotion, the second for penetration into its mysteries, and for full response to the grace it offers. The first method, employed in official histories,[8] has by now accomplished its work of clarification; the second is at present being used to extend the significance of the Devotion into ever wider ranges of the spiritual life. In this book the second method will be generally followed, while every care will be taken to make the distinctions necessary for a true historic perspective.

As the documents here offered are drawn from many sources, they testify to the Devotion in a variety of ways, some more fundamental than others. It must never be overlooked that:

The foundations of the Devotion are not to be discovered in private revelations which are only of an historical—not a doctrinal—significance. . . . Devotion to the Sacred Heart rests on a four-square doctrinal foundation: the theology of the Incarnation as found in the treatise *De Deo Incarnato;* the corpus of texts of Sacred Scripture containing the divinely inspired words on Christ's love for man; papal documents; and the Sacred Liturgy.[9]

The writings of holy men and women here presented, as well as those of commentators and historians, all rest securely upon the same four-square foundation. It is beyond the competence of this book to explore this foundation; its underlying presence will simply be indicated. Theology and Scripture are, of course, all-pervading throughout these pages; the rise of the Liturgy is traced; official documents, including the great Papal Encyclicals, are given in abridged form in their chronological place. All the works quoted bear the authentic stamp of the Devotion, while their very diversity in value, content and tone witnesses to the overshadowing action of the Holy Spirit, at first secret, then brilliantly manifest, drawing together through the centuries the elements of Devotion to the Sacred Heart to their final crystallization in an official cultus of the Church and to their final glorious expression in the *Haurietis Aquas* of our Holy Father Pope Pius XII.

It is a great thing to follow a divine thought which is slowly fulfilled in a soul under the action of the Holy Spirit. It is a still greater thing to follow a divine thought which is developed in the Church for the sanctification of the elect, by the irresistible force of the eternal will.[10]

The Holy Spirit accomplishes the thoughts of God for the whole body of the Church as for its individual members. He who proceeds as substantial Love from the Father and the Son, He who formed the human nature of Christ, animates the *totus Christus;* for "as Christ is the head of the Church, so is the Holy Spirit her soul."[11] The unfolding through time of the Devotion to the Sacred Heart, source and symbol of love, and its dynamic role in the present day, is His work, for "the Church is accustomed most fittingly to attribute . . . to the Holy Spirit those works in which love excels."[12]

NOTES

1. Eph. 4,13.
2. Ps. 32, 11.
3. Pius XII, *Mystici Corporis* (New York, America Press, 1943), p. 7.
4. Emmanuel Cardinal Suhard, *Growth or Decline? The Church Today* (Montreal, Fides, 1948), p. 29.
5. This is the method followed by Jean Bainvel, S.J., in *Devotion to the Sacred Heart,* and by A. Hamon, S.J., in *Histoire de la Dévotion au Sacré Coeur,* in which the authors, by distinguishing between the literal and metaphorical use of terms and by stressing the necessity of reference to the heart of flesh, show clearly where the Devotion as such is *not* to be found. Both writers admit the value of the second method in studying the Devotion as a whole, with a view to releasing its full powers in the spiritual life. The second method is followed by François Charmot, S.J., in *The Sacred Heart and Modern Life,* and by Dom Aelred Watkin, O.S.B., in *The Heart of the World.*
6. Some earlier accounts of the Devotion claim that it did not exist in the analytic sense before the eleventh century. But as Reverend John A. Hardon, S.J., has observed, this view is no longer tenable in the light of the Encyclical *Haurietis Aquas.* He says: "In as much as the formal object is now clearly stated to be the love of Christ (in its three-fold manifestation) this love was an object of Christian devotion from the dawn of Christianity. The symbolic element of the Heart, to signify Christ's love, is indeed a later innovation. But the latter does not constitute the formal object. Pope Pius XII says that the divine love for us is 'the principal reason for the devotion.' The original Latin for 'principal reason' is *ratio princeps* which may be rendered as 'essence,' so that since divine love is the essence of the devotion to the Sacred Heart, and this has been repeatedly revealed

in the Old and New Testaments, it follows that the Devotion itself, *quoad rationem principem,* goes back to the origins of Christianity and, in fact, to the first supernatural manifestation of God's infinite love."

7. See Job 7, 17.

8. Chief among these are: A. Hamon, S.J., *Histoire de la Dévotion au Sacré Coeur* (Paris, Beauchesne, 1924–49, 5 vols.) and J. Bainvel, S.J., *Devotion to the Sacred Heart* (New York, Benziger, 1925, translated from the French). For histories of special periods, see the bibliography.

9. François Charmot, *The Sacred Heart and Modern Life,* trans. by Kathryn Sullivan (Kenedy, 1952), p. 51.

10. Hamon, *op. cit.,* Vol. II, p. v.

11. Leo XIII, *Divinum Illud* (New York, America Press, 1944), p. 10.

12. *Ibid.,* p. 6.

CHAPTER II

THE HEART OF TIME

"My Heart is Love itself."

The heart of time is the moment in which the Eternal stepped into the temporal and took the Heart of man. In a city of Galilee named Nazareth an angel spoke to a woman named Mary, and under the overshadowing of the Spirit of Love the Word was made flesh; the Heart of Christ had come into being, and one human adorer paid devotion. "Among the external operations of God the highest of all is the mystery of the Incarnation of the Word . . . and this is rightly attributed to Him who is the Love of the Father and of the Son."[1] As St. Thomas says:

The nature of God is goodness. . . . But it belongs to the essence of goodness to communicate itself to others. Hence it belongs to the essence of the highest good to communicate itself in the highest manner to the creature, and this is brought about by "His so joining created nature to Himself that one Person is made up of these three—the Word, a soul, and flesh."[2]

Of this flesh was the Heart of Christ. The moment of the Incarnation marks the beginning of its life; the mystery of the Incarnation is the foundation of the homage paid to it. Devotion to the Sacred Heart is inseparable from the root-dogma of Christianity.

Few men knew, in the first years of His life, that the Child growing up in Nazareth was God, but the Child knew all that was in man. He knew, too, all that was in Himself. Had a stranger, pausing in the hillside town and noticing the boy's grave eyes, stopped Him one day by the well to ask: "What are you?" the answer would have been twofold: "I am a man like you," and "I am who am." Two natures, two sources of action, were in Him; He was

human and He was divine. But if the astounded stranger had followed his question with another still more searching, and had
asked: "Who are you?", the answer could only have been onefold:
"I am the second Person of the Trinity." There is nothing human
in the personality of this small human being who answers to the
name of Jesus. The "who" in Him is the Word of God, Son forever
of God the Father, co-spirator with the Father of God the Holy
Ghost. For the rest of his life that bold seeker who asked the
"who" and "what" of a chance-met child could say to his friends:
"I spoke to God once, and He answered in a Galilean accent."
The divine and the human are bound in Him by hypostatic union,
for "the human nature in Christ . . . is in union with a completed thing, the whole Christ as He is, God and man."[3] As personality is the source of attribution for all that makes up a Person,
the very hands and Heart of Christ can, like Himself, be adored
with the adoration of latria. The adoring stranger of Nazareth
might well have been drawn to ask one more question, "Why?
Why are you what you are—a God-man?" The answer would have
been simple: "God is love." The stranger, after that, might never
have gone away, for man had "come to a deep heart"[4] in the Son
of Man.

His Mother had come to it first, and had understood its silence in
the days before her Son could speak. She pondered the things said
of Him in her own heart till it too was fit to become, one day, the
object of a great Devotion. She watched His human faculties un-
fold. As the Child grew His created mind reached out through experience to meet the infused knowledge which came from the fulness of grace that was in Him as the highest of creatures, knowledge that could reflect but not exhaust the omniscience that was
already His as God. The silent, pondering mind lived in a world of
thought that went to the ends of the universe and into its laws and
causes, and each thought was the prayer of God contemplating
God while busy at a carpenter's bench. His mode of knowing, like
Himself, was twofold: divine and human. And so was His mode of
willing. His human will was constantly expressing itself in acts of
free choice—which is intellectual love—and these choices echoed
the divine will which was His from everlasting. The Son had come
to Nazareth precisely to say "yes" by His mortal life to the will of
the Father. As His thirtieth year came close and He knew that it

was time to take to the road of His mission, His human nature was already saying "not my will but Thine be done." Yet all through His life, from Incarnation to Ascension, this human soul possessed the Beatific Vision, living in heaven while on earth.

The body that had been shaped for the most beautiful of the sons of men, united to His divine personality by the same hypostatic bond as His soul, grew tired as the miles lengthened, and fell asleep in Simon's boat. When He awoke and calmed the storm, Simon adored Him, body as well as soul. The passions that are alive in every human composite as part of its bodily texture were alive in Him in their full potency for good, incandescent with sanctity; He marvelled, grieved, grew angry and desired with desire, and His Heart recorded each emotion in its beat. Through three years of give-and-take with His fellow mortals He experienced those physical and moral weathers that make up every lifetime, and His Heart experienced the full range of human feeling, for Himself or for others. His friends, only half understanding, had heard its voiced appeal. The wretched, the forgotten, the sick and the bewildered turned to it unerringly; they clamored after Him in the streets, broke into His nights of prayer, and He could not say "no." He bore the burden of His love in silence till the moment came to share it; then, one day at the height of His preaching life, He gave Himself away and told His secret. "Learn of Me," He cried, "for I am meek and humble of Heart."[5] Thus He Himself gave to His Heart the significance of the divine "I" for which it would later come to stand. Like His entire humanity, of which it was a vital part, it was *instrumentum conjunctum divinitatis*.

The words of Life pass always into deed, and the time came for the final giving away. He had said and done all that He could; He would now let it be done to Him. When Life hung dead on the cross under a sky without light, His Mother and the friend who had rested on His Heart the night before stood by Him, silent. He could give no more, but He could still accept a blow; John saw it given. "And one of the soldiers with a spear opened His side, and immediately there came out blood and water. . . . And he that saw it hath given testimony."[6] Through the open wound the spear reached to the Heart, and in that same hour "the Church was born from the side of our Savior on the cross."[7]

The lifeless but still divine body with its pierced Heart was buried behind a sealed stone, but on the third day Life awoke in the sunrise of the resurrection garden and once more walked and spoke and ate with men. Then Thomas recovered his lost faith by putting his hand into the open side. The Devotion had begun its work. And after forty days the Desire of the Everlasting Hills stood on a hill of His native land and showed how far the Work of Love must reach: "Go ye into the whole world and preach the Gospel to every creature."[8] The whole of time would be passed in doing it; after that there would be no more reason for time.

When His mortal body had been taken to heaven the Church was revealed to the world on Pentecost. All that He had done in His brief years of life according to mortal mode was to expand through a longer life led in the lives of other men incorporated into His Body through grace. His Heart would be there in the *Corpus Mysticum,* still desiring with desire, and calling for an answering love from His members.

Long before His coming to earth, and in every age since, human custom, answering to the human need of expressing the invisible in the terms of the visible, had made the bodily heart into a symbol, a focal point, a single name for the many-levelled reality of love. This needed no Revelation; nature and poetry were enough to make such a symbol universal among all peoples, primitive or cultured. It rested upon a simple fact of experience; the heart is the physical recorder of emotions, and all emotions revolve around love. When the Son of God became the Son of Man His Heart was like the hearts of all His fellow men; it could stand metaphorically for the whole of His affective, interior life. It was the *cor* which is the "core" of personality[9] (in Him divine) knit to nature (in Him human and divine); it was the physical source of the lifeblood (in Him the price of redemption); it was the register of the movement of the bodily appetitive faculties (in Him the keenest ever known); it was the symbol of His love in all its forms (in Him from everlasting, but expressed through time). It is as the symbol of the specifically human love of the God-man that we honor the physical Heart of Christ as "the Sacred Heart," for again by virtue of the hypostatic union, this human love is divine. Thus, as Christ's Vicar in our own day has so luminously stated, this Heart is the index and symbol of the threefold love with which the Incarnate Word loves His Father and His fellow men: first, the divine love which He shares with the Father and the Holy Ghost, then the love infused into His soul which sanctifies His human will (whose action is directed by His beatific and infused knowledge), and finally the sensible love centered in His human body.[10]

Thus all the elements of what was later to grow into the clear and dynamic synthesis of spirituality known as the Devotion to the Sacred Heart were present from the beginning of Christianity, undefined but vital. Centuries of history were needed to give it a form and a name. Like the Church itself, the cultus of prayer and of practice in which the Devotion is now expressed lay pressed into that Gospel-told human life, the great tree in the mustard seed. Church History is simply the biography of the whole Christ, and each element of the Devotion that holds "the thoughts of His Heart from generation to generation" was alive already in Galilee, in One who said: "I am with you all days."[11]

The first epoch of that history is measured by the life-span of the Apostles, who, having known Him "whom our hands have handled, the Word of Life,"[12] set out for the ends of the earth to do His bidding, while the Evangelists committed to writing the life of Him who had "loved them unto the end."[13] By the close of the first century the See of Peter had been fixed at Rome; Saint Paul had done his missionary work; and Saint John had heard in vision the final harmonies of the end of time. With the writing of John's Gospel Revelation was complete and the Canon of Scripture closed.

As all dogmas can be traced to Scripture, in which they are at least implicitly contained, and from which they are drawn and developed by Christian tradition, and devotions grow from dogmas, it follows that the roots of any fundamental devotion are likewise to be found in Scripture. As devotions develop and take distinct forms of their own, they continue to draw their life from new adaptations of the Word of God, which thus, conversely, becomes enriched by ever fuller interpretation. This illustrates the theological adage: "Lex orandi est lex credendi"; and if the law of prayer is the law of belief, then faith itself becomes more luminous as devotions pass from their implicit to their explicit form.

In the case of Devotion to the Sacred Heart this cycle is clearly marked in the long curve that sweeps from the dogmatic exegesis brought to bear on scriptural texts in the Patristic Ages, through the contemplative commentaries of the mediaeval cloisters, on through the dynamic controversies that followed the message of Paray-le-Monial, to full expansion in a Liturgy proper to the Sacred Heart in recent times.

As the Devotion progresses, the texts from which it draws its life appear in ever greater numbers, texts first pondered in solitary hearts, then woven into writing by eager pens until they enter the prayers and the daily speech of the many, and are finally consecrated to their special use in the Divine Office and the Mass. For besides the literal and typical meanings of any given text, meanings upon which the authoritative teaching of the Church can alone pronounce, there is also the accommodated meaning: a liberty allowed to individual interpreters in applying the text. Accommodation is used by the Fathers and Doctors in the exposition of truth, often by way of allegory; by mystics in the expression, often poetic, of their experiences; and by the Liturgy in the voicing of public prayer, in which case the Church sets her sanction upon an accommodated sense which, while not declared revealed in the strict sense, draws its grace from Scripture. Through all these ways, the Devotion to the Sacred Heart has now become a searchlight whose beam, turned back upon the pages of the Bible, picks out the gleaming line of God's love running through it from Genesis to the Apocalypse.

The searchlight moves first towards the impenetrable edges of eternity: "I have loved thee with an everlasting love, therefore have I drawn thee";[14] it is Love Uncreated "moving towards incarnation." In dealing with His chosen race, God as Father will not cease to send the whirlwind "until He shall have performed the thoughts of His Heart."[15] Even under the law of fear, "when the Lord beheld the wickedness of man upon earth He was touched with sorrow of heart."[16] The songs of David, "man after God's own heart,"[17] were sung in prophecy of the Christ to come in the flesh, whose "Heart expected reproach and misery,"[18] while the eyes of Solomon saw Him "crowned in the day of His espousals, the day of the joy of His Heart."[19] Isaias saw that generations to come would "draw waters with joy out of the Savior's fountains,"[20] and these, says the Liturgy looking back, are His wounds, and the greatest is the wound in the Heart. That Heart did not exist under the Old Covenant, but its love was foreknown, and had already been expressed. The New Testament witnesses to the love of God Incarnate, whose life of self-giving the Gospels record. And the first Christians had, in that love, "but one heart and one soul."[21] Of Saint Paul, Apostle to the Gentiles, it could be said: "Cor Pauli, Cor Christi."[22] He who knew so well "the charity of Christ which surpasseth all understanding,"[23] wrote: "How I yearn for you all in the Heart of Christ."[24] And all this love "is poured out in our hearts, by the Holy Ghost who is given to us."[25]

The Litany of the Sacred Heart,[26] compiled in the eighteenth century, sweeps the searchlight from the beginning to the end of the Sacred Book, touching thirty-three facets of the jewel-like Heart of the King in its invocations. It begins before time, seeing the "Heart of Jesus, Son of the Eternal Father"; it moves through His human virtues and sufferings till it comes to the end when the Heart of Jesus shall be the "delight of all the saints." Scripture as a narrative written by God's finger is the record of history that moves through time; as the source of a Devotion it weaves all times together.

One familiar figure stands at the fountainhead of Church History, "John the Gospeller, Christ's darling,"[27] longest-lived of the Apostles, who wore himself out repeating: "Little children, love one another." The disciple whom Jesus loved may well be called the patron saint of the Devotion to the Sacred Heart. It was he who gave formal testimony to the piercing of Christ's side, "and he knoweth that he speaketh true, that you also may believe."[28] His account became the central text from which later friends of Christ drew the full light of the Devotion thus adumbrated. His Gospel and his Epistles are ablaze with the love drawn from the Heart upon which he had once rested his head. As the centuries passed, he whose words had closed Revelation played his part also, many times and in a most marked fashion, in the private revelations made to holy souls at the moments most significant in the Devotion's development. By his presence to souls, in vision and in prayer, he has seen to it continually that "the Scriptures may be

fulfilled," those Scriptures of which the ever-active Spirit of Love
is the author.

NOTES

1. Leo XIII, *Divinum Illud*, p. 7.
2. *Summa Theologica*, III, q. 1, a. 1.
3. *Ibid.*, q. 2, a. 3.
4. Ps. 63, 7.
5. Matt. 11, 29.
6. John 19, 34.
7. Pius XII, *Mystici Corporis*, p. 14.
8. Mark 16, 15.
9. See Dom Aelred Watkin, in *The Heart of the World* (London,
Burns, 1954), pp. 6 f.: "With this ultimate knowing and loving we
reach the very core of our being. How easily does the word 'heart'
leap to the mind. The heart in the sense of being the heart and core
of life; the heart in the sense of that ultimate expression and experience
of personality in knowing and loving. And both senses are one. . . .
The heart is, then, the symbol which we give to this core of our
personality."
10. Pius XII, *Haurietis Aquas* (America Press, 1956). For the
text, see below, p. 222.
11. Matt. 28, 20.
12. I John 1, 1.
13. *Ibid.*, 13, 1.
14. Jer. 31, 3.
15. *Ibid.*, 30, 24.
16. Gen. 6, 6.
17. I Kings 13, 14.
18. Ps. 68, 21.
19. Cant. 3, 11.
20. Is. 12, 3.
21. Acts 4, 32.
22. St. John Chrysostom, *Homily* 23, 3, on the Epistle to the Ro-
mans. P.G. LX, 680.
23. Eph. 3, 19.
24. Phil. 1, 8. This is the translation of the Westminster version,
which uses the word "heart" for the *viscera* of the Vulgate. This
illustrates the vital symbolism which underlies both the popular idea of
"heart" and the Devotion to the Sacred Heart itself. Many expressions
in Scripture, and in the Greek and Latin literature of the Church
which refer to other organs of the body, can be rendered "heart,"

and thus be related to the Devotion, because of their connection with the affective life of man.

25. Rom. 5, 5.

26. See *Appendix,* p. 237, "Sources of the Litany of the Sacred Heart."

27. Aelfric, "The Assumption of St. John," in M. Williams, *Word-Hoard* (New York, Sheed, 1940), p. 405.

28. John 19, 35.

CHAPTER III

THE SHAPING CENTURIES
100–800

"Draw near to My wounds."

The ages of chaos in Europe, from the second century to the seventh, were also creative ages when again "the Spirit of God moved over the waters." As the Roman Empire gave way before the "barbarians" from the North, the new Rome rose from the cellars and graveyards of the old to stand on the seven hills; the City of God was shaping. The faith, which had reached the farthest boundaries of the Empire under the stress of ten persecutions, stood erect when these ceased after Constantine's Decree of Toleration. The leaven of the supernatural could then do its work in the world. It began by elevating and revivifying the ancient culture of Greco-Roman civilization that was perishing; classic languages, art and learning were used to express the new vigor of Christian thought in age-old forms in the schools of Africa, Byzantium, and the Roman provinces. Then it met and subdued the onrush of the new races by sublimating their ideals and blending them with the settled richness of the old.

The first task of the Church in these ages was an intellectual one: to answer the question "What think you of Christ?" The dogma of the Incarnation is her cornerstone, and the great Christological and Trinitarian truths were laid in place in the first Councils in which the language of theology was forged. The Christian world was torn by heresies on these fundamental points: by Arianism, which denied Christ's divinity; by Nestorianism, which separated Him into two persons; by Eutychianism, which reduced His humanity to a shadow. At Nicaea (325) it was proclaimed that "the Son is of one substance with the Father";[1] at Ephesus (431) that Mary is the Mother of God "because she is mother according to the flesh of the Word of God made flesh";[2] at Chalcedon (451) that "the two natures of Jesus Christ are united in one Person without confusion, change, division, separation or suppression."[3] Theology grew rich on the spoils of these battles in which truth won, and by the close of the Patristic Age the Roman world could say with the Centurion who stood on Calvary and witnessed the piercing of His Heart: "Indeed this was the Son of God."[4]

Thirteen hundred years later, when a new theological battle arose over the question of the official recognition by the Church of the Devotion to the Sacred Heart, the victory would be won by showing that the Christological formulas of the Fathers were not contradicted but vindicated by those who worshipped the Divine Heart. The advocates of the Devotion had been called Nestorians for adoring a heart of flesh; Pius VI answered: "In reality they adore the Heart of Jesus as it is, the Heart of the Person of the Word to whom it is inseparably united."[5] Thus the doctrinal roots of the Devotion of love reach down into the strong, creative ages of the Church, endowing it with the same intellectual clarity and power with which the Church shaped her Creed in the first Councils.

In the years between Councils the work of exegesis went on, as the Fathers expanded Scripture and Creed alike in their massive commentaries and controversies. These works open the moral and mystical as well as the dogmatic treasures of the Church. Prayer draws upon them as freely as does philosophy. These intellectual giants were also men of intense feeling, and their work is suffused with a warmth of language and a vibrant sense of desire which can come only from minds moved by the heart. What Saint Gregory of Nyssa said of Saint John the Evangelist might be said of each of the Fathers of the Church: "He who rested upon the breast of the Lord at supper, steeped his heart like a sponge in the fountain of life, filled with an unspeakable sense of the mysteries of Christ."[6] Thus, scattered through their works are passages which have a significance beyond the immediate and reveal many elements of the Devotion to the Sacred Heart, unsynthesized as yet but ready to move, by their own dynamic power, down the thought-lines of the Church to their point of fusion in the Heart to be venerated in its own time in public worship.[7]

Early in the second century an earnest young pagan wandered from one philosopher of Asia Minor to another, seeking the truth from Stoics and Platonists and finding only its shadows. He found its reality at last in Christianity. He taught school in peripatetic fashion under the porticoes of Athens and finally reached Rome, where he laid down his life for Christ (c. 165). Saint Justin Martyr was the first of the Apologists, seeking in his Greek writings to harmonize philosophy and theology and to bend pagan wisdom to the divine. In his *Dialogue with the Jew Trypho* he commented upon the Psalms and there in prophecy saw the Heart of Christ, a heart that knew fear as only our humanity can know it, a heart that records in physical movement the fluctuations of passion:

"I am poured out like water and all My bones are scattered; My Heart is become like wax melting in the midst of My bowels." By these words He declares what happened in that night when they came against Him on the Mount of Olives. . . . For His sweat broke out like drops of blood and poured from Him, while He prayed and said: "If it be possible, let this chalice pass from Me"; and clearly His Heart trembled with fear, and His bones trembled. But the Heart became like wax melting within Him, that we might surely know that the Father willed His Son to be brought into such fears, lest we should think that because He was God He did not feel the things inflicted upon Him.[8]

These words were written while persecution was still scattering "the blood of the martyrs, seed"[9] of the Church, blood which is the strongest answer that can be given to the call of the love of Christ, who first laid down His life for His friends. Martyrdom is the testimony of heart made to Heart. In the year 177 a group of Gallo-Romans, "captained by the grace of God," witnessed to the faith by torture and death in Lyons. Among them was young Saint Sanctus, who was "strengthened by the spring of living waters that flowed from the Heart of Christ."[10] The fear suffered by the Son of Man had become the fortitude of His followers.

In the meantime Christian scholarship did not wait for the end of the storm to take root and grow. In the School of Alexandria, the crossroads of the East and West, Origen (185–253) brought Greek philosophy into play upon Scripture. He, intellectual wrestler and lover of the martyrdom that was not granted him, grew serene as he penetrated into "the unsearchable riches of Christ."[11]

In a treatise on the symbolism of bodily members, he developed the exegesis of the word "heart," making it stand (as common language has always done) for the whole interior life of man, but enriching the concept with distinct shades of meaning for the synonyms of "heart." For the Heart of the God-man he shaped the wonderful phrase *principale cordis Jesu,* giving as its mystical meaning: knowledge with love and experience. In Origen the word "heart" is to be taken in an intellective rather than an affective sense; thus the Heart of Jesus is the source of His thoughts and sentiments, the storehouse of the secrets of divine love. This savoring knowledge, knowledge that loves in the very act of knowing, is wisdom; and wisdom, after love itself, is the divine attribute most closely linked to the Devotion to the Sacred Heart. Saint Thomas says that the gift of wisdom corresponds to charity. For "it belongs to wisdom to consider the highest cause,"[12] and this judgment is reached through the Holy Ghost. When, in the eighteenth century, artists drew a heart and within it the image of a small child, symbol of wisdom, they were expressing the thoughts of Origen:

Thy Heart, O my Spouse, the dogmas that are held in Thee, the grace of doctrine. . . . In this way it is said that John rested in the inner Heart of Jesus, and in the inner meanings of His doctrines, there searching out and knowing thoroughly the treasures of wisdom and knowledge hidden in Christ Jesus.[13]

No one can understand the Gospel of John unless he has rested as John did on the breast of Jesus, or has received Mary from Jesus to be his own mother.[14]

I think that if John was then symbolically lying in the breast of Jesus, thus chosen because his Master thought him worthy of special love, this symbolizes that he—leaning upon the Lord, the Son of God, greatly cherished by Him and resting in His deep secrets—was lying in the bosom of the Lord as the Word Himself is in the bosom of the Father, as it is said: "The only-begotten Son of God who is in the bosom of the Father, He hath declared Him." And now that we have learned that he whom Jesus loved rested on the breast of Jesus, let us so act that we also may be judged worthy of special love; then we too shall rest in the bosom of Jesus.[15]

As for the physical Heart of Christ, it lay behind the open wound of the Crucified; it was reached by the tip of the soldier's spear, and blood and water came from it. The Fathers of the Church, both

Eastern and Western, without speaking of the Heart as such, see in the wound the gateway of grace, of the sacraments, of the Church itself.

Saint John Chrysostom (347–407) who, in the midst of his golden preaching and of ceaseless schisms and upheavals in Constantinople, was able to cleanse the Church by "sweeping the stairs from the top down," yet found time to contemplate the wounded side:

The soldiers came and broke the legs of the others, but not those of Christ. Yet to please the Jews they pierce His side with a lance, and treat the dead body contemptuously. O wicked and accursed crime! But be not troubled nor cast down, my Beloved. For while they wrought with evil will they fought for the truth. For it had been prophesied: "They shall look upon Him whom they pierced." Still more, this crime revealed the truth even to unbelieving ones who were to come after, to Thomas and to those like to him. For thus was the unspeakable mystery consummated: "And there came forth blood and water." Not without cause, not by chance did these fountains flow, but because the Church was formed from them both.[16]

Saint Ambrose (340–397) who, as Bishop of Milan, stood steady in the midst of the chaotic backwash of the Roman Empire, who humbled Theodosius and kept the Arians at bay, was a poet who gave the Church her first hymns. This lyric note is heard in his Commentaries:

After the Passion of the Lord, what else could follow save that a river flowed from the body of the Lord, when there poured from His side blood and water, by which He brought joy to the souls of all, since in that river He washed away the sins of the whole world?[17]

No corruption came from His wounds, as from those of other men, but a fountain of eternal life welled up, as Scripture teaches us, saying: "Water shall spring with joy from the Savior's fountains." Therefore water sprang from His wounds, that we might drink our health. All sinners of earth shall drink, that they may lay aside their sins.[18]

He is the vine, He is the grapes; the vine clinging to the trees, the grapes pierced by the soldier's lance, pouring forth blood and water. For so says John: "There came forth blood and water," water for our washing, blood for our purchasing. The water cleanses us, the blood redeems us.[19]

Saint Augustine, the most affective of intellectuals (354–430), went further still. He watched with eyes of a philosopher-historian the building of the City of God upon earth; he defended as a theologian the doctrine of grace against Pelagius; but all the time he was sounding the deep places of the human heart through knowledge of his own. He learned from experience what the Heart of Christ had also learned from experience, and he followed this knowledge till it led him to see the Church also emerging from "the deep Heart."

Man shall come to a deep Heart, and God shall be exalted. They said: Who shall see us? The searchings of the searchers failed, their evil counsels. Man himself came to those same counsels; He suffered Himself to be held as a man. For He could not be held unless He were man, nor seen unless a man. Thus as a man He came to all those sufferings, which would have availed nothing in Him unless He were a man. But if He had not been a man, man would not have been set free. Man had come to a deep Heart, that is, a secret Heart, subjecting man to human forms, hiding within Him the form of God in which He is equal to the Father, and showing the form of a servant in which He is less than the Father.[20]

John leaned upon the breast of the Lord, and drank from that breast what he has given us to drink.[21] . . . John the Evangelist received a special gift from the Lord, upon whose breast he leaned at supper, by which is signified that he drank in the deepest secrets of the inward Heart.[22]

Adam slept that Eve might be made; Christ died that the Church might be made. Eve was made from the side of the sleeping Adam; the side of the dead Christ was struck by a lance that the sacraments might flow forth, from which the Church is formed.[23] . . . The Evangelist, according to his wont, is careful of his words. He does not say that the lance struck the Lord's side, or wounded it, but rather that it opened His side, that thus the door of life might be opened whence the sacraments of the Church flowed forth, without which that life which is the true life cannot be entered.[24]

It is this last passage that Saint Thomas echoed later when he wrote:

That they might testify to His death one of the soldiers opened His side. And with reason does the Evangelist say "opened" not "wounded," because through this side there is opened to us the doorway to eternal life. "After that I saw a door opened." This is the door in the side of the ark through which those living creatures entered who were not to perish in the flood. And this door is the cause of salvation.[25]

Two other fifth-century saints witnessed to the wounded side in its impassible glory after the resurrection. Saint Peter Chrysologus (406–450), Bishop of Ravenna under Leo the Great, wrote in a sermon:

"Bring hither thy hand and put it into My side, and be not faithless but believing." This He said that those wounds which had poured forth water for cleansing and blood for redeeming all men, might, on being opened again by thee, pour forth faith upon the whole world. Thomas answered and said: "My Lord and my God." Let heretics come and hear, thus said the Lord: "Be not faithless but believing." For lo, at the cry of Thomas He not only shows His human body, but through what that body suffered He shows that Christ is Lord and God. And truly is He God who lives after death, who rises after wounds.[26]

And Saint Paulinus (354–431), from his retreat at Nola where he had fled "from all the noisy crowding up of things,"[27] wrote further:

We are helped, and so is the Gospel, by the blessed speed of that young Apostle, by means of which, through running together with Peter who was slower with the weight of age, he who had leaned upon the Lord's breast came first to the sepulchre to see the resurrection. For from the deep places of that breast he had drawn forth two fountains, the Apocalypse and the Gospel, which he poured over the whole earth.[28]

Pope Saint Gregory the Great (540–604), the last of the Western Fathers, was the architect of the coming Middle Ages. Under the pressure of his task of forming the new nations of Europe into members of the Christian commonwealth, his busy soul was lonely for the serenity of contemplation, and he found it without leaving his business. He found the Heart of Christ in the love-song of the Canticle, the most frequently used source of mystical expression:

"Arise, my love, my sister, and come, my dove in the clefts of the rock, in the hollow places of the wall." By the clefts of the rock I mean the wounds in the hands and feet of Christ hanging freely on the cross. By the hollow places in the wall I mean the wound in His side made by the lance. And it is well said that the dove is in the clefts of the rock and the hollow places of the wall, for in remembering the cross she imitates the patience of Christ, while she calls to mind the example of His wounds. Like the dove in the rock the simple soul finds in these wounds the food that will strengthen her. Also by the clefts may be signified the sacraments.[29]

Saint Bede the Venerable (672–735) in his studious round of monastic life at Jarrow was one of the links between the Patristic Age and mediaeval times; he could say: "I wholly applied myself to the study of Scripture, and amidst the observance of regular discipline and the daily care of singing in the church, I always took delight in learning, singing and writing."[30] He echoed Gregory, the Pope who had brought about the conversion of his nation:

"Thou hast wounded my heart, my sister, my spouse." This word is to be taken simply, for by mentioning the wounded Heart it expresses the greatness of the love of Christ for the Church.[31]

During all these centuries there was as yet no trace of a public cultus to the Sacred Heart. They were times of "long and austere struggle in the defence of the faith, when Christian piety tended to be more intellectual than affective, when Christ our Savior, even in the ignominy of His Passion, was universally beheld as God rather than as man."[32] They were times when the Liturgy, coming out of the catacombs, was reaching its full splendor; the chief liturgical symbol was a gold cross, at first without corpus, then bearing a serene figure in crown and priestly robes. Christian art was a symbolic expression of the high truths of faith; it had not yet found the realistic forms which would move the emotions to pity for the suffering Savior. Such was part of the divine plan; the Spirit of Wisdom then guided men to think of the heart as a metaphor for wisdom; truth precedes love.

Later on when souls, by contemplative prayer, found themselves dwelling within the very Heart of Christ, those tremendous doctrinal concepts which earlier had seen in the wanton act of a soldier the very origin of the Church became closely woven into the Devotion to the Sacred Heart.[33] The Postulator of the Cause, in defending the first petition for the introduction of the Feast of the Sacred Heart in 1697, emphasized the value of this Patristic tradition when he wrote:

The institution of a Feast in honor of the Sacred Heart of Jesus has to do with a matter which is serious, true, useful, and in accord with custom; by it the hearts of the faithful are stirred to the love of Christ the Lord. It is in keeping with faith, because the memory of the Passion is recalled; it is in harmony with Sacred Scripture in which this Devotion is implied; it follows the example and teaching of the Holy Fathers.[34]

The full significance of this theological outlook of early times was brought out when the final Liturgy for the Feast was composed in the twentieth century. Then in the Divine Office at Matins for the Feast and during the Octave, passages from Saint John Chrysostom, Saint Cyril of Alexandria, Saint Augustine and Saint Gregory the Great were interwoven with passages from anonymous mediaeval writers, from later doctors such as Saint Bernardine of Siena and Saint Peter Canisius, and from the *Miserentissimus Redemptor* of Pius XI, in which the price of salvation is seen "coming from the hidden fountains of the Heart."

It is as though the doctrinal bedrock of the Church laid so firmly in the Patristic Age had been struck by the rod of prayer in later times, till the sweet waters of devotion flowed from it. "Arise, then, O soul, place thy lips there and drink,"[35] says Mother Church, who was not young then and is not old now, and who sees her end in her beginning.

NOTES

1. H. Denziger, *Enchiridion Symbolorum* (St. Louis, Herder, 1937), p. 30.

2. *Ibid.*, p. 57.

3. *Ibid.*, p. 71.

4. Matt. 27, 54.

5. From the Bull condemning the heretical Synod of Pistoia, 1794, see p. 137.

6. *Homilia I, in Cantica Canticorum*, P. G. XLIV, 786.

7. The organic Heart of Christ, the proximate object of the Devotion, is not clearly indicated in these passages, although it is implied indirectly. As Hamon puts it: "No one then penetrated the mystery of the wounded side." See: *Histoire de la Dévotion au Sacré Coeur*, Vol. II, p. 82. Bainvel says that these texts "open up the way for the Devotion. They are the materials of which it will make use." See: *Devotion to the Sacred Heart*, p. 353.

8. P. G. VI, 717.

9. Tertullian, "Apology," *Fathers of the Church* (New York, 1950), Vol. X, p. 125.

10. Eusebius, *Historia Ecclesiastica*, V, 1.

11. Eph. 3, 8.

12. *Summa Theologica*, II, q. 45, a. 1.

13. *Homilia I, in Cantica Canticorum*, P. G. XIII, 87.

14. *In Joannem*, P. G. XIV, 31.

15. *Ibid.*, P. G. XIV, 800.

16. *In Joannem*, LIX.

17. *Commentary on Psalm XLV*, P. L. XIV, 1194.

18. *Commentary on Psalm XXXVII*, P. L. XIV, 1073.

19. *Liber de Benedictionibus Patriarcharum*, P. L. XIV, 715.

20. Treatise on Psalm XLIII, *Breviarium Romanum*, Lesson IV of Matins on Holy Saturday.

21. *In Joannis Evangelium*, P. L. XXXV, 1382.

22. *Ibid.*, 1536.

23. *Ibid.*, 1463.

24. *Ibid.*, 1953.

25. *In Joannem*, P. G. XIX, 34.

26. *Sermo XXXIV*, P. L. LII, 439.

27. From Paulinus' poem "Non inopes animi," *Mediaeval Latin Lyrics*, trans. by Helen Waddell (New York, Holt, 1933), p. 35.

28. *Epistola XXI*, P. L. XVI, 251.

29. *Expositio super Canticam*, P. L. LXXIX, 499.

30. *Ecclesiastical History of the English People*, Everyman Library, p. 283.

31. *In Canticam*, P. L. XCI, 1139.

32. Hamon, *op. cit.*, Vol. II, 81.

33. That the Devotion to the Sacred Heart draws its dynamism in succeeding ages from the doctrinal bases laid in the Patristic Ages is recognized in many present-day studies of its history. For example: "This Devotion is essentially a reaction against the danger of removing the humanity of Christ from the center of spirituality, and a restoration of the perfectly balanced doctrine defined at Chalcedon." C. Moeller, "Devotion to the Sacred Heart," in *Theology Digest*, II:80 (Spring 1954).

34. Nilles, *De Rationibus Festorum Sacratissimi Cordis Jesu* (Oeniponte, 1875), p. 24.

35. *Breviarum Romanum*, Lesson VII, Matins for the Feast of the Sacred Heart. The Octave is no longer observed.

CHAPTER IV

THE CLOISTERED WAY
800–1200

"I will reveal the riches of My Heart."

The early Middle Ages were energetic and constructive times when
men strong in body and objective in mind were building Christendom, not without the noise of fighting. Yet, paradoxically, the
élite among them went into cloisters, "driven by the Spirit" as
Christ was when He hid in the wilderness. "Turning within" was
the first movement needed to find the Heart of Christ, and this, in
time, led to a new outpouring of the Spirit upon the Church. In a
Pentecost sermon preached in 1180, a German priest, Konrad, declared that "Christ is Himself the Holy divine Truth. Therefore
rightly is the Spirit that proceeds from His Heart called the Spirit
of Truth. When the Holy Ghost who went forth from His Heart
came upon the disciples, they understood all Scripture."[1] And the
ages which first synthesized the elements of Devotion to the
Sacred Heart, did so in harmony with the principles of the *philosophia perennis* which was forming in the twelfth century in scho-
lastic disputations. Already rooted in Patristic dogma, the Devotion then drew its vigor no less from ascetical theology.

All "devotions" take their name from the virtue of devotion,
which is an act of the virtue of religion, the highest of all virtues
because of its object, which is God Himself. Devotion is thus fundamental to the spiritual life; it is strong, simple, rudimentary, appetitive in its nature, the mark of the athlete soul. Yet clear and
practical as devotion is in its energizing power, it springs from a
hidden and deeply silent cause: the contemplation of God's goodness. Saint Thomas deals with it as follows:

Devotion is nothing else than the will to give oneself readily to things
concerning the service of God. . . . It is an act of the appetitive part

of the soul and is a movement of the will. . . . Now the will moves
the other powers of the soul to their acts. Wherefore, since devotion is
an act of the will whereby a man offers himself for the service of God,
who is the last end, it follows that devotion prescribes the mode of human acts.

It belongs to the same virtue to will to do something and to have the
will ready to do it. Now it is evident that to do what pertains to the worship or service of God belongs properly to religion. Wherefore it belongs to that virtue to have the will ready to do such things; hence devotion is an act of religion.[2]

It is written: "In my meditation a fire shall flame out."[3] But spiritual fire causes devotion. Therefore meditation is the cause of devotion. The extrinsic chief cause of devotion is God. But the intrinsic
cause on our part must needs be meditation or contemplation. For devotion is an act of the will to the effect that man surrenders himself
readily to the service of God. Now every act of the will proceeds from
some consideration, since the object of the will is a good understood.
Consequently meditation must be the cause of devotion, in so far as
through meditation man conceives the thought of surrendering himself
to God's service. Therefore a consideration of God's goodness and loving kindness leads to this, for such consideration leads to love which is
the proximate cause of devotion.

Matters concerning the Godhead are in themselves the strongest
incentive to love, and consequently to devotion, because God is supremely lovable. Yet such is the weakness of the human mind that it
needs a guiding hand not only to the knowledge but also to the love of
divine things by means of certain sensible objects known to us. Chief
among these is the humanity of Christ, according to the words of the
Preface: "that through knowing God visibly we may be caught up to
the love of things invisible." Wherefore matters relating to Christ's humanity are the chief incentive to devotion, leading us thither as with a
guiding hand, although devotion itself has for its object matters concerning the Godhead.[4]

The direct and principal effect of devotion is spiritual joy of the
mind . . . though its secondary effect is sorrow according to God.[5]

It would seem to follow from this exposition that "devotions,"
those distinct modes of prayer and practices of virtue which
center on some special truth of faith, could only grow from the
root virtue of devotion in the measure in which the Church found
leisure for contemplation in her expanding life. This came to pass
when the early Middle Ages succeeded the more strenuous times

of the Fathers, and monasticism arose to offer a cloistered way
to peace.

While theologians were writing their books in the cities where
culture and controversy flourished noisily, ascetics were fleeing to
the soundless deserts. After a lifetime of solitude Saint Anthony
sought out Saint Paul the Hermit in a cave in the Thebaid (c. 342),
and the two wondered aloud, as they ate the bread brought by a
raven, "if new roofs be risen in the ancient cities."[6] Thus charity
and a common striving drew hermits together, and by the fourth
century monasteries began to replace the solitary huts of the wilderness. The first monastic Rule was compiled by Saint Pachomius.
Monasticism was then carried to the East by Saint Basil, and to the
West by Saint Martin of Gaul, and by Saint Patrick of Ireland,
using the palm-green Island of Lerins as its steppingstone, and
reaching to the tidal rocks of the North Sea. Then Saint Benedict
(480–553) chose a mountain cliff in Italy for his populous solitude. At Monte Cassino he was granted a vision of God, and in
Him "the whole world gathered together as it were under one beam
of the sun."[7] In the light of that vision he wrote the Rule upon
which all Western monasticism was to be built, the Rule in which
"the heart becomes broadened, and with unutterable sweetness of
love the way of the commandments of the Lord is run."[8] In this
Benedictine atmosphere there crystallized "a new expression of
Christian tenderness," in devotedness to the Heart of Christ; Eternal Wisdom spoke in terms of human love, and woke an answering love in cloistered hearts.

It is difficult to trace the development of the Devotion across the
earlier centuries (7th to 11th) of those restless times in which the
new nations of Europe were converted and the patterns of Christian civilization were first drawn. The missionary builders and the
educators of the new kingdoms were all monks, Saint Patrick for
Ireland, Saint Martin for France, Saint Augustine of Canterbury
for England, Saint Boniface for Germany. Everywhere, in forests,
villages or cities, the monasteries made a center of learning, and
gave the newly converted peoples an alphabet and parchment on
which to write their own heroic traditions sublimated by faith into
the first expression of Christian humanism.

Thus while there are no references, even indirect, to the Divine
Heart in the Latin writings of those days, there appears in a ver-

nacular poem written by an unknown monk of the ninth century
a direct and simple revelation of one of the most fundamental
notions connected with the Devotion: that the human sentiments
of the God-man are known by the motions of His Heart. The
anonymous *Heliand* is an Old Saxon epic of the life of Christ,
ringing with the heroic language of the Teutonic tradition. It is
full of the strong, masculine spirit of the North that had brought
new life into the decadent Roman Empire; it is a hero-worship-
ping poem and the hero is the Son of God. The learning of the
monasteries had reached out among the people to shape from
their own national ideals and imagination a vivid story of the life
of "God's kingly Son," who had made Himself a leader of men. In
this poem it is by the Heart that we know Him; in its sweeping
alliterative measures we see for the first time in literature the
truth of what Gerard Manley Hopkins later said: "The Sacred
Heart is Christ's most perfect character": [9]

The Sermon on the Mount:

> There sat the Shepherd of the land
> among His flock;   God's own Son
> would speak to them   with many a thoughtful word,
> teaching His people   how they God's praises
> should work out   in this world-kingdom.
> First He sat there and was silent;   long He gazed at them,
> in His Heart bore grace towards them,   the holy Lord,
> mild in His Heart. . . .   Blessed are the mild,
> thanes meek of heart;   to them the holy God,
> the mighty one, will be mild.   Blessed likewise among the
>   throng
> those that are pure in heart; the Ruler of the heavens
> they shall see in His kingdom.

The raising of Lazarus:

> To Him, born of God,
> Mary said sorrowing   how full of care,
> full of grief was her heart,   how bitter her affliction
> for the loss of Lazarus,   the beloved man.
> With sobs she wept,   until God's Son
> felt His Heart touched,   and hot tears
> escaped the weeping one.

The Passion:

Then gazed the Lord Ruler
towards Jerusalem,   the Best One among all the good.
He saw the town-rampart shine   and the buildings of the
    Jews,
. the high mead-halls,   and the house of God,
most blissful of blessed things.   Then in Him stirred
His Heart in His breast;   the holy Son of God
could not stop His tears.   With many words He spoke
grievously sorrowing   with a heavy Heart: . . .
            "To me are come
pain and terror-agony;   I must now for this world
suffer, and for this people."   Then to His thanes He spoke,
the holy Lord,   and His Heart became saddened,
His soul darkened. . . .
John the good,   who by the Son of God
among the faithful ones   was the best beloved,
most close to the mind   of the mighty Christ,
was made to rest on His bosom,   to lie on His breast,
leaning with his head there,   where many holy secrets
and deep thoughts he learned. . . .
The Son of the Lord   bent Himself down,
the strong One bent in kneeling-prayer,   mightiest among
    kings.
Falling down   to the Father of all men
He greeted Him then   with grieving words,
in deep sorrow.   His Heart was saddened,
and in His humanity   His mind was moved. . . .
But then He went   yet another time
up the mountain   to pray there,
the mighty Lord,   and He spoke there still
many good words.   God's angel came now,
the holy one from heaven   to fasten His Heart,
to strengthen it for the bonds. . . .
            Then sent Him back
Herod the king,   to whence He had come
in the midst of the rabble   who spoke slander against Him,
insolent malice,   the bound One
overheaping with mockery.   His Heart was glad,
for all these things   He suffered in meekness.[10]

There are passages in Old English poetry of that early date in
which flashes of devotion to the wounded side of Christ are expressed in the same heroic language of Teutonic tradition.
Christ and Satan is a poem stemming from the biblical paraphrases of Caedmon (c. 680), the inspired goatherd who sang
to the Abbess Hilda of Whitby the things that he had heard in a
dream. It deals with the apparition of Our Lord to the Apostles
on Easter, and reflects the thoughts of Saint Augustine:

> Some could not believe,   know in their hearts.
> Such was the loved man,   Didymus he was named,
> until with his hands   he took hold of the Healer,
> touched His very side   whence blood had poured,
> falling to the earth,   the bath of Baptism.
> Fair was that fight   that the noble Lord
> suffered for us,   our Leader.
> He mounted the beam,   poured out His blood,
> the good One on the gallows,   through His ghostly might.[11]

Cynewulf, a monk of Mercia (c. 750–829), wrote in his native
tongue the thoughts gathered from his Latin studies. His tremendous symphonic poem *The Christ* pictures the Healer coming
at the end of the world, and speaking thus to the multitudes
gathered on the edge of eternity:

> Then was I hung   on a high beam,
> fastened to the rood.   There the ruling ones
> with a spear poured out   blood from My open side,
> falling dark to the earth.   It was done that thou
> mightest be set free   from devils' hard rule,
> and I, sinless,   suffered such pain
> and heavy evil, until I, all alone,
> sent forth the living soul   from My own body.
> See now the fearful wounds   made long ago
> in My hands   and in My feet
> by which I hung,   hard fastened.
> Here too canst thou see,   even now marked plain,
> the bleeding wound   here in My side.
> How uneven the reckoning   between us two!
> I bore thy sore,   that thou in bliss
> might taste of joy   in My high realm;
> and dearly by My death   I bought for thee

a long life   spent ever in light
dwelling in beauty   shadowless.[12]

While the Teutonic and the Roman spirits were thus being
forged together, feudalism called for armed alertness. Then the
first Crusade stirred the new order of chivalry to holy warfare;
priests and knights were kept on the march. Lay investiture cor-
roded both spiritual and temporal affairs by confusing the nature
of each. Then strenuous voices were raised in the turmoil, when
fearless men of prayer dared to speak out for all ranks of society
to hear the truths that they had mastered in contemplation. Abbot
Willram (c. 1075) wrote boldly to the Emperor Henry IV, who
had risen against Pope Gregory VII in the matter of investitures;
he makes Christ say to His Church:

Come from Libanus, My Spouse. Hasten to Me in the purity of thy
baptism. If thou keepest thyself as pure as thou art become by baptism,
thou shalt behold what grace I will bestow on thee even in this world. I
will cause Emperors and Kings who now sit on their thrones and rise
against thee like panthers and lions with cunning and strength, to honor
thy footsteps and be converted to Christian piety. Thou hast wounded
My Heart, my sister, My spouse, thou hast wounded My Heart.[13]

Yet during these times a network of monasteries, centers of
peace, was being woven over Europe. The Divine Office had
been taking shape under the pressure of monastic life since the
days of the Desert Fathers; blended with Gregorian music, by
the eleventh century it rang the changes of the liturgical year
from choir to choir, from sunrise to sunset and through the night
again. It was the voice of the *Corpus Mysticum* praying aloud;
from its public splendor contemplative souls drew thoughts for
their private pondering. Art too shaped those thoughts. The figure
of the vested King of Glory that had stretched its arms in Byzantine
majesty on the ceremonial crosses of earlier ages was now replaced
by the figure of Christ suffering. A realistic rather than symbolic
crucifix brought home the humanity of the Redeemer, and with it
His love. The Passion stirred souls to pity and compunction.
The time was ready for an awareness of a Heart of flesh to awaken
in souls of prayer; the road to it led through the wound in the side.

Saint Anselm (1033–1109) was such a soul. He drew in the
contemplative spirit at the monastery of Bec, where he taught

and prayed hidden from the world; he gave it out in the warfare of his work as Archbishop of Canterbury. He was the militant defender of the rights of the Church; he was the philosopher weighing proofs for the existence of God while he sat, an abstracted guest, at the table of King Henry I. But more than both he was the saint perpetually homesick for the cloister, who found the answer to his question "Cur Deus Homo?" in love. He wrote:

Jesus is sweet in the bowing of His Head and in death, sweet in the stretching out of His arms, sweet in the nailing together of His feet with one nail.

Sweet in the bowing of His head; for bending down His head from the cross He seems to say to His loved one: "O My beloved, how often hast thou desired to enjoy the kiss of My mouth, declaring to Me through thy comrades, 'Let Him kiss me with the kiss of His mouth.' I am ready, I bow My head, I offer My mouth to be kissed as much as thou wilt. And say not in your heart, 'I seek not such a kiss which is without beauty and loveliness, but I seek a glorious kiss which the angelic citizens of heaven seek ever to enjoy.' Be not thus mistaken, for unless you kiss that first mouth you will never reach to that other. Kiss therefore the mouth that I now offer to you, for though it be without beauty or loveliness it is not without grace."

Sweet in the stretching out of His arms; for in extending His arms He reveals how He desires our embraces, and seems to say: "O all you that labor and are heavy burdened, come and be refreshed within My arms. See how I am ready to gather you all within My arms; then come, all. Let no one fear to be repulsed, for I desire not the death of the sinner but that he be converted and live. My delights are to be with the children of men."

Sweet in the opening of His side; for that opening reveals to us the riches of His goodness and the charity of His Heart towards us.

Sweet in the nailing of His feet with one nail, for by that He says to us: "Lo, if you think that I must flee from you, and so are slow to come to Me, knowing that I am swift as the hart, see that My feet are fixed by a nail, so that I can in no wise flee from you, for mercy has Me bound fast. I cannot flee from you as your sins deserve, for My hands are fixed by nails."

Good Jesus, humble Lord, dear Lord, sweet in mouth, sweet in Heart, sweet in ear, unknowably and untellably pleasant, kind and merciful, mighty, wise, benign, generous but not rash, exceedingly sweet and gentle! Thou alone art the highest good, beautiful above the sons of men, fair and comely, the chosen of thousands and all-desirable! Fair things become the fair. O my Lord, now my whole soul desires Thine arms and Thy kiss. I desire nought but Thee, as though no reward were promised. If hell and heaven were not, yet would I long for Thee, for Thy sweet good and for Thyself. Thou art my constant meditation, my word, my work. Amen.[14]

In the meantime another household was forming within the Benedictine family. Led by Saint Bernard (1090–1153), the new Cistercian monks built their home by the clear waters, Clairvaux. Their abbey became the fountainhead of many streams. The austere Cistercian churches rose in valleys and forests as remote as possible from the courts, castles and schools where the twelfth-century Renaissance was gathering force. Paradoxically, Saint Bernard himself was a counselor of kings, a preacher of the Crusade, a disputant in the University of Paris, but in the chapter room at Clairvaux he put into words the science of love, mysticism. He had learned it in silence, and spoke of it for his brothers' sake. He knew by experience the secrets of the *Canticle of Canticles*. His conferences on it bring into full play the power of accommodating the sacred text, of making it live in each age and in each place where souls turn to it for the bread of their daily life:

"Arise, my love, my spouse, my dove in the clefts of the rock." . . . When you think, as here, of lovers, think not of man and woman but of the Word and of the human soul. And if I speak of Christ and of His Church, it is the same thing, save that by the Church is meant not one soul but the union of many, or rather their oneness. . . .

Someone, in dwelling on this passage, has interpreted the "clefts of the rock" as the wounds of Christ. And rightly, for the rock is Christ. O good clefts which strengthen our faith in the resurrection and in the divinity of Christ! "My Lord and my God," cried Saint Thomas. And whence did he draw this cry but from the clefts of the rocks? In them "the sparrow has found herself a house and the turtle a nest for herself where she may lay her young." In them the dove lies in safety and unafraid watches the circling hawk. And again it is said: "My dove in the clefts of the rock," and again the voice of the dove cries: "He hath exalted me upon a rock," and again: "Our feet have stood upon a rock." The wise man builds his house upon a rock, for there he fears not the violence of wind and flood. What better than the rock? On a rock I stand high, on a rock secure, on a rock firm. There I am safe from the enemy, strong against falling, because I am lifted up from the earth. For all earthly things are failing and unstable. Let our conversation but be in heaven and we shall fear no fall and no overthrow.

Thus he was wrong who said: "My sin is greater than may be forgiven," unless it be that he was not one of Christ's members, and had no share in Christ's merits that he might claim them and call them his own, as a member may use what belongs to the head. But as for me, I shall take to myself what is lacking to me from the Heart of the Lord, for mercy flows from it, nor are there wanting openings through which it may flow. They dug His hands and His feet; they opened His side with a lance. And through these clefts I may suck honey from the rock and oil from the hard stone; that is, I may taste and see that the Lord is sweet. He was thinking thoughts of peace, and I knew it not. For "who hath known the thoughts of the Lord, and who hath been His counselor?" But the key that unlocks is the key that pierced Him for me, that I may see the will of the Lord. Why should I not look through the cleft? The key cries out, the wound cries out that God indeed makes peace with the world through Christ. The iron pierced His soul, and His Heart has drawn near to us, that no longer should He not know how to compassionate my woes. The secrets of His Heart lie open to me through the cloven body; that mighty sacrament of love lies open, *viscera misericordia Dei nostri,* in which the Orient from on high has visited us. Why should not the Heart lie open through the wounds? For what shines out more surely from Thy wounds but the truth that "the Lord is sweet and merciful and full of pity"? For greater mercy than this no man hath, that he lay down his life not for his friends but for his foes, men doomed to death. . . .

It is said: "And His back parts are as the paleness of gold." Did He not grow pale in death? But better is pale gold than glittering brass, and "the foolishness of God is wiser than men." Golden is the Word; golden is Wisdom. This gold grew pale, hiding the form of God and showing the form of a servant. It discolored the Church as well, who says: "Do not consider me that I am brown, for the sun hath altered my color." And her back parts too show pale gold, for she is not ashamed of the shadow of the cross, nor has she shrunk from the disgrace of the Passion, nor fled from the livid wounds. She dwells lovingly on them and hopes that her own last end may be even so. She hears the words "My dove in the clefts of the rock," for she ponders over the wounds of Christ and lingers ever there in her meditation. From there comes the strength of her martyrs, their strong faithfulness to God most high. For no martyr should fear to lift up his bloodless and livid face to that face by whose bruises he is healed, and to show a glorious likeness to that bitter death that is the paleness of gold. Why should he fear

when the Lord says to him: "Show Me thy face"? And to what end
does the Lord so bid? I think it is because He wishes to be seen. He
would rather be seen than see. For what does He not see? He has no
need that anyone show himself to Him, from whom nothing is hidden,
nothing unrevealed. He wishes then to be seen; this gracious Captain
desires that the face and eyes of His devoted soldier should be lifted
up to those wounds, that his soul may stand erect and he may draw
from the sight strength unshakable. For gazing on those wounds he
shall not feel his own. The martyr stands fearless and in triumph,
though his body be torn. While iron pierces his side he watches, not
only with strength but with joy, the blood that pours out from his flesh.
Where then is the soul of the martyr? It is safe; it is on the rock; it is in
the Heart of Jesus, whose wounds were opened to let it in.[15]

Some of Saint Bernard's sons followed the hidden way for
which he longed in the midst of his busy popularity. Abbot
William (1085–1148) of the Benedictine monastery of St. Thierry,
an active opponent of Abelard in the controversy concerning the
Trinity, finally withdrew to a Cistercian monastery to give his
last years to pure contemplation. There he wrote the life of Saint
Bernard, and in the *Liber de Contemplando Deo* followed the
secret path into the Sacred Heart pointed out by his father in God:

The voice of Thy testimony shall answer me deep in my soul and in my
mind, crying out within me, stirring the depths of my being; and my
inner eyes are blinded by the lightning of Thy truth, bringing home to
me that no man can see Thee and live. For truly until now I, full of sin,
have not availed to die to myself that I might live to Thee; yet by
Thine own command and by Thy gift I stand on the rock of my trust,
of Christian trust, in a place which is within Thyself, where, as best I
can, I shall wait patiently, where I shall clasp and kiss Thy right hand
that covers and protects me; and then I look up, gazing often and
striving to see even afar the One who sees me, and following the
footsteps of the humanity of Christ Thy Son. But when I strive to come
to Him, whether like the woman with the issue of blood I try by stealth
to reach for His touch or His garment to bring healing to my ailing
and miserable soul, or whether like Thomas, that man of desires, I too
desire to see and to touch Him wholly, I want still more. For I long to
come to the most holy wound of His side, that door in the side of the
ark, that I may put in not only my finger or my whole hand, but enter
wholly into the very Heart of Jesus, into the Holy of Holies, the ark of
the covenant, into that golden urn, the soul of our humanity that holds
within itself the manna of His divinity.

But alas! It is said to me: "Do not touch Me," and again, in the Apoc-alypse: "Out with the dogs!" Thus driven back and away by the lash of my just conscience, I am forced to bear the sorrow of my unworthiness and presumption. Then again, taking my stand on the rock, which is the refuge of hedgehogs, full of the thorns of sin, once more I clasp and kiss Thy right hand that covers and protects me, and because of what I had glimpsed and felt, I long more ardently, scarce able to wait till Thou take away that covering hand and pour in Thy enlightening grace until, according to the words of Thy truth, dead to myself and alive to Thee, I begin to see Thy face by the light of its own unveiling, and to be joined to Thee in the vision of Thy face.[16]

In the English Abbey of Swineshead another Cistercian, Gilbert of Hoyland (d. 1160), saw the Heart of Christ as it is in His Mystical Body: the source of loving contemplation:

"In the day of His espousals and of His joy." Note the order of things. One day sees His espousals and His crowning. If you know this, you are blessed if you follow it. You change His plan if you wish to be espoused before being crowned, if you seek first the joy and quiet of being conquered by Christ before conquering with Christ. It is a blessed anticipation, but not in order, if you wish to rest before that triumphant espousal, if you seek joy before work. For but one day is appointed for these three: the diadem, the espousals, and the joy of heart.

What is the Heart of our Solomon? You are, He says, the Body of Christ—members of member. Happy indeed is every member of such a head; but he who is the heart, he is of the noblest member. And lo, is not he the heart who is cherished in the inner heart of God's secret places, in the vital heat of His affections, in the depths of His meditations? From the heart come thoughts, not works. Rightfully is he the heart who dwells in spiritual thoughts, in the fatness of grace, in the breast of truth, in the womb of wisdom, as Solomon did in type. And indeed the Church is all this; she is His soul, His crown, His heart, His bride; she is the crown for His head, the spouse by His side, the heart in His breast. How then could we be better placed, and shall we not rejoice? Go forth, then, daughters of Sion, and see, that you too may pass into the deep thoughts of His Heart, with the grace of a spouse, with the beauty of a diadem.

"Thou hast wounded My heart, My Sister, My Spouse." The wound of His Heart shows the vehemence of His love. O Heart truly sweet that is moved by love of us to show the beatings of its love! . . .

What marvel is this, my brothers? Shall we not call that soul blessed

which pierces with the arrows of love the very Heart of Our Lord
Jesus Christ? Sharp and sure and truly violent is that movement of
love which availed to stir Thy love, good Jesus. Great and violent is
the strength of charity, reaching and piercing God Himself, and like an
arrow piercing His Heart. What wonder if the kingdom of heaven suf-
fereth violence? The Lord Himself bears the wound of violent love.
But see with what dart it is wounded. He says: "Thou hast wounded
My heart with one of thine eyes, with one hair of thy neck." Do not
cease, O spouse, to seek out thy Beloved with such darts. The glances
of love are like so many arrows to both. Be not slack in this warfare;
be not content to wound thy Beloved once, but give wound after wound.
Happy art thou if thine arrows are fixed in Him, if thine acts of love
strive with Christ, if thine eyes rest unwearied upon Him. O blessed
wound from which virtue goes forth! The woman touched but the hem
of His garment, and Christ felt virtue go forth from Him. How much
more is it when His Heart is not only lightly touched, but is wounded.[17]

The humming Augustinian Abbey of Saint Victor in Paris was
a center of theological activity in the years when the University
of Paris was beginning its turbulent career. The Victorines were
experts in the allegorical method of interpreting Scripture, and
Richard of Saint Victor wrote as follows on the words of the *Canticle,* "He shall eat butter and honey":

Honey, it is said, comes down from heaven; butter, as we know,
comes from flesh. Thus is honey from heaven by means of dew, and
butter from flesh by means of milk. What else is butter but the fat
of milk, and what else is honey but a certain sweetness, or, I might
say, the fat of dew? By milk, because of its sweetness, is rightly signified sweetness of heart; in butter, because of its origin, is rightly
signified joy of heart. Butter is made from milk, and from true joy
of heart comes true sweetness of heart. The more milk we have the
more shall we abound in butter. So, according to the abundance of
our kindness will be the abundance of our joy. If we look at the
Heart of Christ, there is nothing sweeter, nothing kinder. Nowhere
can there be a creature sweeter than His Heart; no heart could more
abound in joy than His.

True joy of heart lies in the testimony of a good conscience. "Our
glory," it is said, "is the testimony of our conscience." The testimony
of a good conscience in our heart does not yield to concupiscence. How
clean must have been that conscience which felt no concupiscence?
What could be sweeter than a heart that no evil has touched, that never
had or could have bitterness or sharpness, and whose sweetness was

measured by the greatness of its joy? Weigh, if you can, the sweetness
of a Heart which no bitterness could disturb or weaken. In the midst
of His suffering, He pitied His enemies more than He felt the pain in
His own members. More than all others, our Emmanuel had a Heart
of flesh to compassionate, for never has there been a heart more
tender in loving kindness. Emmanuel alone could rejoice in full and
lasting sweetness, and this was the butter drawn so abundantly from
the flesh by means of milk. For what was His banquet of butter? It
was His constant rejoicing in inward sweetness.[18]

A *Manuale,* probably written by Jean de Fecamp (c. 1190),
echoes more succinctly the lyric flow of Saint Bernard:

God came through love to men; He came among men, He was made
man. The invisible God, through love, was made like to His servants.
He was wounded by love for our sins. Safe and strong is the rest offered
to the weak and to the sinful in the wounds of the Savior. There I
dwell secure; through the wounds the depths of His Heart lie open to
me. What is lacking to me I shall take to myself from that Heart, for
His mercies flow forth, and there is no lack of openings through which
they may flow. Through the gaping holes in His body the secret places
of His Heart are revealed to me; the sacred mystery of His love lies
open, the mercy of our God in which the Orient from on high has
visited us. The wounds of Jesus Christ are full of mercy, full of sweetness and charity. They have dug His hands and feet, they have pierced
His side with a lance. Through these clefts it is permitted me to taste
how sweet is the Lord my God, for in truth He is sweet and mild and
of great mercy to all who call on Him in truth, to those who seek Him
and who greatly love Him. Plentiful redemption is given to us in the
wounds of our Savior, the floodtide of sweetness, the fullness of grace,
the perfection of virtue.[19]

The *Vitis Mystica,* a treatise on the Vine and the branches, has
been attributed both to Saint Bernard and to Saint Bonaventure;
it is, perhaps, better that it remain anonymous, that we may hear
in it the collective voice of the early mediaeval mystics who have
found "the bright treasure" within the wounded side. In chapter
three the essential elements of Devotion to the Sacred Heart emerge
in all their warm and luminous beauty. It is significant that passages from this chapter have been woven by the Church into the
Divine Office,[20] making perpetual the voices of those cloistered
lovers whose prayers are thus placed on the lips of the *ecclesia
orans* in later and busier centuries:

O kind Jesus, true Vine, tree of life which is in the midst of Paradise, whose leaves are unto healing, whose fruits are unto eternal life; blessed flower and fruit of the most chaste Virgin Mother, without whom nothing has savor, since Thou art the wisdom of the eternal Father: deign to refresh my mind, strengthless and dry, with the bread of knowledge and the water of wisdom, that hidden things may lie open to me by Thy unlocking, O Key of David, and shadowed things may be lightsome by Thy shining, O true Light, to me Thy humble servant; and that through the showing and revealing of Thyself we may all—both those who speak and those who listen—have everlasting life. . . .

The Vine has a ditch dug about it. By this ditch is meant the guilt of the wicked, since he who digs a ditch works to deceive someone. . . . But when the diggers saw that they could in no wise harm the Vine, they dug the more, till they themselves fell in. They toiled to dig around the Vine, and to pierce it, that it might at least, like other trees, become forever dried up. They dug and they pierced not only His hands and His feet but His side also, and with the lance of fury they pierced through the depths of the most holy Heart, which had long since been wounded with the spear of love. For the spouse says in the Canticle: "Thou hast wounded My Heart, My spouse, My friend, My sister." Why should it be wounded further than by Thine enemies? Why give a second wound, since the Heart of the sweet Jesus is already wounded? Do you not know that a heart dies when stricken by one only wound and that the dead Heart of the Lord Jesus felt nothing, being already wounded? It had borne the wound of love, it had undergone the death of love, the Heart of our Spouse Jesus. . . .

We come then, once for all, to the most sweet Heart of Jesus, and good it is for us to be here. Not easily shall we let ourselves be torn from Him of whom it is written: "Those who withdraw from Thee are written in the earth." What then of those who come to Him? Thou Thyself teachest us. Thou hast said to those approaching Thee: "Rejoice that your names are written in heaven." Let us rejoice together, for if it is thus with those who are written in heaven, what shall they do who are written in the earth? They shall mourn indeed. But who would not rather choose to rejoice? Then let us draw near to Thee, and let us exult and be glad in Thee, remembering Thy Heart! A good treasure it is, a good pearl, O good Jesus, Thy Heart that we have found in the dug field of Thy body. Who would throw away this pearl? Rather will I give all things; I will sell the thoughts and desires of my mind and buy it for me, casting all my care in the Heart of the Lord Jesus, and without fail it will care for me.

Towards this temple, towards this Holy of Holies, towards this ark of the Testament, I will adore, and I will praise the name of the Lord, saying with David: "I have found my Heart, that I may pray to my God." And I have found the Heart of the King, of my brother and my friend, the loving Jesus. And shall I not adore? I shall adore indeed. For His Heart is with me, and still more boldly I can say it, for He is indeed my head. For even as the eyes of my bodily head are truly my eyes, so also this spiritual Heart is my heart. Well it is with me. For truly I have but one heart. Thus with Thy Heart and with mine, most sweet Jesus, I will seek Thee out and pray to Thee, my God. Let my prayers come into the sanctuary of Thy most merciful hearing; draw me wholly into Thy Heart. Even though the twisting of my sins may trip me up, yet is that Heart grown great and wide with incomprehensible love, and Thou art He who alone can make clean that which is conceived of unclean seed, so that when my bundle of wrongs is laid down, I may pass through the pierced opening. O Jesus supremely lovely above all others, wash me yet more from my sins, and cleanse me from my iniquity, that purified by Thee I may draw near to Thee the most pure, and may be worthy to dwell in Thy Heart all the days of my life and may prevail ever to see and to do Thy will.

To this end was the side pierced, that a door might be opened to us. For this was Thy Heart wounded, that we might dwell in it and in Thee, freed from all outward restlessness. For nought else than this was it wounded, that through the visible wound we might see the invisible wound of love. How better could He have shown His own ardent wish than by yielding not only His body but His Heart to be pierced by the lance? Thus His fleshly wound shows forth His spiritual wound. Perhaps He foreshadowed this by His own words in which it is twice said: "Thou hast wounded." Of each wound His sister and spouse is the cause, as if the Lover had clearly said: "Because thou hast wounded Me with the dart of thy love, I am wounded also by the soldier's spear." For who would allow his heart to be wounded with a spear unless it had first received the wound of love? And so He says: "Thou hast wounded My Heart, My Sister, My Bride, thou hast wounded My Heart." . . .

Who would not love a heart so wounded; who would not give back love to such a love? Who would not embrace one so chaste? She loves that wounded one indeed who, wounded deeply by such love, can say: "I am wounded by charity." Does she not return the love of her loving Spouse when she says: "Tell my Beloved that I languish with love"? Love embraces her beloved in brotherly wise when she

says: "Who will give Thee to me as a brother, sucking the breasts of
my mother, that I may find Thee without, and embrace Thee and kiss
Thee, and no man may now despise me?" And who is he that is
without? I think, he that is out of the body. As long as we are in this
body we are walking towards the Lord. Who can bear this journey
patiently? It is full of the pain of past things, of the labors of things
present, of the fear of things to come. And in this way, although our
Spouse gives the grace of consolation to everyone, none the less He
stands long as behind a wall; this body of sin is a barrier between us
and Him, nor does He yield Himself easily to be touched and kissed,
save by that soul who knows—though rarely indeed—that she has
by some means taken hold of Him, and cries out: "I have found Him
whom my soul loves; I have held Him and will not let Him go."

But no one rises easily to such a height. As for us who dwell within,
that is, who are yet in the body, let us love Him and return His love;
let us embrace our wounded one, for wicked husbandmen have dug
His hands and His feet, His side and His Heart. And let us hold ourselves ready, that He may deign to bind with the bonds of His love
those hearts which till now have been hard without repentance.[21]

The transition from such lyric prose into poetry is easily made;
vibrant prayer is apt to break into song. The earliest-known hymn
to the Sacred Heart is the *Summi Regis Cor Aveto* in which, for
the first time, the Heart of Christ is directly addressed and invoked, as "the core" of His personality. If an author for this
poem can be found, it is most likely to be the gentle sacristan of a
Premonstratensian monastery at Cologne, Blessed Hermann
Joseph (1150–1241). In steady, pulsing lines, tense and lingering,
clean cut and sharply rhymed, it sings to the Heart of Christ,
personifying the symbol of love as the Lover Himself.

> I hail Thee, kingly Heart most high,
> As my happy heart draws nigh.
> All my joy is to enfold Thee,
> All my heart delights to hold Thee;
> Thou dost move me now to speak.
>
> What love could bring Thee to this doom,
> What sorrow fold Thee in its gloom
> To make Thee pour Thy life out thus,
> Giving all Thou hast for us,
> Out of death our souls to seek?

O how bitter was Thy death,
How strong, how hungry that last breath!
How it pierced the sacred cell
Where the world's life willed to dwell,
Tearing through Thee, most sweet Heart!

By the death that Thou didst bear
When Thou for me hung suffering there,
Heart, my own heart's dear delight,
Keep my love within Thy sight.
Thee I choose for my own part.

O sweet Heart, chosen over all,
Clean my heart, so prone to fall,
So hardened in its vanity;
Make it love and fear but Thee,
Shaking off its cold and shame.

Through the marrow of my heart,
—Guilty, sinful, set apart—
May Thy love flow swift and strong,
Till my heart, thus borne along,
Lies wounded in that loving flame.

Open, open wide and fair,
As a rose of fragrance rare;
Join my heart to Thine anew,
Heal, then once more pierce it through.
Can a heart that loves feel pain?

Such heart knows never what to do;
It cannot keep the balance true,
It cannot measure, count the sum.
He whom love has overcome
Longs to die and die again.

My heart's strong voice cries out, O hear,
Gentle Heart, I love Thee dear.
To my own heart bend, incline,
Till that heart can cling to Thine
Devoutly, pressing close to Thee.

Let it live in love so deep
That it falls not into sleep.
Let it pray Thee and implore,
Let it honor and adore,
Joying all the time in Thee.

Open, open wide, Heart-rose,
Thou whose fragrance ever grows.
Make my heart grow large and great
With a thirst that will not sate,
In the flame of my desire.

Let us live so, Heart to heart,
Wounded, Jesus, as Thou art.
Heart to Heart shall grow alike
If through my heart Thou wilt but strike
With shame's arrow, sharp and dire.

Put my heart deep in Thine own,
Hold me, leave me not alone;
Joy and sorrow mingled be,
Beauty with deformity
Here, where all my life is spent.

Here my heart shall live and die,
To Thee ever drawing nigh;
Strongly would it thirst for Thee,
Jesus, say not no to me,
That it may rest in Thee, content.[22]

This hymn brings the story of the Devotion to the Sacred Heart
to about the year 1200, the turning point from the early into the
later Middle Ages. Behind the studious monastic authors already
quoted was a host of other fervent souls who witness to the wide
permeation of the Devotion into the prayer-life of those vigorous
times, so turbulent in action and so serene in thought. The Devotion had been learned in the living by "studying beautifulness,
dwelling in peace in their houses";[23] it was ready to pass from
the cloister to the wider life of the Church.

Where and by whom was made the synthesis of these various
elements that integrate the devotion to the Sacred Heart? We cannot
tell. And it is probable that whoever did so was unconscious that he

had introduced any new idea into the Church. Can it even be said that any one person has done it? It has, as it were, been formed spontaneously in the social consciousness of the Church under the influence of the Holy Ghost who abides in her. . . . This synthesis is the fruit of meditation on the wound of the side. Through devotion to the wound of the side the wound of the Heart has been known; devotion to the wound of the Heart has perceived therein the symbol of the Heart wounded with love. From these discoveries of love has sprung the devotion to the Sacred Heart.[24]

Never would it lose touch with its contemplative origin, any more than a plant becomes severed from its roots when it rises above ground. Church History is not made by a series of changes from external causes succeeding each other in time; it is the growth of a continuous life that holds within itself the cause of each change. Devotion to the Sacred Heart, as an integral part of that life, follows the same law. The first souls to discover and to pray to the Divine Heart were contemplatives who had fled from the world for the world's own eventual good. Their rigorous cloister let them see the wide horizons of love. The thoughts that moved them and the words they used have come down to us by those traditions, vital though scarcely perceptible, which are to the members of the Mystical Body of Christ what the laws of heredity are to the whole human race; they make the soul's life what it is. The Devotion to the Sacred Heart, in our own day a source of missionary zeal and social action, has never lost its cloistered character; it can only live by prayer. It is still true that "meditation is the cause of devotion."

NOTES

1. A. C. Schonbach, *Old German Sermons*, III. Quoted in K. Richstaetter, *Illustrious Friends of the Sacred Heart* (St. Louis, Herder, 1930), p. 31.

2. *Summa Theologica*, II-II, q. 82, a. 1.

3. Ps. 38, 4.

4. *Summa Theologica*, II–II, q. 82, a. 3.

5. *Ibid.*, a. 4.

6. St. Jerome, "Life of St. Paul," in *The Desert Fathers*, trans. by Helen Waddell (New York, Holt, 1936), p. 48.

7. *Dialogues of St. Gregory*, Bk. II, P.L. LXVI, 196.

8. *Rule of St. Benedict*, P.L. LXVI, 218.

9. G. M. Hopkins, *Note-Books and Papers* (New York, Oxford, 1937), p. 299.

10. *Heliand,* Karl Simrock, ed. (Berlin, 1882).

11. *The Junius Manuscript,* P. Krapp, ed. (New York, Columbia, 1931), pp. 152, ll. 540 ff.

12. *The Christ of Cynewulf,* A. S. Cook, ed. (Boston, Ginn, 1894), p. 54, ll. 1446 ff.

13. Richstaetter, *op. cit.,* p. 26.

14. *Meditation X, P.L.* CLVIII, 761.

15. *Sermo in Cantico LXI,* P. L. CLXXXIII, 1070.

16. P.L. CLXXXIV, 368.

17. *In Cantico,* Sermon XXII, P.L. CLXXXIV, 113, 155. The passage on "the Heart of our Solomon" was quoted by the Postulator of 1697 as evidence of explicit Devotion to the Sacred Heart in the twelfth century, though the heart of flesh is only referred to implicitly.

18. *De Emmanuale,* P.L. CXCVI, 655.

19. P.L. XL, 960. This treatise has often been attributed to Saint Augustine, a tribute to the warmth of his heart and of his style.

20. Lessons VIII and IX of Matins for the Feast of the Sacred Heart.

21. *Vitis Mystica,* P.L. CLXXXIV, 635. From the Prologue and Chapter III.

22. P.L. CLXXXIV, 1322. In the MSS this hymn called "Ad Cor" appears as one section of a longer work entitled *Rhythmica Oratio ad Unum Quodlibet Membrorum Christi Patientis.* Internal evidence points to separate composition, probably at an earlier date than the compilation. Migne places it among the works of Saint Bernard; for its attribution to Bl. Hermann Joseph, see Bainvel, *op. cit.,* p. 166, and Richstaetter, *op. cit.,* p. 40.

23. Ecclus. 44, 6.

24. Bainvel, *op. cit.,* p. 133.

CHAPTER V

A FIRE SHALL FLAME OUT
1200–1417

"My Heart is yours."

As the Middle Ages drew to their high point in the thirteenth century the life of the Church became more and more closely woven into the earth-rooted lives of hearty, healthy men and women who were securely conscious of the fact that the frontiers of this goodly world are heaven and hell. Their year was calendared by the Liturgy, their swords were hilted by a cross. Christ in His humanity, anointed by the Spirit with every virtue that could elevate the ways of men, walked among them. He could be found in the leper or in the knight, and His Mother took her sunlit place as queen in cathedral windows. The familiarity that took divine things for granted could be abused; the sermon of Innocent IV "On the Five Wounds of the Church" amply recognized the fact. But where this same familiarity kept the sacramental outlook which sees the things of sense as obvious symbols of things of the spirit, there sanctity flamed high. Warm realism was stronger than abstract thought in meditation; the lovers of Christ were exceedingly familiar with His Heart.[1]

The writings of the preceding centuries sound today like a bell calling to prayer, followed by the far chanting of monks whose faces are hidden in their cowls. In the thirteenth and fourteenth centuries the sounds are more individual; men and women of strong personality are sharply etched not only in their cloisters but in their gardens, and some of them are on the open roads. Their thoughts on the Sacred Heart are recorded not only in treatises but in prayers and in confidences made one to another, even in conversations with the divine Lover which the listeners of a later age can overhear. Of the voices heard speaking, one is human and one divine; the God-man Himself is inviting familiarity.

The human speaker in the first of such conversations to be recorded is a Cistercian nun of Aywières, in Brabant, Saint Lutgarde (1182–1246). As a young girl she had been turned from worldly affections by a vision of Christ showing her the wound in His side "as though freshly bleeding," and saying: "Here you shall contemplate forever what you love and why you love." A contemporary biographer, Thomas à Cantimpré, relates that she once asked Our Lord to take away from her the miraculous understanding of the Psalter that He had granted, and

. . . to give her a better gift. And the Lord said to her: "What do you want?" "I want," said she, "Thy Heart." And the Lord said: "I, rather, want *your* heart." And she: "So be it, Lord. But take it in such wise that the love of Thy Heart may be mingled in the love of mine, and that in Thee I may possess Thy Heart, at all times secure in Thy protection." And thus was made that intercommunion of hearts in which, rather, there is union of spirit between the created and the Uncreated, by an exceeding grace; and this is that of which the Apostle spoke: "He who clings to God is one spirit with Him." Hear, O reader, while I tell a marvel: from that day on, as a nurse with a fan watches an infant in the cradle, lest the buzzing of flies should annoy it, so Christ guarded her safely in the hollow of His Heart.

And once, when she was hurrying weak and ill to Matins in the middle of the night:

At the door of the church Christ appeared to her, nailed to the cross and bleeding. And lowering one arm He caught her as she went by, and drew her mouth to the wound in His right side. And there she drank such sweetness that ever after she was stronger and readier in the service of God.[2]

Saint Lutgarde is the first, as far as is known, to whom mystic revelations concerning the Heart of Christ were granted. From that day to this no period in the history of the Devotion to the Sacred Heart has been unmarked by phenomena extraordinary even in the supernatural order. Especially have two of the manifestations granted to the Flemish Saint—the mystical exchange of hearts between the Lover and the beloved, and the call to drink from the streams that flow from the Heart's wound of the Crucified—been repeated again and again. No dogmatic teaching of the Church has ever been allowed to rest on a private revelation; no act of faith in any matter so revealed, or in any mystical manifestation such as visions, ecstatic states or the stigmata, has ever been required of the faithful. Yet, slow and scientific as the Church may be in admitting such manifestations as facts, she has always granted their possibility; and she implicitly accepts their actuality when she canonizes those who have received these purposeful graces, or when she extends her liturgical cycle because of them. Her devotional life has thus been so enriched that each of her members comes to share, in a measure, in the gifts given to the few. Such favors seem most at home in the warm familiarity of the mediaeval cloisters where they were first granted, yet the various mental climates of the centuries following have neither chilled nor checked them. Through them Devotion to the Sacred Heart reached out from the cloister to take on the ways and tones of the lay world.

Not long after the death of Saint Lutgarde, a five-year-old girl named Gertrude (1256–1302) was brought to the monastery at Helfta, clothed in a small Benedictine habit, and entrusted to the care of Mechtilde von Hackeborn whose sister, another Gertrude, was then Abbess. Under the latter's guidance Helfta had reached its golden age; it was lovely with gardens that invited spiritual joy, it was wise with books where the best of classical and theological learning lay stored, and it was holy with the perfection of the liturgical worship that rose from its choirs. It was holy also in its many saints, of whom the child Gertrude swiftly became the greatest. In her youth a passion for books and learning almost halted her, but the sight of Our Lord's face when He met her in the corridor one evening drew her wholly after Him. Before long she was praying: "Through Thy wounded Heart, dearest Lord, pierce my heart so deeply with the dart of Thy love that it may no longer be able to contain earthly things, but may be governed by the action of Thy divinity alone." The prayer was answered; Our Lord said to another of His familiar friends, "If you look for Me, you will find Me in the heart of Gertrude."[3]

It was the Sacred Heart as it is in heaven that drew her upward with abounding joy; and in figures drawn from the Liturgy and

from her own poetic soul she wrote of what she saw, sometimes
in spontaneous poetry:

> O everlasting summer;
> Safe dwelling;
> O house replete with all delight;
> O Paradise of undeparting joy.
> Flowing streams of indescribable pleasures.
>
> Enticing verdure of all beauty,
> Filled with flowers;
> Soothing with sweet murmurs;
> Nay, with the sweetly moving melody of ordered notes;
> Refreshing with the odorous breath
> Of life-giving spices;
> Exhilarating, with the melting sweetness
> Of savors inwardly perceived,
> With wonderful caresses which pass not.
> Oh, what he sees, what he hears,
> What he smells and tastes and feels!
> Though everything an angel knows,
> And all a man can understand
> Became our knowledge,
> Unshakable, serene,
> The instrument could never shape
> A single sentence to express
> Thy excellence,
> Thy eminence,
> O divine Heart.[4]

Almost as poetic is the prose of her *Legatus Divinae Pietatis,*
partly written by her own hand and partly collected from her say-
ings by her sisters, in which this "Saint of the holy Humanity"
recorded her austerely radiant inner life:

As Gertrude offered her heart to God in the following manner:
"Lord, behold my heart, which is detached from all creatures; I offer
it to Thee freely, beseeching Thee to purify it in the sanctifying waters
of Thy adorable side, and to adorn it with the precious Blood of Thy
sweetest Heart, and to unite it to Thee by the odors of charity," Our
Lord appeared to her and offered to the eternal Father her heart,
united to His own, under the form of a chalice, the two parts of which
were joined together by wax. The saint, perceiving this, said with

extreme fervor: "Grant me the grace, most loving Lord, that my heart may be always before Thee like the flasks which princes use, so that Thou mayest have it cleansed and filled and emptied according to Thy good pleasures, whenever and however Thou willest." . . .

"But is it possible," she said, "that Thy deified Heart is suspended like a lamp in the midst of mine which is, alas, so unworthy of its presence when at the same time I have the joy of finding in Thyself this very same source of all delight?" "It is even so," replied the Lord; "when you wish to take hold of anything, you stretch forth your hand and then withdraw it again after you have taken it, so also the love I bear towards you causes Me to extend My Heart to draw you to Me, when you are distracting yourself with exterior things; and then when you have recollected yourself I withdraw My Heart, and you along with it, so that you may enter into Me; and thus I make you taste the sweetness of all virtues."

Then, as she considered on one hand with exceeding wonder and gratitude, the greatness of the charity God had for her, and on the other her own nothingness and the great number of her faults, she retired with profound self-contempt into the valley of humility, esteeming herself unworthy of any grace, and when she had remained therein for some time, He who loves to pour forth His gifts on the humble seemed to make a golden tube come forth from His Heart, which descended upon this humble soul in the form of a lamp, making a channel through which He poured forth on her the abundance of all His marvels; so that when she humbled herself at the recollection of her faults, Our Lord poured forth on her from His Sacred Heart all the virtues and beauty of His divine perfection, which concealed her imperfection from the eyes of the divine Goodness.[5]

Jesus Christ once appeared to the saint and, showing her His Heart, said to her: "My Beloved, give Me your Heart." And as she presented it to Him with profound respect, it seemed to her that He united it to His by a canal which reached to the ground, through which He poured forth abundantly the effusions of His infinite grace, saying to her: "Henceforth I shall use your heart as a canal through which I will pour forth the impetuous torrents of mercy and consolation which flow from My loving Heart on all those who shall dispose themselves to receive it by having recourse to you with humility and confidence."[6]

These experiences, so simply and richly worded, were woven into the pattern of the Church's year as it moved from feast to feast, till other devotions and mysteries were made part of the central mystery of the love of Christ's Heart:

In the evening [of the Feast of the Assumption] at Vespers, the saint beheld Our Lord drawing into His Heart all the praises which had been chanted in honor of His Blessed Mother, and thence pouring them forth upon her in an impetuous torrent. As the antiphon *Ista pulchra est* was chanted, Gertrude offered the words to Our Lord through His Sacred Heart in memory of the sweet caresses He had bestowed on His Blessed Mother by the same words; and this devotion, passing through the Heart of Jesus to the Heart of Mary, encircled her like a cincture of stars, consoling her in a marvelous manner. Many of these stars appeared to fall to the ground, but the saints gathered them up, presenting them to Our Lord with joy and admiration. This signified that all the saints obtain ineffable joy, glory and beatitude from the superabundant merits of the Blessed Virgin. . . .[7]

As Saint Gertrude prayed very devoutly on the Vigil of Pentecost that she might be prepared to receive the Holy Ghost, she heard Our Lord saying these words to her interiorly with great love: "You will receive the virtue of the Holy Spirit who is coming to you." But while she felt extreme joy and satisfaction at these words, she thought also of her utter unworthiness, and it appeared to her as if a cave were made in her heart, which became deeper and deeper as this sentiment increased in her soul. Then she saw a stream of honey coming forth from the Heart of Jesus, and distilling itself into hers, until it was entirely filled. From this she understood that it was the unction and grace of the Holy Ghost which flowed thus sweetly from the Heart of the Son of God into the hearts of the faithful. . . .

After she had communicated, she offered the whole life of Jesus Christ to God the Father in satisfaction for her fault of never having made a sufficiently worthy preparation to receive Him into her heart, even from the hour of her regeneration in baptism. Then she saw the Holy Ghost in the form of a dove, descending from heaven upon the adorable Sacrament with an impetuous flight like that of an eagle; and seeking the sweet Heart of Jesus He appeared to enter therein and find there a most agreeable abode.[8]

Gertrude came at last to share with Saint John, as another "disciple whom Jesus loved," the intimacies of the Last Supper:

Then Our Lord made her rest on His Heart so that her soul touched it, and as she remained there some time she felt two most sweet and admirable movements therein. Then the Lord said to her: "Each of these movements operates the salvation of man in three different manners. The first operates the salvation of sinners; the second that of the just. By the first I converse continually with My eternal Father; I appease His anger against sinners and incline Him to show mercy. By the second I speak to My saints, excusing sinners to them and urging them, with the zeal and fidelity of a brother, to intercede with God for them. By the third, I speak to sinners themselves, calling them mercifully to penance and awaiting their conversion with ineffable desire.

"By the second movement of My Heart, I invite My Father to rejoice with Me for having poured forth My precious blood so efficaciously for the just, in whose merits I find so many delights. Secondly, I invite all the heavenly host to praise My providences, that they may return Me thanks for all the benefits which I have granted them, and that I may grant them more for the future. Thirdly, I speak to the just, giving them many salutary caresses and warning them to profit faithfully by them, from day to day and hour by hour. As the pulsations of the human heart are not interrupted by seeing, hearing or any manual occupation, but always continue without relaxation, so the care of the government of heaven and earth and the whole universe cannot diminish or interrupt for a moment these two movements of My divine Heart, which will continue to the end of ages."[9]

Saint John himself, on his feast day, led her to the most significant of all her revelations, one in which the role of the Devotion to the Sacred Heart in the life of the Church found clear expression:

This Apostle appeared to the saint as she assisted at Matins on his feast, when she applied herself with special fervor to her usual exercises. Gertrude then recommended some of the religious of whom she had charge very fervently to him; he received her prayer very lovingly and said: "I am like my Master in this—that I love those who love me." The saint inquired: "What grace then, and what benefit, can I hope for, who am so unworthy, on your dear Feast?" "Come," he replied, "come with me, thou elect one of my Lord, and let us repose together on the sweetest bosom of the Lord, in which all the treasures of beatitude lie hidden." Then, taking her up in spirit, he presented her to our loving Savior, and having placed her on His right, he placed himself on the left and reposed there. Then he exclaimed, pointing reverently to the bosom of Jesus: "Behold, this is the Saint of saints who draws to Himself all that is good in heaven and on earth." She then inquired of Saint John why he placed himself on the left hand and had given the right to her. He replied: "It is because I have become one spirit with God, and am able to penetrate where flesh cannot enter, but you are not yet able to penetrate into such high things because you are still in the flesh. I have therefore placed you at the opening of the Divine Heart, from whence you may drink in all the sweet consolations which flow from it with such impetuous abundance that it is capable of satisfying all who desire to taste thereof."

Then, as she felt the constant pulsations of the Divine Heart, and rejoiced exceedingly thereat, she said to the saint: "Beloved of God, didst thou not feel these pulsations when thou wert lying on the Lord's breast at the Last Supper?" "Yes," he replied, "and this with such plenitude that liquid does not enter more rapidly into bread than the sweetness of these pleasures penetrated my soul, so that my spirit became more ardent than water under the action of a glowing fire." "And why," she inquired, "have you neither said nor written anything of this for our edification?" He replied: "Because I was charged with instructing the newly formed Church concerning the mysteries of the uncreated Word, that these truths might be transmitted to future ages as far as thou wouldst be capable of comprehending them, for no one can comprehend them entirely; and I deferred speaking of these divine pulsations until these latter days, that the world might be aroused from its torpor and animated, when it had grown cold, by hearing of these things."[10]

Thus Saint John made known what he had learned in the Cenacle, that souls still in the flesh may penetrate by prayer through the open wound of the Heart into the love of the Godhead, and draw from it the fire that alone can kindle a torpid world. Thus is the divine Heart the source of both prayer and apostolate. The expression "these latter days," *tempore moderno,* refers directly to the times in which Saint Gertrude lived; it indicates with equal clearness that the Devotion to the Heart of fire holds the graces of regeneration with equal plenitude for our own "modern times."

Gertrude found understanding souls at Helfta with whom to share her secrets. To Mechtilde of Magdeburg Our Lord had also granted visions of His Heart. "In my great sufferings," she wrote, "God revealed Himself to my soul, showed me the wound of His Heart, and said: 'See how they have hurt Me.'" From the prayers and poems of Mechtilde von Hackeborn in the *Liber Specialis Gratiae* it is evident that Devotion to the Sacred Heart was beginning to offer a way of life to those who penetrated its spirit, with definite practices through which virtue could grow strong, and the day be sanctified from the morning salutation to "the Heart of thy heavenly Friend," through the aspirations which, at each striking of the clock, commended "to Thy Divine Heart all that I have done in the hour that is gone," to a prayer for "needful sleep" at night.

The life at Helfta followed the ancient Benedictine pattern, but in the meantime the Church had renewed her youth in the fervent advent of the new Mendicant Orders that had come into being in the early thirteenth century (1209). When Saint Francis of Assisi took to the roads as God's minstrel, he drew all manner of men after him, even to the heights of Mount Alvernus where his flesh was pierced with the wounds of Christ in hands and feet and side. In his followers the Devotion to the Passion was marked by an immediacy that came of living close to the human Christ, as starkly poor as He, as tenderly compassionate, as courageous for suffering.[11] If they could not give their blood in return for His, they gave Him the pity of blood-brothers. It was a matter of heart to Heart, for the Franciscan nuns as well as for the "brothers of the birds and fishes." Many times a day Saint Clare saluted and adored the Divine Heart in the Blessed Sacrament. Saint Margaret of Cortona (d. 1297) would say to those who sought her: "Lay thy hands on the wounds of His hands,"[12] and be led to His Heart, while Angela of Foligno (d. 1309), wrestling with the mysteries of contemplative union in prayer, found that "the Heart of our most sweet Jesus was full of these things, and overflowing, infinitely more so than He showed in His body."[13] Saint Anthony of Padua, through mention of the divine Heart, brought the beat of warm affection into the elaborate metaphors of his sermons. But it was Saint Bonaventure (1221–1274), "Seraphic Doctor" because his spirit was one of burning love, and Minister General of his Order, who was the first of the Franciscans to stand in spirit by the Crucified after death and wait for the piercing of His Heart. The *Lignum Vitae* was a treatise on mysticism, in which he found that the "eighth fruit" of the Tree of Life is victory in the struggle with death:

At last, when the innocent lamb who is the true sun of justice had hung for the space of three hours on the cross, and for the same length of time the visible sun, compassionating its Maker, had hidden its rays of light, then, when all things were consummated, the very

Fountain of life ran dry, when Jesus, God and man, with a great cry and with tears, showing the depths of His mercy and declaring the power of His divinity, died, giving His soul into the hands of His Father. Then "the veil of the temple was torn from the top to the bottom, the earth shook, the rocks were rent, and the graves opened." Then the centurion knew Him for the true God. Then those who had gathered to jeer at the sight of Him went back, beating their breasts. Then the most beautiful of the sons of men made a fragrant holocaust in the sight of His Father's glory, "that He might turn away His wrath from us."

Look down then, O Lord, holy Father, from Thy sanctuary in the high dwellings of heaven; look down, I say, upon the face of Thy Christ; this holy host which our High Priest offers to Thee for our sins, and be placated for the wickedness of Thy people. And thou also, O redeemed man, think who, what, and how great is He who hangs for thee on the cross, whose death gives life to the dead, at whose passing heaven and earth mourn, and hard stones are rent as by natural pity. O human heart, thou art harder than any stone if at the memory of such love thou art not struck by terror, not moved by compassion, not torn by grief nor softened by love!

Then was it decreed by divine ordinance that one of the soldiers should pierce this sacred side, opening it with a lance, that from the side of Christ sleeping upon the cross the Church might be formed, and the Scriptures might be fulfilled which said: "They shall look upon Him whom they pierced"; and that the price of our salvation might be poured out in blood mingled with water, which from that fountain, the secret depths of His Heart, would give power to the Sacraments of the Church to give the life of grace, and would be for those who live in Christ the cup of living waters, springing up unto life everlasting. Lo, now indeed that lance, by the wickedness of Saul, of the reprobate Jewish people, has, by divine mercy, through the wide wound opened in that partition, made a cleft in the rock and a hollow place in the wall, as a dwelling place for doves.

Arise then, friend of Christ, be like the dove making a nest in the depths of the hole; there, like the sparrow that has found herself a house, watch without ceasing; there like the turtle hide the eggs of chaste love; there place thy mouth, that thou mayest draw water from the Savior's fountains. For this is that fountain flowing in the midst of Paradise which, dividing into four streams and poured out into a devoted heart, waters and makes fruitful the whole earth.[14]

Saint Bonaventure wrote also a treatise of direction to some nuns, entitled *On Perfection of Life:*

Since the fervor of devotion must be nourished and kept alive in man through frequent remembering of Christ's passion, it is necessary that he who would have unquenchable devotion in himself must often and always see with the eyes of his heart Christ dying on the cross. For this the Lord said in Leviticus: "The fire on my altar ever burns, which the priest feeds by throwing on wood each day." Listen, most devout Mother, the altar of God is thy heart; on this altar must ever burn the fire of fervent devotion, which thou must feed each day with the wood of the cross of Christ, and with the memory of his passion. Thus says the Prophet Isaias: "You shall draw water with joy out of the Savior's fountains," as though to say: "whoever desires of God the waters of grace, the waters of devotion, the waters of tears, let him draw them from the Savior's fountains, that is, from the five wounds of Christ."

Draw near then, O handmaid, with the footsteps of thine affection, to Jesus wounded, to Jesus crowned with a garland of thorns, to Jesus fixed to the gibbet of the cross; and not only see in His hands the mark of the nails with Blessed Thomas the Apostle, not only put thy fingers into the place of the nails, not only put thy hand into His side, but enter in wholly by the door of the side to the very Heart of Jesus. There transformed into Christ by most ardent love of the Crucified, fastened by the nails of divine fear, transfixed in thine inmost heart by the lance of love, pierced through by the sword of deep compassion, seek nothing else, desire nothing else, will to be consoled by nothing else than this: that thou canst die on the cross with Christ. Then with the Apostle Paul thou wilt cry out and say: "With Christ I am nailed to the cross. I live now not I, but Christ liveth in me."[15]

While the Franciscans were following Lady Poverty from town to town, the Dominicans had enlisted in a holy war against heresy. They had been founded (1216) as a result of Saint Dominic's crusade against the Albigensians, and it was soon seen that book-learning and zeal-bright theology were to be their best weapons in the wars of the Church. It was the Dominicans who in the four-teenth century first celebrated a Feast in honor of the Five Wounds, with a proper Office, the ninth lesson of which told how the lance of Longinus had "opened a way into the Heart of the Lord."[16] They were found before long, in every country, as spiritual directors in convents, including Helfta itself; thus, to a very large extent, the outpouring of mystical graces that marked those years was controlled, recorded, and often inspired by the intellectually trained Dominicans who, in their devotion to the Gift of Wisdom, found it, as Saint John had done, while resting upon the Heart of Christ.

Saint Albertus Magnus (1206–1280), teacher of Saint Thomas and, after him, greatest of Dominican scholars, brought the inquiring mind of a scientist into his prayer. He marvelled that blood could still have flowed from a heart already cold in death, and he found the answer in that heart's deathless love. It is he who, at the time of the institution of the Feast of Corpus Christi, first connected the Devotion to the Sacred Heart with the Blessed Sacrament, marking how in the Heart of Our Lord "is preserved the manna of grace which dispenses the Holy Eucharist to us. . . . Goodness, and gentle condescension, affection and sympathy, love and pity have induced the Divine Heart to bestow this gift upon us."[17] Blessed Henry Suso, "minnesinger of God," was writing prose lyrics in his *Little Book of the Eternal Wisdom,* in which he revealed how to prepare for Communion: "Ah, sweet Lord, that I might receive from the open wounds of my Beloved, from His Heart, a single small drop of blood." And Eternal Wisdom answered him: "The soul should sing Me a song of Sion, that is, a song of praise, then will I embrace her and she shall lean on My breast."[18] While the fourteenth century was bringing the coldness, abuse and scandal of which Saint John had spoken to Saint Gertrude, two other great souls were holding up the flame of the spiritual life while worldliness was quenching it where it should have shone brightest: in the lives of churchmen in high places. One, John Tauler, was a Dominican preacher, the other, Saint Catherine of Siena, a Dominican tertiary.

Tauler (1300–1361) sought the root cause of the mysteries of the life of Our Lord, and found them in the Sacred Heart. He was a popular preacher, earnest and quiet, who yet "set the whole world aflame by his fiery tongue," said those who heard him. He strove in his theology to find a way by which the sanctified man might reach even in this life, be it but fleetingly, the *visio essentiae Dei* for which he himself longed; but while his mind scaled these high and perilous places—and the accuracy of his theological views concerning them may be questioned—his heart found comfort in the passion-mysticism where he knocked at the "tenderly disclosed Heart and the opened side of Our Lord."

Christ's side was also, doubtless, opened that we might have access and entrance into His Heart. . . . It was opened, and straightway there flowed forth the sacraments. From this is seen Christ's incomprehensible love towards us, since He hath spent His whole self upon us. Nothing hath He hidden in His Heart which He hath not wholly given to us. What more could He have done for us than He hath done? His own Heart He hath opened to us, as His most secret chamber, wherein to introduce us as His elect bride. For His delights are to be with us; and in the peacefulness of silence and in silent peacefulness, to take His rest among us. He hath given us, I say, His Heart fearfully wounded, that we may dwell therein until, utterly purified and cleansed and conformed to His Heart, we may be made fit and worthy to be led with Him into the divine Heart of the eternal Father. He giveth us His own Heart to be our dwelling, and asketh in return for ours, that it may be His dwelling.

He giveth us, I say, His Heart, even as a bed adorned with the red roses of His own purple blood, and He asketh in return our own heart, even as a bed decorated for Him with the white lilies of clean works. Who will dare to refuse Him what He Himself, in His rich bounty, hath bestowed upon us? Behold! He inviteth us into His sweet wounds, and into His loving and open side, even as into a rich wine-cellar flowing with all delights, saying to us in the words of the Canticle: "Come, My Sister, My dove, into the holes of the rock," that is, into My sacred wounds. Who hath a heart so iron and so stony as not to be touched by such love and kindness, when He who is the King almighty, immense, eternal, embraceth us with such mighty love, who are but dust and ashes? And yet, Oh the shame and the sorrow; we turn our back upon Him and despise so great a majesty. This is why Augustine crieth out in the person of Christ: "Weigh with thyself, O man, of what kind and how great was the suffering which I underwent for thy salvation. When thou wert still My enemy I led thee back into My Father's favor. When thou wert wandering as a lost sheep, I sought thee for long and with much sweat and labor, and when I had found thee I brought thee back upon My shoulders with great suffering to My Father. I submitted My head to the crown of thorns, I laid My hands and feet open to the nails, I bent My whole body patiently to scourges; I shed My blood even to the last little drop; I gave My soul for thee that I might join thee unto Me by love; and yet thou withdrawest and art separated from Me. Lastly, I opened My Heart to thee, and gave thee the rosy blood of My Heart to drink. What more askest thou of Me? Tell Me, I pray thee, how I

may soften and turn and draw thee to My love, and of a truth I will
do it unto thee."[19]

The year 1370 was a dark one in the life of the Church; Pope
Gregory IX was in Avignon, not Rome, and the shadow of
schism hung over Christendom. It was a turning point in the life
of Saint Catherine of Siena (1347–1380). She had lived as a hermit in her father's house, then emerged as an apostle in her artistic, gay and factious city. On July 10, 1370, she was granted a
vision in which Our Lord drew her to Himself and made her drink
long from His Heart. Then He took her heart from her breast and
put His own in its place. Transformed by this exchange she lived
from then on in unbroken union with Him, spending herself for
the Church and for souls. She wrote (or rather dictated, for she
was unlettered) in the strong Tuscan that had just come into its
own as a literary language, and even in a letter would break
spontaneously into prayer:

In Thy nature, O eternal God, I recognize my own nature. And
what is my nature, O unthinkable Love? It is fire! For Thou art but
the fire of love, and this nature Thou hast given to man. Then my
soul, seized by desire, entered wholly into His side, and there I acquired such knowledge of the divinity and experienced so much sweetness, that I cannot understand why my heart was not broken by the
strength of love. . . .[20]

Her *Dialogue* or *Treatise on Divine Providence* has been called
the mystical counterpart of Dante's *Divine Comedy*. While her
letters, spiritual as they are, reflect the tumultuous history of both
Church and State in her own time, the *Dialogue* turns full-face to
eternity; it is a series of colloquies between the soul of Catherine
(which is the soul of Everyman) and the Eternal Father. Uniting them is the heart-centered humanity of Christ. These dialogues
are real conversations, enthusiastic outpourings of questions, answers and exclamations, in which homely, bold (and sometimes
mixed) metaphors strive with each other to explain the inexplicable.

Then the eternal God, to enamour and excite that soul still more
for the salvation of souls, replied to her and said: "First, as I have
shown thee that which thou didst wish, and ask Me, I will now explain
to thee the nature of this Bridge. I have told thee, My daughter, that

the Bridge reaches from heaven to earth; this is through the union which I have made with man, whom I formed of the clay of the earth. Now learn that this Bridge, My only-begotten Son, has three steps, of which two were made with the wood of the most holy cross, and the third still retains the great bitterness He tasted when He was given gall and vinegar to drink. In these three steps you will recognize three states of the soul, which I will explain to thee below. The feet of the soul, signifying her affection, are the first step, for the feet carry the body as the affection carries the soul. Wherefore these pierced feet are steps by which thou canst arrive at His side, which manifests to thee the secret of His Heart, because the soul, rising on the steps of her affection, commences to taste the love of His Heart, gazing into that open Heart of My Son with the eyes of the intellect, and finds it consumed with ineffable love. I say consumed, because He does not love you for His own profit, because you can be of no profit to Him, He being one and the same thing with Me. Then the soul is filled with love, seeing herself so much loved. Having passed the second step, the soul reaches out to the third—that is, to the mouth,—where she finds peace from the terrible war she has been waging with sin. On the first step, then, lifting her feet from the affections of the earth, the soul strips herself of vice; on the second she fills herself with love and virtue; and on the third she tastes peace. So the Bridge has three steps, in order that, climbing past the first and second, you may reach the last, which is lifted on high, so that the water, running beneath, may not touch it; for in my Son was no venom of sin. This Bridge is lifted on high, and yet, at the same time, joined to the earth. Dost thou know when it was lifted on high? When My Son was lifted up on the wood of the most holy cross, the divine nature remaining joined to the lowliness of the earth of your humanity.

"For this reason I said to thee that, being lifted on high, He was not lifted out of the earth, for the divine nature is united and kneaded into one thing with it. And there was no one who could go on the Bridge until it had been lifted on high, wherefore He said: '*Si exaltatus fuero a terra, omnia traham ad meipsum,*' that is, 'If I am lifted on high, I will draw all things to Me.' My Goodness, seeing that in no other way could you be drawn to Me, sent Him in order that He should be lifted on high on the wood of the cross, making of it an anvil on which My Son, born of human generation, should be remade, in order to free you from death and to restore you to the life of grace; wherefore He drew everything to Himself by these means, namely, by showing the ineffable love with which I love you, the heart of man being always attracted by love. Greater love, then, I could not show you, than to lay down My life for you; perforce, then, My Son was treated in this way by love, in order that ignorant man should be unable to resist being drawn to Me. . . ."[21]

"Open the eyes of thy intellect and see perfect souls running by the Bridge of the doctrine of Christ crucified, which was their rule, way and doctrine. They place none other before the eye of their intellect than Christ crucified, not the Father, as they do who are in imperfect love and do not wish to suffer pain, but only to have the delight which they find in Me. But they, as if drunken with love and burning with it, have gathered together and ascended the three steps, which I figured to thee as the three powers of the soul, and also the three actual steps, figured to thee as in the Body of My only Son, Christ crucified, by which steps the soul, as I told thee, ascended, first climbing to the feet, with the feet of the soul's affection; from thence arriving at the side, where she found the secret of the Heart and knew the baptism of water, which has virtue through the blood, and where I dispose the soul to receive grace, uniting and kneading her together in the blood. Where did the soul know of this her dignity, in being kneaded and united with the blood of the Lamb, receiving the grace in holy baptism, in virtue of the blood? In the side, where she knew the fire of divine charity. And so, if thou rememberest well, My Truth manifested to thee, when thou didst ask, saying: 'Sweet and immaculate Lamb, Thou wert dead when Thy side was opened. Why then didst Thou want to be struck and have Thy Heart divided?' And He replied to thee, telling thee that there was occasion enough for it; but the principal part of what He said I will tell thee. He said: 'Because My desire towards the human generation was ended, and I had finished the actual work of bearing pain and torment, and yet I had not been able to show, by finite things, because My love was infinite, how much love I had, I wished thee to see the secret of the Heart, showing it to thee open, so that thou mightest see how much more I loved than I could show thee by finite pain. I poured from it blood and water, to show thee the baptism of water, which is received in virtue of the blood. . . .

" 'This is in virtue of the infinite divine nature, united with the finite human nature, which human nature endures pain in Me, the Word, clothed with your humanity. But because the one nature is steeped in and united with the other, the eternal Deity drew to Himself the pain which I suffered with so much fire and love. And therefore can this operation be called infinite, not that My pain, neither the actuality of the body be infinite, nor the pain of the desire that I had to complete your redemption, because it was terminated and finished on the cross, when the soul was separated from the body; but the fruit which came out of the pain and desire for your salvation is infinite, and therefore you receive it infinitely. Had it not been infinite, the whole human generation could not have been restored to grace, neither the past, the present, nor the future. This I manifested in the opening of My side, where is found the secret of the Heart, showing that I loved more than I could show with finite pain. I showed to thee that My love was infinite. How? By the baptism of blood, united with the fire of My charity, and by the general baptism given to Christians, and to whomsoever will receive it, and by the baptism of water, united with the blood and the fire, wherein the soul is steeped. And, in order to show this, it was necessary for the blood to come out of My side. Now I have shown thee (said My Truth to thee) what thou askedst of Me.' "[22]

By 1378 the Great Western Schism had broken out, and Saint Catherine spent her last strength in the cause of the rightful Pope, Urban VI. In Rome, she felt herself literally crushed to the earth one day under a great weight, and it was made known to her that the bark of Peter was resting on her prayers. The exchange of her heart for the Heart of Christ had made her a co-redeemer of her times.

It is the nature of love to fulfill itself as soon and as completely as possible, and the Devotion of love has done just this in the lives of many who have lived it fully. Beginning with Saint Lutgarde (and who knows how much earlier?) divine Love has shown itself to the senses under the most tangible of symbols—a living heart. At times this Heart takes possession of another heart with a completeness that has more in it of heaven's fulfillment than of earth's strivings, though ever deeper pain may still follow. It has overridden the barriers of flesh, and in radiant disregard of mortal condition has fulfilled itself in union of hearts here and now. This union, spiritual and invisible, is made visible in the incomprehensible simplicity of mystic experience. The records of these experiences give the tone of high poetry to the story of the Devotion to the Sacred Heart, as the saints try in lyric language to tell what it is to have the body share before its time in the transformations of a soul going from grace to grace. "For if, while you are thus in the Heart of Jesus, divinity absorbs you, blessed are you."[23]

NOTES

1. See Richstaetter, *op. cit.*, for a wealth of illustrative quotations from mediaeval manuscripts.

2. *Acta Sanctorum* for June 11. For a modern biography of Saint Lutgarde, see: Thomas Merton, *What Are These Wounds?* (Bruce, 1950).

3. This tradition is echoed by the Liturgy in the Collect of the Mass for the Feast of Saint Gertrude: "O God, Who didst prepare for Thyself a pleasant dwelling place in the heart of blessed Gertrude, do Thou, through her merits and intercession, mercifully wipe away from our hearts every stain of sin and grant us to enjoy her companionship."

4. *O Beata Trinitas*, trans. by Rev. John Gray (Sheed, 1927), p. 75.

5. *Life and Revelations of Saint Gertrude* (Burns, 1870), pp. 190, 184.

6. *Ibid.*, p. 257.

7. *Ibid.*, p. 435.

8. *Ibid.*, p. 414.

9. *Ibid.*, p. 236.

10. *Ibid.*, p. 315.

11. Later, on October 4, 1673, feast of Saint Francis, Saint Margaret Mary was granted a vision of the Poverello, "clothed with light and with incomprehensible splendor . . . because of his love of the sacred Passion, because of which his crucified Lover impressed His own sacred wounds upon him; this made him one of the most favored friends of His Sacred Heart." Our Lord then indicated to Saint Margaret Mary that Saint Francis was to be her guide in the ways of love. *Vie et Oeuvres* (Paris, 1915), Vol. II, p. 161.

12. Richstaetter, *op. cit.*, p. 73.

13. *Visions and Instructions of Blessed Angela of Foligno* (Benziger, 1903), p. 319.

14. "Lignum Vitae," in *Sancti Bonaventurae Opera Omnia*, Quaracci, ed. (1898), Vol. VIII, p. 79. This passage has been woven into the Liturgy of the Feast of the Sacred Heart as Lesson VII of the Office of Matins.

15. *Ibid.*, p. 120.

16. This Feast was celebrated on the day which Our Lord Himself later indicated to Saint Margaret Mary as the day which He desired for the Feast of His Heart: the Friday after the Octave of Corpus Christi.

17. Richstaetter, *op. cit.*, p. 120.

18. *Ibid.*, p. 135.

19. *Meditations on the Life and Passion of Our Lord Jesus Christ,* trans. by A. Cruikshank (Benziger, 1925), p. 326. Tauler's authorship of these sermons has been questioned. They are, in any case, indicative of the awareness of the Sacred Heart in the German countries in the fourteenth century.

20. From a letter. See: A. Walz, "Sainte Catherine de Sienne et le Sacré Coeur," in *Vie Spirituelle,* LXXVI, 891.

21. *The Dialogue of St. Catherine of Siena,* trans. by Algar Thorold, rev. ed. (Newman, 1950), pp. 77–79.

22. *Ibid.,* pp. 170–172, 173–174.

23. From an anonymous fourteenth-century treatise, quoted in Hamon, Vol. II, p. 227.

CHAPTER VI

"TO MAKE US MERRY"
1200–1417, Continued

*"To go into His Heart is
heaven here and now."*

In the ages of a common faith every educated man in Europe
was bi-lingual. He thought and spoke in his own vernacular, he
read and wrote and most often prayed in Latin. Latin was the
lingua franca of the nations because it was the tongue of their
mother, the Church. It was the language of prayer because the
Liturgy was sung in it; it was the language of learning because the
Universities taught in it. Churchmen saying their Breviaries on
muleback, and wandering scholars, lightheartedly singing for their
supper, carried it back and forth in their journeying over vague
frontiers. It was a healthy Latin that easily passed into colloquial
speech; thus gradually, through translations, paraphrases and lusty
parodies the opulence of Latin passed into the national languages.

Devotions, because they were first expressed in Latin, followed
the same path. When they appeared in the common tongue it was
a sign that people in the castles and villages were sharing what
was treasured in the cloisters. The casual, unobtrusive way in
which references to the Divine Heart first appear in popular religious or even secular literature is significant of the all-pervasive
character of the Devotion, which was found here, there and everywhere before it had time to become conscious of itself. Its terms,
even when colloquial, are theologically sound because they were
first expressed in disciplined Latin. Already, at the end of the
twelfth century, the unknown author of the *Chanson d'Aspremont*
related how, at the court of Charlemagne, a noble duke told the
story of the Savior to a Saracen ambassador:

"A Jew tormented Him on the cross,
And His Heart was run through by a great sharp sword."[1]

At the beginning of the thirteenth century, Walter von der Vogelweide, the arch-minnesinger, was straying from court to court, lamenting the passing of beauty, criticizing those in high places, and calling for a crusade. He sang best when he sang of love, light or lasting, and very poignantly when it was the love of the Heart pierced by the lance, for "Christ His Heart in sorrow broke."[2] Walter's fellow poet, Gottfried von Strasbourg, was then writing his *Tristan,* the immemorial story of fatalistic, pagan love; but to him is also attributed the "Hymn of Praise to Jesus and Mary," in which he turns from sin to "Jesus, the lovely Emperor," who "gives us bliss through His wounded Heart," wide open like His arms to receive back sinners.[3] It is the authentic mark of the Devotion to the Sacred Heart thus to see the physical and not merely the metaphorical Heart of Christ as the symbol of His love for men. These lighthearted livers of their own lyrics found the right theological formula as they thumbed their small harps.

A few years later, in Italy, a turbulent and worldly lawyer named Jacopone da Todi became a Franciscan and turned his enthusiasms into mystical song. His *laude* in the Umbrian dialect are like love-dialogues between his soul and Christ, who said to him:

> Look on My wounded side,
> Pierced and wounded for thee,
> O look on the spear-thrust wide
> Deep in the Heart of Me!
> For there thy name shalt thou see
> Writ on My Heart forever
> By love insatiate.[4]

He has also put into words another unspoken dialogue, held between the Hearts of the Mother and her Son on Calvary:

> Christ: Lady, take My broken Heart
> For thine own to share apart.
> John, beloved as thou art,
> Shall be to thee a son.
>
> Mary: Son, Thy spirit hath gone forth!
> Son of most stupendous worth!

My sight is of its vision dearth,
And bloodless is my heart!

Hear me, Son most innocent,
Son of splendor o'er me spent,
Passing to Thine element,
With darkness for my part.

Son of whiteness and of rose,
Son unrivalled as the snows,
Son my bosom held so close,
My heart, why hast thou gone?

Son of beauty and of gold,
Son whose eyes all gladness told,
Son, why hath the world so cold
Thee cast scorn upon?

Son so gentle and so meek,
Son to all the sad and weak,
O how bitterly they wreak
Evil on Thy head!

John, my nephew, look and see;
Dead thy brother now must be;
For I feel the sword through me
As the prophet said.

Slain are mother here and Son,
Stricken by this blow as one,
Clasped in final union
On the cross of dread.[5]

In England, about 1225, three young girls left the Plantagenet court and formed a small community somewhere in Dorset, claiming to be anchoresses though they were three, not one, behind the window with its cross-marked curtain that kept them free from the excitements of the nobility. In their zeal and inexperience they asked their director (possibly the wise-hearted Dominican, Friar Robert Bacon) to write a rule for them. So he wrote, with some trouble to himself as he took pains to tell them affectionately, the famous *Ancren Riwle*. Its warm, friendly, sparkling style went straight to the soul through the heart. It was in two parts: a rule for the inner life that "rules the heart and makes it all even and smooth," and a rule for the outer life that saw to it that "anchoresses shall have no beast but one cat."

One section is entitled "why men ought and must love Jesus Christ, and what takes His love from us and keeps us from loving Him." The anchoresses may have been aloof from men, but they were of their times, which were the times of knighthood. Prayer as well as warfare was chivalrous, exciting in its valor and pageantry. Cloistered souls as well as courtly had their knight, who won them with the blood of His Heart, as we read in "The Parable of the Knight and the Lady":

God hath won our love in all kinds of ways, and hereto belongs a tale and a veiled parable.

A lady there was who was beset all about with foes, and her land destroyed, and she was all poor within her earthen castle. Yet a mighty Knight's love was turned upon her, so immeasurably strong that for the wooing of her He sent His messengers one after the other, and often many together. He sent her baubles both many and fair, and means of livelihood, and the help of His high army to hold her castle. She took it all as a thing of no account, for she was so hard-hearted that He could never come near to her love. What wilt thou more? He came at last Himself, and showed her His fair face, that He was the fairest of all men to behold, and spoke so sweetly and with words so merry that they might have raised the dead from death to life. And he wrought many wonders and many deeds before her eyes and showed her His might. He told her of His kingdom, and promised to make her queen of all He owned. All this availed nought. Is not such scorn to be wondered at? For she was never worthy to be His slave. But through His debonaireness love had so overcome Him that He said at last: "Dame, thou art warred upon, and thy foes are so strong that thou mayest in no wise without my succor flee from their hands, lest they do thee to a shameful death. I will, for love of thee, take this fight upon myself and save thee from them that seek thy death. I know in sooth that I shall receive among them wounds unto death, and I will it heartily, to win thy heart. Now I beseech thee, for the love that I show thee, at least to love me dead after that death whom living thou wouldst not love." The King did all this. He freed her from her foes, and was cruelly ill-treated, and slain at last. Would not that lady be of evil nature if she did not love Him over all things thereafter?

This king is Jesus Christ, God's Son, that in such wise wooed our souls that the devil beset. And He, like a noble wooer, after many messengers and many good deeds, came to prove His love and show by knightship that He was love-worthy, as knights used sometimes to do. He went into tournament and for His sweetheart's sake raised His shield in fight as a keen knight pierced on every side. This shield that covered His Godhead was His dear body that was stretched on the rood, broad as a shield above in His outstretched arms and narrow beneath; for one foot, as men ween, was set upon the other foot. . . . This shield shields us not only from evil, but it doth yet more; it crowneth us in heaven. But Lord, thou sayest, whereunto? Might He not with less grief have rescued us: Yes, surely, full lightly, but He would not. Wherefor? To take from us every excuse for not giving Him our love that He so dearly bought.

Men buy lightly what they love little. He bought us with His Heart's blood—a dearer price was never—to draw our heart's love to Him that cost Him so dear. In a shield there are three things: the wood, the leather and the painting. All these were in the shield: the wood of the rood, the leather of God's body, and the painting of the red blood that made Him fair. Again a third reason: after a keen knight's death men hang his shield high in the church as a remembrance. And so is this shield, the crucifix, set in church, in the place where men may soonest see it, to think thereby of the knightship of Jesus Christ that He showed on the rood. His sweetheart beholds thereon how He bought her love and let His shield be pierced, that is, He let His side be opened to show her His Heart, and to show her openly how inwardly He loved her, and to draw her heart. . . .

He saith: "If thy love is to sell, I have bought it with love beyond all other. And if thou sayest that thou wilt not set it so cheap but wilt have more, name what it shall be; set the price of My love. Thou shalt not say so much that I will not give for thy love much more. Wilt thou have castles and kingdoms? Wilt thou rule all the world? I shall do thee better; I shall make thee with this queen of heaven. Thou shalt be seven-fold brighter than the sun; no evil shall harm thee, nothing shall vex thee, no joy shall be wanting thee; all thy will shall be wrought in heaven and on earth, yea, and in hell". . . .

Lo, thus Our Lord wooeth. Is she not too hard-hearted whose love such a wooer cannot win to himself? And especially if she thinks of these things: what He is, and what she is, and how great is the love of one as high as He is for one as low as she. For thus saith the Psalmmaker: "Non est qui se abscondit a calore ejus." There is none who can so hide himself as not to love Him. The true Sun was for this raised up on the rood in the noon-tide, to spread over all His hot love-gleams. Thus zealous was He, and for this He died, to kindle His love in His lover's heart. "I am come," He says in the Gospel, "to bring fire into earth, that is, burning love into earthly hearts, and what yearn I for but that it blaze? . . .

Now you have heard, beloved sisters, how and why God is to be mightily loved. And to kindle you well, gather wood thereto with the poor woman of the town of Sarepte, which signified the kindling of fire. "Lord," said she to Elias the holy prophet, "lo, I gather two sticks." These two sticks betoken the beam that stood upright and that other also that went crosswise over the dear rood. With these two sticks you shall enkindle the fire of love in your hearts. Look often towards them. Think if you ought not easily to love the King of bliss that so spreads His arms towards you and, as begging a kiss, bends downwards His head.[6]

The fourteenth century was a time of stress in England as it was all over Europe, the time of the Hundred Years' War, the Black Death, the Peasants' Revolt; the time too when the Monk of the *Canterbury Tales* "loved a roast swan best of anything," and the Pardoner tried to pass off his "pygges bones" as relics upon his fellow pilgrims. Yet even the lighthearted Chaucer, who satirized these abuses with a shrug, saw the earnest Heart of Christ for one moment, in the stanza for the letter X of the *A.B.C. to Our Lady* that he translated from the French of de Guilville:

> Xristus, thy Son, that in the world alit
> Upon the cross to suffer His passion,
> And so that Longinus His Heart split
> And made His Heart's blood to run down.[7]

Chaucer's contemporary, the rough-clad William Langland, blood-brother to the poor, spent his crowded but lonely days brooding over the mystery of "the field full of folk" and of Piers the Plowman who must see them all home to God. In the turbulent dream-allegory in which he follows the pilgrims through eleven dreams that have the quality of vision, he sees the fragments of life fitted into the pattern of eternity. His poem is the epic of the Mystical Body of Christ growing to its full stature in a world of sin and failure; its theme is "doing the truth in charity." Here and there flash out lines which witness to a popular awareness of the Heart of Christ on the streets of London. Holy church,

seen as a lady "lovely in face and in linen clothes," says to the
dreamer:

> Truth telleth that love   is the treacle of heaven;
> No sin may be seen in him   that useth that spice.
> And all his works Truth wrought   with love as it pleased
>   Him,
> Taught it to Moses, the dearest   and most like to heaven,
> And the plenitude of peace,   most precious of virtues.
> For heaven might not hold it,   it was so heavy of itself,
> Till it had of the earth   eaten its fill;
> And when it had of this land   flesh and blood taken,
> Was never leaf upon linden   lighter thereafter,
> Portable and piercing   as the point of a needle,
> So that no armor stops it,   and no high walls.
> For this is love a leader   of the Lord's folk of heaven,
> And a mean, as the mayor is,   between the king and the
>   commons.
> Right so is love a leader   and the law shapeth;
> Upon man and his misdeeds   mercy he asketh.
> And to know its nature: it cometh by might,
> And in the heart there is its head   and its high well.
> For in kind knowing by the heart,   there might beginneth,
> And that falleth to the Father   that formed us all.
> He looked on us with love,   and let His Son die
> Meekly for our misdeeds,   to amend us all.
> Yet He wished them no woe   that wrought Him that pain,
> But meekly with His mouth   mercy He sought,
> To have pity on the people   that put Him to death.
> Here may thou see example,   in Himself alone,
> That He was mightful and meek,   and granted mercy
> To them that hung Him on high   and pierced Him through
>   the Heart.[8]

The dreamer ponders over her words:

>   On Holy Church I thought
> That took me at the font   for one of God's chosen;
> For Christ calls us all   to come if we would,
> Saracens and schismatics,   and so He did the Jews;
>   *Vos omnes sitientes, venite ad aquas,*
> Bade them suck for sin   safely at His breast,
> And drink healing for their ills,   whosoever can draw it.

> And may all Christians come, quoth I,   and claim there
>   entry,
> By the blood that He bought us with,   and baptism
>   after. . . .
> God became man of a maid,   and *metropolitanus*,
> And He baptized and bishoped   with the blood of His
>   Heart
> All that willed and would,   with inner-wit believe it;
> Many a saint since   hath suffered death,
> And to bring the faith there   in many countries died.[9]

In the overpowering Holy Week vision that climaxes the poem, the dreamer sees the events of Good Friday in terms of the mediaeval legend which honored under the name of Longinus the soldier who pierced Our Lord's side, finding good excuse for his deed:

> There came forth a knight   with a keen spear ground,
> Named Longinus, as letters tell,   who had long lost his sight.
> Before Pilate and other people   in the place he rose;
> In spite of his teeth   he was made at that time
> To take his spear in his hand   and joust with Jesus.
> For they were all unhardy   that rode on horse or stood
> To touch Him or taste Him,   or take Him from the rood.
> But this blind fellow then   bore Him through the Heart.
> The blood sprang down the spear   and unsealed the knight's
>   eyes.
> Then fell the knight upon knees   and cried for mercy:
> "Against my will it was, Lord,   to wound You so sore,"
> He sighed and said,   "Sore it grieves me,
> The deed that I have done;   I put me in Thy grace.
> Have ruth on me, rightful Jesus."   And right with that he
>   wept.[10]

Because this poem is as realistic as it is visionary, and carries the breath of the streets along the way to heaven, it testifies that overfamiliarity had played with the expression "Heart of Christ" and made of it an expletive:

> They shot against Him with shots,   many a sheaf of oaths,
> Broad hooked arrows,   "God's Heart and His nails,"
> And almost had unity   and Holy Church brought down.[11]

While Chaucer laughed at the world and Langland stormed over it, a third poet was looking straight into heaven. The nameless author of *Pearl* relates in his own dazzling dream-allegory how he fell asleep in his garden "in August in the high season," and of how the lost daughter for whom he grieved appeared to him. She led him from pain to peace, along the banks of a shining river into sight of the New Jerusalem. He watched her there in "a light more bright than sun or moon," till his eye was caught by the glorified wound over the Heart of Christ the Lamb:

> With delight they fared together there
> On the golden streets that gleamed as glass;
> Hundreds of thousands I knew there were,
> And all alike their livery was;
> 'Twere hard to choose those of gladdest cheer.
> They saw the Lamb then proudly pass
> With seven horns of red gold clear,
> Robed in pearl-white, as one who has
> All loveliness. Many a gracious lass
> Pressed to the throne before His sight;
> Mild as modest maidens at Mass
> So drew they on with great delight.
>
> Delight to see Him there appear
> Was far too great for me to tell.
> The Elders all, when He drew near,
> Grovelling at His feet they fell
> Legions of angels together were,
> Scattering incense of sweet smell.
> With glorious glee and new cheer
> All sang the praises of that gay Jewel.
> That voice might have struck through earth to hell
> That the Virtues of heaven raised so bright,
> Where the Lamb's own Hosts His praises swell.
> Iwis I was caught in great delight.
>
> Delighted on this Lamb to gaze
> My mind marvelled wonderingly.
> Best was He, blithest, most to praise
> Of any that we know to be.
> White His robes were, simple His ways
> And calm His looks, but I could see

A wound wide and wet always
Over His Heart, rent terribly.
From His white side the blood poured free.
Alas, thought I, who did that spite?
Burned alive should that foe be
Ere in such a thing he took delight.

The Lamb's delight we well may ween,
Though He was hurt and wide wounds had.
In His face pain was never seen;
Glorious was His glance, and glad.
I looked among His servants sheen;
Fulness of life was on them laid.
And there I saw my little Queen
Who I thought was near me in the glade.
Lord, much of mirth she there made
Among her comrades clothed in white.
Across the stream I longed to wade
For love-longing and great delight.[12]

History has focussed more sharply on the rascally, tavern-haunting friars of fourteenth-century England than on the hidden ascetics and mystics who lived unnoticed in their huts, anchorholds or monastic cells. The homely holiness of these more than compensated for some of the Canterbury pilgrims. Those were paradoxical days in which the most flagrant abuses were balanced by the blunt yet unearthly beauty of many hidden lives. The same flowering of mystical experience and expression that gave Catherine of Siena to Italy and John Ruysbroeck to the Low Countries gave Richard Rolle to England. This hermit, wearing a habit made haphazardly from two of his sister's gowns, sang continually under the pressure of all but unbearable joy. His prayer-songs are scattered through many anthologies of popular lyrics, among them a *Querela Divina*:

O mankind, have in mind
My pains' smart.
Behold and see that is for thee
Pierced My Heart.

These lines are accompanied by a rough drawing of Christ, who points with one hand to His side, while beneath the other

hand is a large heart with a gaping wound, around which is
written: "This is the measure of the wound that Jesus Christ suffered for our redemption." Devotion to the Sacred Heart had
found its way into popular literature, forthright, unpolished, tender. Of the school of Richard Rolle is the following:

> Sweet Jesus, now will I sing
> To Thee a song of love-longing.
> Make in my heart a well-spring,
> Thee to love over all thing. . . .
>
> Sweet Jesus, my heart's delight,
> Thou art my day without a night.
> Give to me both grace and light
> For to love Thee all aright.
>
> Sweet Jesus, my heart's gleam,
> Brighter than the sun's beam,
> As Thou wert born in Bethlehem
> Make Thou in me Thy love-dream. . . .
>
> Sweet Jesus, Lord good,
> For me Thou sheddest Thy blessed blood.
> Out of Thy Heart it came in flood;
> Thy Mother saw it with dreary mood.
>
> Jesus, Sweetheart, Thou art so free
> That Thou didst all love for me;
> What shall I give back to Thee?
> Thou carest for nought but love of me. . . .
>
> Jesus, of love I see tokening;
> Thine arms spread out for love-clasping,
> Thy head bowed down for sweet kissing,
> Thy side all open for love-showing.
>
> Jesus Lord, my sweeting,
> Hold me ever in Thy keeping.
> Make of me Thy darling,
> That I love Thee over all thing.[13]

The tone of song is heard in the following:

> Lovely tears of lovely eyes—
>   Why dost thou me such woe?
> Sorrowful tears of sorrowful eyes—
>   Thou breakest my heart in two.
>
> Thou grievest sore;
> Thy sorrow is more
> Than man's tongue can tell;
> Thou singest of sorrow,
> Mankind to borrow
> Out of the pit of hell.
>
>   Lovely tears. . . . etc.
>
> Thy mother seest
> How woe Thou beest,
> Therefore she years apart;
> To her Thou speakest,
> Her sorrow Thou slakest;
> Sweet prayer won Thy Heart.
>
>   Lovely tears . . . etc.
>
> Thy Heart is rent,
> Thy body is bent
> Upon the rood tree;
> The tempest is spent,
> The devil is rent,
> Christ, by the might of Thee.[14]

When these hidden mystics wrote down their thoughts in prose they did so in the richly simple, image-starred speech of the villages, revealing not only their own experiences of prayer but also the theological traditions reaching back to patristic days. The expressions of Saint Augustine and of Saint Anselm appear with fresh savor and certainty with no sense of quotation in the following anonymous "Meditation on the Five Wounds." A tradition unconsciously possessed can ring with originality:

Behold especially in the five most notable wounds: two in His blessed hands and two in His blessed feet, and the most open wound in His right side. Into these wounds of Christ's most blessed hands and feet, with Thomas of India put in thy fingers, that is to say, thy most subtle thoughts and desires. And in the wound of Christ's blessed side, since it is the largest and deepest, put in all thy hand, that is to say, all thy life and all thy works, and there feel Christ's Heart so hot loving thee, and also there feel the water of Christ's side streaming as of a well of life, to wash thee and mankind of sin. And there fetch up water of everlasting life without end of these five most open wounds of Christ as out of five wellsprings. . . .

Out of the largest and deepest well of everlasting life in the most open wound of Christ's blessed side, fetch up deepest and heartliest water of joy and bliss without end, beholding there inwardly how Christ Jesus, God and man, to bring thee to everlasting life suffered that hard and hideous death on the cross, and suffered His side to be opened, and Himself to be stung to the Heart with that grisly spear. And so with that doleful stroke of the spear there gulched out of Christ's side that blissful flood of water and blood to ransom us, water out of His side to wash us, and blood of His Heart to buy us. For love of these blessed wounds creep into this hot bath of Christ's Heart-blood, and there bathe thee, for there was never sin of man nor of woman, thought nor wrought, that was laved with lovely sorrow and heartly repentance, that there was not in this well full remission to buy it and water of life fully to wash it and cleanse it. Then rest thee here, comfort thee here, live in Christ's Heart without end.[15]

Best known and loved among the anchorites is Dame Juliana of Norwich, a refreshingly wise and witty woman, "lovely and homely" like the Lord she loved, who, "greatly stirred in charity for her even-Christians," wrote down for their comfort "the Revelation of love that Jesus Christ, our endless bliss, made in sixteen showings," in a day and a night of 1373. In the tenth showing she entered the open Heart of Our Lord, and there learned that in all things "love was His meaning."

Then with a glad cheer Our Lord looked into His side and beheld, rejoicing. With His sweet looking He led forth the understanding of His creature by the same wound into His side within. And then He showed a fair, delectable place, and large enough for all mankind that shall be saved to rest in peace and in love. And therewith He brought to mind His dear-worthy blood and precious water which He let pour out for love, and with the sweet beholding He showed His blissful Heart even cloven in two.

And with this sweet enjoining He showed unto mine understanding, in part, the blessed Godhead, stirring then the poor soul for to understand, as it may be said; that is, to think on the endless love that was without beginning, and is, and shall be ever. And with this our good Lord said full blissfully: "Lo, how that I loved thee," as if He had said: "My darling, behold and see thy Lord, thy God that is thy maker and thine endless joy; see what liking and bliss I have in thy salvation, and for My love enjoy now with Me."

And also, for more understanding, this blessed word was said: "Lo, how I loved thee! Behold and see that I loved thee so much ere I died for thee, that I would die for thee. And now I have died for thee and suffered willingly what I may. And now is all My bitter pain and all My hard travail turned to endless joy and bliss to Me and to thee. How should it now be that thou shouldst anything pray that liketh Me, but that I should full gladly grant it thee? For My liking is thy holiness and thine endless joy and bliss with Me."

This is the understanding, simply as I can say, of this blessed word: "Lo, how I loved thee." This showed our good Lord for to make us glad and merry.[16]

Dame Juliana, unlike Saint Catherine of Siena, did not leave her solitude in response to her visions. Her role was to remain hidden, entrusting to a piece of parchment what had passed between her heart and the Heart of her "courteous Lord Jesus." Because of Him she could be glad and merry in times that were dark for Mother Church. Devotion to the Sacred Heart keeps a place of fruitful peace for those who know it, for to such were the light burden and the sweet yoke promised. In times of crisis there will always be anchorholds for which the world is unknowingly the better.

NOTES

1. Quoted in Hamon, *op. cit.*, Vol. II, p. 106.
2. Quoted in Richstaetter, *op. cit.*, p. 47.
3. *Ibid.*
4. *Jacopone da Todi*, E. Underhill, ed. (London, Dent, 1919), p. 261.
5. *The World's Great Catholic Poetry*, James J. Walsh, ed. (New York, Macmillan, 1942); used with the publisher's permission.
6. *Ancren Riwle*, J. Morton, ed. (Camden Society 57, O.S.), p. 388.
7. *Complete Works*, W. W. Skeat, ed., p. 270.

8. *Vision of Piers Plowman,* W. W. Skeat, ed. (Oxford, 1888), B Text, Passus I, ll. 146 ff.

9. *Ibid.,* Passus XI, ll. 112 ff.

10. *Ibid.,* Passus XVIII, ll. 76 ff.

11. *Ibid.,* Passus XX, ll. 224 ff.

12. *Pearl,* I. Gollancz, ed. (London, Chatto, 1921), Stanzas 93–96.

13. *Richard Rolle of Hampole,* C. Horstman, ed. (London, 1896), Vol. II, p. 9.

14. *Religious Lyrics of the Fourteenth Century,* C. Brown, ed. (Oxford, 1924), p. 87.

15. *Richard Rolle of Hampole,* Vol. II, p. 440.

16. *Revelations of Divine Love,* Dom G. R. Hudleston, ed. (Westminister, Newman, 1952), p. 44.

CHAPTER VII

THE SWORD OF THE SPIRIT
1417–1620

> *"True strength is
> in My Heart."*

During this sweep of time the Devotion to the Sacred Heart began to emerge from private into public life and to play a role more visible, active, definite and astringent than before, ready under the impulse of the Holy Spirit to "renew the face of the earth."

For by the time Dame Juliana had closed her eyes in her anchorhold to open them upon the last and most blissful of all "showings," the Middle Ages were giving way under the shock of the Renaissance; the next century marked the beginning of modern times. The fifteenth was a century of transition, complex and contradictory, provoking the sixteenth century into Reformation and Counter-Reformation. The election of Martin V in 1417 brought an end to the Western Schism, but not to strife; the Turks took Constantinople and were beaten back in Hungary. Above the sputter of newly-invented gunpowder was heard the steadier clatter of the printing press, as artists and writers around the Vatican turned towards Humanism, Christian or pagan. The ships of Columbus found a new world for the Church, in compensation for the thousands of members torn from her as the revolt of Luther spread through the old world, weakened by the dry-rot of scandal and abuse. Forces of true reform sprang to the challenge, and after the Council of Trent the Church could look the new ages in the face.

That the Devotion to the Sacred Heart was by then a public concern is proved by the visible traces that it left in the places where men gather most freely, their homes and their churches. In 1415 a bleeding Heart in which three nails were fixed was

carved on the tomb of an English abbot.¹ From then on it
appeared with ever greater frequency: in stained glass, on embroidered vestments, on manuscript miniatures, on fonts and over
doorways, on household silver and furniture. As the emblem became distinctive and familiar, so the prayers in honor of the Heart
itself became more specific, personifying It and addressing It directly.

In 1535 a Paris bookseller put out a board before his shop on
which passers-by could read: "At the sign of the Heart of Jesus."
Practices of virtue were suggested in the elaborate Litanies and
"Little Hours"² that were drawn up, and thus Devotion to the
Sacred Heart took on a definitely ascetical character as it reached
out to penetrate all walks of life in the years of transition that
searched and purified the Church. In 1492 the sultan Bajazet
sent the relic of the lance that pierced the Savior's side to Pope
Innocent VIII; it gave new impetus to the devotion to the Five
Wounds through which the blood of His Heart was poured out,
the blood so lavishly portrayed in fifteenth-century art.

Poggio, spokesman for pagan humanism, scoffed at the name
of Jesus, but Saint Bernardine of Siena (1380–1444), apostle of
the Holy Name, made reparation. Tireless tramper of the roads of
Italy, ringing preacher to the multitudes, and theologian of the
sacred humanity, Bernardine set fire to his hearers, kindling love
and turning their vanities literally into heaps of ashes. He saw the
Heart of Christ as a mystic censer, and on one Good Friday,
holding up a crucifix, he cried out:

O love that melts all things, what have You done to those who
love You? The bottomless deep has opened upon us, that a flood of
fire may sweep over the earth. The deepest mysteries of the Divine
Heart have been revealed to us, sparing nothing; the cruel lance
has gone within. . . . The open side reveals the Heart, the Heart
that loved unto death. We are called to enter into this ineffable love
which made Him come down to us. Let us go to the Heart of Jesus,
deep Heart, secret Heart, Heart that forgets nothing, Heart that
knows all, Heart that burns with love. The violence of love has
opened the door; let us go in, loving like Jesus; let us pierce the
divine secret hidden from all eternity. The wound in the side has
shown us the eternal temple of eternal joy.³

It was a woman of manly courage who led the way into the suffering Heart. Camilla Varani (1458–1527) was a princess of a family whose blood flowed hot with the excitements of the Renaissance. Wealth and pleasure glittered around her childhood and she took them both with a laugh, but every Friday she loyally forced herself to think of the Passion until she could "shed one tear, and then run off without waiting for a second." But the Lord of the Passion followed her and won her brave heart for His own. She entered a convent of Poor Clares at Urbino, taking the name Battista, and let the world of courtiers and humanists go on without her. But she suffered for that world, and her experiences of the suffering of the Sacred Heart were needed to purify the violent beauty of the Quattrocento. In answer to her own daring prayer she shared the inner anguish of the Redeemer, and in 1488 wrote from experimental knowledge her treatise "Of the Mental Suffering of Our Lord Jesus Christ in His most Sacred Passion." As she said:

There is the same difference between a soul that meditates on the mental sorrows of Jesus, and another which goes no further than the sufferings of His sacred body, as between honey and balsam enclosed in a vessel and that which exudes from it and covers its exterior. He who wishes to draw full nourishment from the sacred Passion should not confine himself simply to tasting the balm on the edge of the vessel; let him enter into the vessel itself, which is the Sacred Heart, and he will there find full satisfaction.[4]

Veiling her identity under the use of the third person, she wrote:

Of the first suffering, of that anguish which the Blessed Christ bore through the souls of the reprobate:

Herein are certain very holy matters touching the sorrows of the Heart of the Blessed Jesus Christ which He, of His goodness and loving kindness, deigned to communicate to a devout religious of the Order of Saint Clare, in the monastery of Urbino. This soul, having an overpowering desire to feed upon and satiate herself with the enrapturing food of the Passion of this most sweet and loving Jesus, after many years of preparation was, through His marvellous condescension, admitted into the mystery of the anguish of His blessed Heart, into that very ocean of bitterness.

Many times had she prayed to God that He would plunge her in that sea of anguish which was His sorrowing Heart, and this the most loving Jesus deigned of His kindness and tender friendliness to do, not once only but over and over again, until she was fain to cry out: "Enough, enough, dear Lord, for so much grief I cannot bear." And in this tender action of His it were easy to believe, seeing how full of sweet and ready response He is to those who crave such gifts of Him with humility, and who ask perseveringly for the same.

This blessed soul, holding herself in prayerfulness and constant watchings, cried to Him one day, in the eager impulse of her heart: "O Lord I pray Thee that Thou wouldst lead me into the innermost sanctuary of the sorrows of Thy soul. Plunge me into the depths of that most bitter sea, for behold, thus would I die, if such desire be not displeasing to Thee, my sweet Life and Love. Tell me, Jesus, Thou hope of my life, how great was this sorrow of Thy stricken Heart." Whereat the Blessed Jesus was pleased to answer her thus: "Wouldst thou know how great was My sorrow? Verily, it was as great as the love which I bear towards My creatures."

Now this blessed soul knew well how great was that love which Christ bears toward His creatures, for many things and beautiful had she told others concerning that love which same I would fain recount here, but I must speak now only of the sorrows which afflicted the Heart of the loving Christ, the measure of which sorrows is the measure of that same love, of which it had pleased God to give her a full understanding.

So it followed that when Our Blessed Lord told her this thing, namely that His sorrow was as great as the love which He bore to His creatures, she, having contemplated the unmeasurable depths of that same divine love, became overwhelmed by the immensity of the sorrows of His Heart. And to so great an extremity was she reduced at this contemplation of the abyss of His sufferings that she became stricken in all her senses and fell to fainting so that she was fain to seek a support for her head through the great sorrow that flooded her heart.

When she had rested a while and gained enough strength to speak, she cried out: "O Lord, since Thou hast shown me how great was Thy sorrow, tell me what were these griefs Thou didst bear in Thy Heart?" Then gently He made answer: "Know, My daughter, these sorrows were without number, because without number are the souls which, being members of My body, are yet through mortal sin separated from Me. And every soul separateth itself from Me each time that it committeth mortal sin. This, therefore, was one of the greatest pains that I bore in My Heart, the separation of My members from My body. . . ."[5]

While Battista was writing with southern fire in Italy, a chain of influences was being set in motion in the north which was to carry Devotion to the Sacred Heart from the cloister into the militant apostolate of the Counter-Reformation, and from a link between its mediaeval and its modern forms.

In the Low Countries the mystic Ruysbroeck had given the impulse towards the primitive simplicity of Christian living which resulted in the foundation in 1380 of the Brothers of the Common Life by Gerard Groote, who thus unknowingly raised a bulwark against the coming of Luther. In the midst of the prevalent laxity their serene, wholesome and gaily austere monasteries were springs of fervor. In the same year in which the Great Schism closed, one of the Brothers of the Common Life was writing the last pages of *The Imitation of Christ*. Its author[6] had chosen for his motto in those tense times: "I have sought rest everywhere and found it nowhere save in little nooks and in little books." The little book which he wrote in his own nook has brought peace to souls in times of tension ever since. As for him and his brothers, "so great was the zeal of their love that they were eager in lowly service one to the other, and charity was shown in deed and humility of heart preserved." This Gospel of charity they learned of the meek and humble Heart. In the *Imitation* itself we read:

If thou fliest to the wounds and to the precious marks of the nails, thou shalt feel great comfort in tribulation. . . . Again, if thou enterest perfectly into the inner heart (*interiora*) of Jesus and there taste but a little of His burning love, thou shalt care no more for thine own convenience or inconvenience.[7]

In his sermons (of whose authorship there is no doubt) Thomas à Kempis speaks at greater length than does the *Imitation* of the divine Heart. There the soul that has thus entered into the "inner places" of Jesus, speaks in familiar conversation with the Beloved:

Vox Christi: I speak to the soul, My dove in the holes of the rock, in the clefts of the cave. To such a soul frequently I speak, as to a beloved disciple. Put thy hand here and know the place of My nails, and be not fearful and trembling, but strong and great-souled in becoming like to Me. He who dares to deny himself and strip himself of affection to any creature will have a single refuge in the open wound of My right side. In the depth of that wound of love it will be given to him more freely to see Me, for he has no care for any created comfort. I draw the depths of his being into Myself, that he may not feel himself who feels My wounded Heart. Make thyself a stranger to all worldly business; put behind thee vain cares; draw away from thy friends and acquaintances; keep thyself pure and free from all, that thou mayest enter into thy Beloved through the door in the wounded side.

Vox Animae: Well do Your words please me, and very well, Lord Jesus Christ. And so I beg Thee, although I am not able perfectly to be like to Thee in all things, grant that I may suffer closely with Thee. I will lift the eyes of my heart to my Lord who hangs naked on the cross; attentively I will gaze upon each wound and each piercing of His body, and with single-hearted love I will enfold and kiss His wounded hands and feet pierced by nails. Lastly I will go into Thy open side as into the bridal chamber of my sleeping Lover; there hiddenly will I live and I shall be safe from all harm. I will linger there in happy quiet and in divine peace. . . .[8]

Enter, enter, my soul, into the right side of thy crucified Lord. Pass through the precious wound to the most loving Heart of Jesus transpierced by love till thou canst rest in the cleft of the rock from the whirlwind of the world. Come, man, to the deep Heart, to the hidden Heart, to the secret Heart, to the Heart of God who opens the door to thee. Come in, O blessed of God; why do you stand without? The veins of life are open to thee, the way of safety, the heavenly ark whence sweet fragrance comes. Here is a place of refuge from the tempting enemy, a place of forgiveness from the wrath of the judgment to come. This is the fountain of oil and of grace everflowing which never ceases to offer mercy to sinners if they will draw near with hearts fully contrite. This is the fountain of that divine river going out from the midst of Paradise to water the face of the earth, to give drink to thirsty minds, to wash away stains, to put out the fire of lust, to quiet the tumult of wrath. Draw thy cup full of love from this fount of the Savior. Draw from the side of Jesus the sweet solace of life, that thou mayest live not in thyself but in Him who was wounded for thee. Give Him thy heart who opened His Heart for thee. Go through the door of the sacred wound to the inner depths of the Redeemer. He asks thee to come, He begs thee to stay with Him, He desires thee to have one heart with Him. "Son," He says, "give Me thy heart."

God asks nothing more of thee. If thou hast given this, thou hast given the most pleasing gift. Give it to Jesus, to none other; give to Christ, not to the world; give thy heart to eternal wisdom, not to vain philosophy. For this He made His side to be opened so broadly and pierced so deeply, that a way might be opened of going to the Heart of thy Beloved, of penetrating to the depths of the Son of God, and of being joined to Him in true union of heart, that all thy affections may be turned to Him, and all thy works done for Him with a simple heart, that thou mayest try to please Him alone, clinging to Him with a pure mind and with all thy strength. . . .[9]

After such a conversation with its Beloved, the soul turns reflectively and speaks to itself; or rather it is à Kempis speaking to the whole world and urging every soul to this intimate "imitation of Christ":

Hasten as fast as thy hungry love will urge thee, lean against the sacred side of Jesus, that thou mayest be sprinkled with blood and water. And, if possible, draw out thy heart and place it next to the Heart of Jesus, that He may keep, rule and possess it, that it may not be drawn abroad or soiled. Reveal to Him thy heart, give thyself trustingly to Him; hand over to Him all thy willing and non-willing. May He be one heart and one soul with thee in God, one in desire and in feeling, in His good pleasure forever. Then thou shalt be in great peace, nor shalt thou be easily disturbed or overshadowed when thou hast given thy heart altogether to Jesus for Him to keep and dwell in forever.

O Jesus, most true, keeper of secrets and living at home in loving hearts! O cross-conformed, gazed on by all contemplatives, O God-conformed, treasure-house of all graces and gifts for all the faithful! Christ, King, Redeemer, whose side was pierced by the sharp point of the lance, open to me, I beg, the door of Thy mercy. Let me go in through the great, wide door of Thy side, into the secret places of Thy most loving Heart, that my heart may be united to Thine with an unbreakable bond of love and vehemently set on fire, that Thou mayest dwell in me and I in Thee, bound to each other forever.[10]

While these lines were being written, a small boy named Nicholas Van Esche was studying with the Brothers of the Common Life at Windesheim. He later left this center of quiet and went to Cologne, hotbed of controversy, where he became a priest. There he opened his house to boys studying at the University which made Cologne the "German Rome," hoping to shelter them against the heresy and corruption that were stalking the streets. Together, master and pupils visited the great Charterhouse of Saint Barbara, founded in 1336. Here the Carthusians lived in the spirit of Saint Bruno, surrounded by city streets instead of mountain gorges, praying as though in a wilderness, and printing books on their own small press for the crowds who came to them; and here was manifest what might be called the first "group devotion" to the Sacred Heart. It was still expressed in the form in which Van Esche had known it at Windesheim, cloistral in character, yet here it was ready to reach out into the restless, changing world, burning into it more effectively than the "bonfires of vanity" lit by the skinny hands of Savonarola.

Among the boys who came with Van Esche to Saint Barbara's was Peter Canisius, future Jesuit and theologian of the Council of Trent. In the library where he browsed were books by Carthusians that gave typically contemplative expression to Devotion to the Sacred Heart, yet looked toward action. There he found *Vita Christi,* by Ludolph of Saxony (1295–1378). In itself it was a résumé of the spirituality of the Middle Ages; in its wide and prolonged influence it was a shaping force of the new age; it reached Saint Ignatius at Manresa and entered into the writing of the *Spiritual Exercises.* The founder of the Jesuits read in it:

The Heart of Christ was wounded for us with the wound of love, that through the opening in His side we may in return enter His Heart by means of love, and there be able to unite all our love with His divine love into one love, as the glowing iron is one with the fire. . . . He has given us wide entrance into His Heart. Therefore let man make haste to enter into the Heart of Christ; let him gather up all his love and unite it with the divine love.[11]

Among those who had lately enriched the library at Saint Barbara's was Dominic of Trèves (d. 1461). His writing on the Sacred Heart was stamped by the ascetic spirit of discipline, a methodical and practical spirit which marked the Devotion in the ages of abuse:

Wilt thou be easily and wholly cleansed from thy sins, freed from thy faults and enriched with all goods? Free thyself first of all from the business that is not strictly necessary, enter thyself as a scholar of the Eternal Love, where the Tutor is the Holy Ghost. Then yield thyself without pictures or fancy—with thy naked understanding and thy will—entirely to the divine will in the Heart of Our Lord Jesus Christ on the cross, our Creator, Redeemer and Lover, that Heart which is wholly filled with love, in which dwells the Holy Trinity and the essential fulness of the Godhead. Through this Heart which embraces in its boundless love all the elect in heaven and on earth, we all have access to God the Father.

To this most merciful Heart of our Lord and our God raise thy heart in spirit when thou hast first well recollected thyself interiorly. This do in all places and at all times, but especially at the Divine Office, and in all thy prayers and work, as the Lord Himself commands: "Come unto Me, all you that labor and are heavy laden and I will refresh you. My Son, give Me thy heart, and let thine eyes keep My ways. Put Me as a seal upon thy heart." To which thou wilt answer earnestly: "My heart is ready, O Lord, my heart is ready. I will praise Thee, O Lord, with my whole heart, and I will glorify Thy name forever."

For in the sweetest Heart of Jesus we find all power, mercy, justice, peace, grace, virtue and everlasting salvation; there find we the living source of full comfort and true light which enlighteneth every man that cometh into the world, but above all those who with intimate confidence take refuge in it in every misery and distress. For whatever of good a man may wish for may be drawn from it in overflowing fulness, and whatever may be bestowed on us of healing and of grace comes to us from the sweetest Heart and from nowhere else. It is the furnace of divine love ever burning with the fire of the Holy Ghost. It cleanses, inflames, and transforms into itself everyone who wills to unite himself with it and cleave to it.

Further, as we have said, all goodness proceeds from the sweetest Heart of Jesus, so must thou refer to it all good things, and all good works which thou sharest with all men, and never attribute the smallest part to thyself. Thou wilt confess thy sins before the same Heart of Jesus, and there implore pardon and mercy; bring to it praise and thanksgiving, not only for thyself but for all those entrusted to thee and for the whole Church, calling from the abyss of our miseries to the abyss of the divine mercy.

Thou wilt also often kiss in thankful recollection the picture of the most kind Heart of Jesus, in which are united all the treasures of the wisdom and foreknowledge of God, ceaselessly and earnestly longing to see it in reality face to face, and lament to it all thy trials. From it thou wilt draw into thy heart its spirit and its love, its mercy and its virtues; thou wilt abandon thyself to it with confidence, in joy as in adversity, hope in it, hold fast to it. In it thou wilt be careful to keep the unity of the spirit in the bond of charity, that in return it may render thee worthy that He should take up His abode in thy heart. Finally thou shalt sleep and rest in peace and tranquility in it. For should the hearts of all men betray thee and desert thee, yet will this truest of Hearts never deceive or forsake thee. . . .

If thou wilt with but little trouble gain great goods and ennoble thy miserable works, appropriate for these Christ's merits, and through thy human works obtain His divine promises; give Him all and thou shalt receive all from Him. For example, thou canst say and desire before or after every action: "Lord Jesus Christ, in union with the love with which Thou hast praised Thy heavenly Father and prayed to Him, with which Thou didst work, and didst suffer such grievous things, grant me perfectly to perform these prayers and works however small they may be, to bear all contradictions with joyful courage to Thy praise and for the prosperity of Thy Church."

As often as thou art distracted or hast fallen under temptation, first implore pardon through the wounds of His feet, then grace and confidence through the wounds of His hands, until at last thou venture to fly to the door of His most merciful Heart, there to beg and to knock in childlike love. In this way thy merits, even the least, may be united to the merits of Christ and transformed and ennobled more than a man can think. So will naught of it be lost, but all, even the smallest, is laid up for thee in the Heart of Jesus, and will be restored to thee with plenteous usury.[12]

The subprior of Saint Barbara's during the years in which Peter Canisius came so often as a student to read in its shadow was named Lanspergius (1489–1539). True to the spirit of the new humanism, he was an editor of ancient manuscripts, not of the pagan classics but of the mediaeval, chiefly the Revelations of Saint Gertrude, whose works were only then becoming widely known. In his own *Pharetra Divina,* he drew heavily upon Dominic of Trèves, enlarging upon the practices suggested by his forerunner, especially that of the use of pictures of the Divine Heart as an aid to devotion, pictures not only on stone or glass, but those small enough to be carried about. It is no wonder that Father Van Esche had a cell reserved for him at Saint Barbara's where he could come with his disciple to open his soul to these "darts of divine love." There Peter read:

Strive to honor the Heart of the most tender Jesus Christ our Lord, which is wholly filled with love and with mercy. Be devout in paying it reverence often; kiss it, enter into it in spirit. Make your requests and offer your exercises through it. It is the depository of all graces, the door by which we go to God and God comes to us. Therefore have a picture of the Divine Heart or of the five wounds, or of Jesus bleeding and all wounded; put it in some place where you often pass, that it may remind you of your practice and your exercise of the love of God. . . . At sight of this . . . raise your heart to God, and in spirit, without sound of words, silently speak to Him, desiring that your heart may be purified, and that your heart and will may be united to the Heart of Christ and His divine will. You may also, if your devotion urges you to do so, kiss this picture—I mean of the Heart of Jesus—as if it were the real and divine Heart of Jesus that you were pressing to your lips, desiring to imprint it on your heart, to plunge therein your spirit, to be absorbed therein, presenting yourself to draw from this gracious Heart into yours His spirit, His graces, His virtues, all that His immensity contains that is salutary for you. For the Heart of the Lord overflows with all this. It is, therefore, profitable and very pious to honor devoutly the Heart of the Lord Jesus. Having recourse to it in all necessities, draw from it consolation and help of every kind. If all hearts abandon you and deceive you, be without fear; this most faithful Heart will neither deceive you nor forsake you.

O most lovable Jesus, when wilt Thou take away my sin-stained heart and give me Thy Heart? When will my heart be fragrant with the odor of Thy virtues, wholly inflamed with the love of heavenly things? Ah, most sweet Jesus, shut up my heart in Thy Heart, dwell therein all alone, be Thou its sole master. May my heart be exalted and adorned with the sublimity of Thy Heart. Imprint, I beg of Thee, on my heart all the wounds of Thy wounded Heart, that so I may read therein unceasingly the immense love of Thy Heart for me, and its intense sufferings.[13]

These "darts of love" reached their mark in the wide-open soul of Peter Canisius, piercing it with the unhealable wound for which the mystics of the Middle Ages had unceasingly prayed. But Peter, like Saint Thomas More, resisted the attractions of the Charter-house. Modern times had begun, and his energies were drawn into the new stream that had broken out so vigorously and was sweeping clean the muddy streets of the City of God on earth. Under the influence of Peter Favre he joined the young Society of Jesus.

But the wound in his heart still called to the Heart of the Crucified, which opened to Him on his profession day. He tells us what then happened in his *Testament:*

My soul fell prostrate before Thee, my dull deformed soul, unclean and infected with many vices and passions. But Thou, my Savior, didst open to me Thy Heart in such fashion that I seemed to see within it, and Thou didst invite me and bid me to drink the waters of salvation from that fountain. Great at that moment was my desire that streams of faith, hope and charity might flow from it into my soul. I thirsted after poverty, chastity, obedience, and I begged to be washed clean by Thee from top to toe, and to be clothed and adorned by Thee. After I had thus dared to approach Thy Heart, all full of sweetness, and to slake my thirst therein, Thou didst promise me a robe woven of peace, love and perseverance with which to cover my naked soul. Having this garment of grace and gladness about me I grew confident again that I should lack for nothing and that all things would turn out to Thy glory.[14]

Saint Peter's life was spent in preaching and in teaching, driven on by that charity drawn from the Heart of Christ. And when, after a long life in the militia of Christ, he lay on his sickbed, he closed each day with aspirations,

in union with the praise which flows from Thee, Lord Jesus, to all Thy saints; in union with the gratitude drawn from Thy Heart, good Jesus, which causes Thy saints to thank Thee; in union with that passion, good Jesus, whereby Thou didst take away the guilt of all mankind; in union with the divine longings which Thou, good Jesus, didst have on earth for the salvation of mankind; in union with every prayer which welled from Thy divine Heart, good Jesus, and flowed into the hearts of Thy saints.[15]

The Jesuits appeared as the free-lances of the Church in those days of intellectual crusade. The new Society was approved in 1540; by 1550 the impact of the Spiritual Exercises was being felt upon countless souls, and they the finest, both in and out of the cloister. These exercises, which kindle generosity of heart and close with the "contemplation for obtaining divine love," are "a very sure way of reaching Devotion to the Sacred Heart." Among the early Jesuits traces of the Devotion flash out. The spirit and the history of the Order prepared it from the beginning for the very definite and all-important role that it would later play in the spreading of the Devotion.

In the meantime the Reformation was running its course in England; the tension led to the first armed uprising in the cause of the old religion. When in 1536 the Lords of North, where "men's hearts were very much grudged with the suppression of the Abbeys," marched on York, the symbol of the Sacred Heart together with the wounded hands and feet appeared for the first time on a banner, the standard of Sir Henry Percy, leader of the Pilgrimage of Grace. The movement failed, as did the second uprising in 1572, led by Sir Thomas Percy, who was finally executed. But his daughter, Lady Mary, carried the banner into the Low Countries where its undefeatable sign was engraved over the door of the Benedictine Abbey which she founded, a sign that calls to the perpetual warfare fought with the Sword of the Spirit.

NOTES

1. Gilbert Dolan, "Devotion to the Sacred Heart in Mediaeval England," in *Dublin Review,* CXX, 373 (April, 1897).

2. Among these were: an "Alphabet" composed by the Franciscan, Father Fridolin, saluting the Heart of Christ as: afflicted, beautiful, chaste, and so through all the letters; and a "Week of the Sacred Heart," composed in the Rhineland, with salutations for Monday, Tuesday, etc. See Hamon, *op. cit.,* Vol. II, Ch. 8.

3. Quoted in Hamon, *op. cit.,* Vol. II, p. 234.

4. *True Devotion to the Passion,* trans. by Enid Dinnis (Kenedy, 1925), p. 38.

5. *Ibid.,* p. 39. New Orders were then founded by saints as familiar as she with the secrets of the Divine Heart: Saint Frances of Rome established the Oblates and Saint Jeanne de Valois the Annonciades. See Hamon, *op. cit.,* Vol. II, pp. 148 ff.

6. Thomas à Kempis is the traditional author of the *Imitation.* Modern scholarship claims that it was written by Gerard Groote and revised by à Kempis.

7. Bk. II, Ch. 1.

8. Thomas Hemerken à Kempis, *Opera Omnia* (Freibourg, 1910), Vol. III, p. 214.

9. *Ibid.,* Vol. V, p. 197.

10. *Ibid.,* p. 199.

11. Ludolph of Saxony, *Vita Christi,* quoted in Richstaetter, *op. cit.,* p. 177.

12. Dominic de Trèves, quoted in Richstaetter, *op. cit.,* p. 179.

13. Lanspergius, *Pharetra Divina,* quoted in Bainvel, *op. cit.,* p. 179.

14. James Brodrick, *Life of Saint Peter Canisius* (New York, Sheed, 1935), p. 125.

15. *Ibid.,* p. 823.

CHAPTER VIII

CROSSCURRENTS
1620–1673

"Love is all."

The mid-span of the seventeenth century, before the Revelations at Paray-le-Monial, was filled with multiple and varied manifestations of the Devotion to the Sacred Heart moving like crosscurrents through those turbulent times. Many influences were at work, seemingly independent of each other. Many devout souls were praying and preaching the Devotion, each in his own fashion. Yet "no man can say 'the Lord Jesus' but by the Holy Ghost,"[1] and the Spirit was abroad in those momentous years, a divine centripetal force drawing the lines of the Devotion towards their focal point.

It is startling to see the working of Providence in a paradox, for this same seventeenth century was an age of centrifugal forces; religious unity had been broken, and the nations, like the thoughts of men, moved further apart along their separate orbits. Patriotism narrowed into nationalism, and the race for power in the new world was on. Catholic-Protestant controversy broke into wars which scarred the countries with slaughter and burning, while two-minded governments tried to bring peace on the disturbing principle that *cujus regio ejus religio,* till unsound tolerance led to fiercer bigotry. Where the "divine right of kings" was enforced, as in England, the king was beheaded. Gallicanism strained away from Rome, and the units of the Holy Roman Empire strained away from each other; the power of the sword no longer served the power of the keys. Deism ignored Revelation; inductive reasoning ignored Scholasticism, while in science the telescope of Galileo turned the universe inside-out. Yet the spirit of cold calculation was met by an opposite tendency towards emotionalism shown in a sort of secular "cultus" of the human heart. As the poetry of John Donne expressed it: "This new philosophy calls all in doubt."[2]

But the Church, revitalized by the shock of challenge, brought her disciplines to bear on the troubles of the hour. She had been poised and balanced by the Council of Trent, and now put out a steadying hand through her freshly organized Tribunals and Congregations. Old Religious Orders were roused by the fervor of the new, while saints arose to be all things to all men in the expanding world and the new social system: a Robert Bellarmine for the learned, a Jean Baptiste de le Salle for the ignorant, a Vincent de Paul for the poor. The Counter-Reformation, through the catechism, through education, through social institutions, built up the Church from within, and by the foundation of the Propaganda Fidei (1622) reached widely into the Orient and the Americas for new members to replace those lost in Europe. Scholars like Mabillon and the Bollandists adopted the methods of the new science to bring back the faith that had been "put in doubt." And it was in this complex century which saw the emergence of so many modern trends from the shaken and purified forces of the past, that Devotion to the Sacred Heart manifested a multiplicity of forms and appeared in many new walks of life and on many new levels of thought, giving the impetus of dynamic holiness to the restless and analytic movements of the age, drawing them into the transcendent unity of love.

The Devotion found expression first in the gracious humanism of Saint Francis de Sales (1567–1622), voice of the Christian Renaissance in spirituality. Geneva was the seat not only of Calvin but also of an apostolic (though necessarily absentee) Bishop who was rugged enough to struggle through mountain snowdrifts to win one soul to the truth, and artistic enough to clothe his classic spiritual teaching in the grace of French prose at its purest. It was not sufficient for him to write a *Treatise on the Love of God;* Saint Francis clothed his own person in that sweet charity, so humorous, benign and self-spending, with which he gave himself away to souls in need, including the highborn, whose hunger is often the most acute. He drew his charity from the Heart of the God-man, with whom he could so truly say "Learn of me, that I am meek and humble of heart" that two centuries later

Pope Pius IX declared in the brief making him a Doctor of the Church:

It is in particular marvelous how, filled with the Spirit of God and drawing near to the Author of sweetness Himself, Saint Francis de Sales sowed the seeds of this Devotion to the Sacred Heart which, in these unhappy times, we have the great joy of seeing marvelously spread, to the great profit of religion.[3]

His most important act for the spreading of religion in his own unhappy times was the foundation of the Order of the Visitation in 1602. As its spirit shaped with practice into a way of life, Saint Francis wrote in 1610 to Saint Jane Frances de Chantal a letter dated, prophetically, on the Friday after the Octave of Corpus Christi:

Good day, my very dear daughter. . . . This night God has given me the thought that our house, the Order of the Visitation, is by His grace noble enough and important enough to have His arms, His blazon, His device and His war-cry. I have thought, dear Mother, if you agree, that we might take for our coat of arms a single Heart pierced with two arrows, and surrounded by a crown of thorns, this Heart serving as the base of a cross that will surmount it and on which will be graven the sacred names of Jesus and Mary. I must tell you, my daughter, when I see you, a thousand thoughts that have come to me on this subject. For truly, our Congregation is the work of the Hearts of Jesus and Mary. The dying Savior has given birth to us in the opening of His Sacred Heart. It is therefore quite just that our heart remain through careful mortification always surrounded by that crown of thorns that rested on the head of our Leader, whilst love kept Him fastened on the throne of His mortal agony.[4]

And again:

O God, dear Sister and beloved daughter, why does it not happen to our hearts as to the heart of the dear Saint whose feast we begin this evening, Saint Catherine of Siena; why does the Lord not take away our heart and give us His own in its place? But will He not rather make our own wholly His, absolutely His, purely and irrevocably His? Oh, may He do so, this sweet Jesus! I beg this of Him, by His own Heart, and by the love that is held in it, which is the love of loves. But if He should not do it (Oh but He will surely do it, since we beg Him to!), at least He cannot prevent us from going to take His own from Him, since He has left His breast open for that. And if we must open ours, in order to take out our heart and put His in its place, shall we not do so? May His holy name be forever blessed![5]

The flashing sophistication of aristocratic life, often covering the dry-rot of moral disintegration, was counterbalanced by the intense spirituality, often reaching a mystic level, of the lives of many of the highborn. The presence of the Carmelites near the court was a powerful magnet to prayer. "States of soul" was a subject of absorbing interest in the days of Fénelon. There were aberrations into Quietism, there was considerable playing at various methods of prayer, but there was also much genuine holiness, intelligent, generous, and God-guided. The Jesuits were the most influential directors of souls both religious and lay, and the fruit of their direction appeared in books, long, illuminating studies of the interior life, which glow with magnificent passages on the love of the Sacred Heart. Meditations, "elevations," and ascetic practices in its honor were developed in the writings of priestly directors like Father Monet, Father Alvarez de Paz, and above all Father Jean Baptiste de St. Jure, whose *Book of the Elect* drew souls to live in the wounded side, and whose *The Spiritual Man* studied "the Sacred Heart and the three steps of the spiritual life," that is, purgative, illuminative and unitive. Meanwhile, in Poland, Father Druzbicki was writing the first complete Manual of Devotion to the Divine Heart, the *Meta Cordium*. These great directors, not yet conscious of the special role of the Jesuits in spreading the Devotion, were kneading it, like a leaven of sanctity, into the restlessly changing social order.

Apostles of the spoken word were also at work. Father Vincent Huby trudged the country roads in districts torn by the religious wars and preached the Spiritual Exercises to throngs of people rapt by the passionate simplicity of his speech and by his abrupt silences. He taught them to say "the rosary of the heart," in which they moved wordlessly over their beads, kissing each in sign of love and reparation, "heart to Heart." In Paris, the famous Father Joseph, "Grey Eminence," swayed diplomatic circles as he did the king, but made more lasting spiritual conquests in the convents of the Daughters of Calvary which he founded, and where he taught the Religious to receive Communion in order "to be nourished by the Heart of Our Lord."

The variety and practicality of the forms taken by the Devotion as it was thus caught in the crosscurrents of the century of division did not drain it of the rich mystical content of earlier days. Souls of every type and in many different countries were favored with the mystical interchange of hearts by which He whose delights are to be among the children of men enters so palpably into the mortal flesh of chosen members of His Mystical Body; they drank from the stream that flowed from the wounded side, they entered the flames that glowed from it. These things happened not only to cloistered nuns like Maria d'Escobar, to whom Our Lord gave "the key of His Heart and of His will," but to ladies of high rank, familiar with the court, like Madame de Neuvilars, who found in the divine flames "her natural element and resting place," and to hard-working and abused servants like Armelle Nicolas, who said to her friends: "If you want to find me, do not look for me anywhere but in the Heart of my divine Love." And in Canada, living a rugged pioneer life among the missionaries to the Indians, Mère Marie de l'Incarnation received "a divine touch" which effected so close a communication between her heart and the Heart of the Son of God that thereafter she spoke to the Eternal Father only through It. This she called "the Exercise of the Sacred Heart of Jesus."[6]

Then, on the Feast of Saint John, 1658, Bossuet himself (1627–1704) preached on the Sacred Heart from the pulpit of Metz. He was then only an archdeacon, not yet the teacher and counselor of kings, the shaper of national policy, the mighty orator and controversialist. But the eye of the future "eagle of Meaux" was already fixing the sun; in his thoughts and studies the Discourse on Universal History was taking shape. Untouched as yet by the intransigeance and errors of his magnificent polemical career, he was already the unswerving champion of tradition whose motto was "Quod ubique, quod semper, quod ab omnibus, credendum est." Misled in practice into the narrowness of Gallicanism, in theory he kept the broad vision that has won for him the name of "theologian of Divine Providence." So even as a young priest, seeing in history the record of God's purpose, he did not hesitate to say, with the superb eloquence of felt truth, that the Sacred Heart holds "the very mystery of Christianity."

It is easy for me to show you, Christians, that John was always the faithful and the well-beloved of His Savior. While He lived among men, none had larger share of His confidence; when He gave back His soul to His father, none of His own received marks of a more tender love; when He gave His body to His disciples, all saw the place of honor that He gave to Saint John near His own person at that holy ceremony.

But what makes me understand still more clearly the strong leaning of the Heart of Jesus towards the disciple of whom we are speaking is the three gifts that He gave him in His Gospel. We find, Christians, that in His life He gave him His cross; at His death, His mother; at the last supper His Heart. What does a living friend desire more than to be united with those whom he loves by doing the same things; and has friendship anything sweeter than this lovable association? The work that Jesus had to do was to suffer; it was what His Father had laid down for Him, the task that He had given to Him. That is why He united Saint John to His laborious and crucified life, and early foretold the sufferings which He destined for him. "You will drink," He said, "of My chalice, and you will be baptized with My baptism." That is the gift that He gave to John during the course of His life. And what better proof can a dying friend give that friendship is precious to him than an ardent desire to leave his heart with his friends even after death, and to live on in their memory? That is what Jesus Christ did with regard to Saint John in so signal a manner that no further proof of love was necessary; for He gave him His divine Mother, as the thing dearest to Him in the world: "Son," He said, "behold thy Mother." But what shows His love still more was the beautiful gift that He gave him at the banquet of the Eucharist; not satisfied with giving to him as to the others His body and His blood to make one body with His own, He took him in His arms and drew Him to His breast. And as if it were not enough to have loaded him with so many gifts, He gave to him the very source of all His bounties, that is His own Heart, upon which He bade him rest as upon a place conquered by right. O truly happy disciple to whom Jesus Christ gave His cross to let him share in His own suffering life; to whom Jesus Christ gave His Heart, to make him to be but one thing with Himself. What was left for you to do, O dear favorite, but to accept these gifts with the respect which is due to the love of your good Master?

I said, O Christians, that it was not enough for the Savior to pour out His gifts upon Saint John. He wished to give him their very source. All gifts come from love; He gave him His love. Love comes from the heart. and so He gave him His Heart; He placed in his hands the root, the fruit of which He had already given him. "Come," He said, "O My dear disciple, I have chosen you before the beginning of time to be the Doctor of charity; come and drink it from its source, come and draw out those words full of sweetness by which you will win My faithful; come to this Heart which lives only for the love of men; and that you may the better speak of My love, come and feel at close hand the burning fire that consumes Me."

I shall not linger now over the privileges of Saint John. But John, since you are its master, open to us the Heart of Jesus; make us aware of the movements caused in it by love only. That is what is revealed by all the writings of Saint John; they all make known to us the Heart of Jesus. His Heart is the summary of the mysteries of Christianity, mysteries of love whose beginning is in the heart, a heart fashioned by love; all its pulsations, all its beatings, come from love. Do you wish Saint John to show you the secrets of this Heart? He goes back even to the beginning, *in principio.* And he comes to this end, *et habitavit,* "He dwelt among us." What was it that made Him dwell with us? Love. "God so loved the world." It is love then that made Him come down to us to be clothed in human nature. But what heart could He have given to this human nature but a heart fully fashioned by love?

It is God who has made all hearts, according to His good pleasure. "The heart of the King is in His hand," as is every heart, *Cor regis in manu Dei est;* that heart of the King, our Savior. What other heart has ever been more completely in the hands of God? It was the heart of a God, which He ruled over closely, the movements of which He controlled. What else could the Divine Word have done in becoming man, save to form for Himself a Heart upon which He stamped that infinite charity which drove Him to come into the world? Give me all that is most tender, all that is most sweet and most human: we must have a Savior who cannot bear misery without being filled with grief, who, seeing the lost sheep, cannot let them wander away. He must have a love which makes Him risk His own life, which makes Him bend down His shoulders to take up the burden of His lost sheep, which makes Him cry out: "If any man thirst let him come to Me and drink. . . . Come to Me all you that labor." Come, sinners, it is you whom I seek. And lastly He must have a heart which makes Him say: "I lay down My life of Myself." Mine is a heart of love that gives itself over to every pain.

And here in his sermon the mind of the preacher moved forward, unknown to his hearers, to touch those points of the Devotion that were to be highlighted in the twentieth century: the divine Heart is the source of that love which flows through the

Mystical Body to make all one; devotion to it is of the essence of Christianity:

See, my Brothers, what a heart is the Heart of Jesus, see what is the mystery of Christianity. That is why the summary of our faith is expressed in these words: "We have believed in the love of God for us." That is the profession of Saint John. . . . But if we believe it, we must so act. The Heart of Jesus reaches out to all the faithful; it is there that we are united, "to be consummated in unity." It was His Heart that spoke when He said: "Father, I will that where I am they also whom Thou hast given Me may be with Me." He makes no exception, He calls all His children, and we must love one another in the love of this divine Savior, *in visceribus Jesu Christi*. Let us therefore take on the Heart of Jesus Christ, a wide-reaching Heart which shuts no one out from its love. It is from this mutual love that we must form a chain of charity that will reach from the Heart of Jesus to every other heart, to bind them and unite them inviolably; let us not break this chain, let us not refuse to any one of our own brothers the right to enter into this holy union in the charity of Jesus Christ. There is room for all. Let us make use without envy of all the good things that come to us from it. We shall not lose them in sharing them with others; we shall possess them all the more surely. They will be the more abundantly multiplied the more generously we share them with our brothers. And why would you tear your brother from this Heart of Jesus Christ? He will not bear such separation; He will vomit you forth, you yourself. He will put up with any weaknesses, if only they are covered by the charity that fills us. Let us then love, in the Heart of Jesus. "God is love, and he that dwelleth in charity dwelleth in God and God in him." Ah, who will give me friends whom I love with true charity? When I pour out my heart upon them, I pour it out in God who is charity. It is not in a man that I place my trust, but in Him in whom that man dwells; and, in my well-founded confidence, I do not fear the changing decisions of human inconsistency.

It is thus that the souls of the Blessed love one another. The love which unites them so closely among themselves grows ever stronger in the mutual exchange of their hearts. They love one another in God, who is the focal point of their union; they love one another for God, who is their only good. They love God in each of their fellow citizens, who they know are only great with His greatness; and keenly conscious of the happiness of their brothers, they themselves are happy to rejoice with them and through them in the gifts which they themselves have not. Or rather, they have all; love gives a universality which makes all gifts common to the whole body, for it consummates them in that holy unity which, by absorbing them in God, puts them in possession of all the goods of the whole heavenly city.

Would we wish to share, my Brother, ever here below in heavenly beatitudes? Let us love one another; let brotherly love fill our hearts: it will make us taste, in the sweetness of its influence, those inexpressible delights which form the happiness of the saints. It will enrich our poverty by giving us a share in goods common to all; and by making us all to be of one mind and one heart it will begin in us that divine unity which will one day be our eternal happiness, and which will be perfect in us when, love having transformed all our powers, God will be all in all.[7]

Although fuel for the French Revolution was heaping up in the form of ruined parishes, untaught children, and direly neglected souls, reform was spreading. The most imperative of all reforms was that of the clergy themselves, "than which there is nothing more saintly or useful in the Church of God," in the words of Cardinal Bérulle, who in 1611 founded the French Oratorians for that purpose. This chaplain of Henry IV, who had brought the Discalced Carmelites to Paris to rebuke worldliness by prayer, was called by the Pope "Apostolus Verbi Incarnati." He wrote a *Discours de l'Etat et des Grandeurs de Jésus* and longed for the institution of a new feast to be called simply "the Feast of Jesus." The young Cardinal was a man of penetrating contemplation, drawn to live in the inner life of the Word Incarnate, to share His "states," meaning by that word the divinely human sentiments of Jesus which center, like those of other men, in a heart. Bérulle, in writing of these "states," revealed an attractive and all-pervasive element of Devotion to the Sacred Heart: seeing the love of Christ shining in all scenes of the Gospel, and through all aspects of His extended life in the members of His Mystical Body. In "Bérullian" asceticism, it is the "spiritual heart" rather than the heart of flesh which is stressed. The expressions "interior life" and "heart" are often almost synonymous in his writings and those of his followers, whose manner of guidance led souls to the prayer of quiet, and to passive mystical experience of "the Heart as Person." Their form of Devotion to the Sacred Heart created a peaceful inward concentration in a century of scattered activities; they rested in "Jésus intériorisé." Bérulle writes:

There are in Jesus Christ both states and actions; both are worthy of honor, and of all the attention and affection of our hearts. But His states should be specially pondered because they are the source of His movements and activities, and because, as states of Jesus, they give infinite homage to God, and are most profitable to souls.

The Incarnation is an enduring state, enduring throughout eternity. Unceasingly God makes gift of His Son to man; unceasingly this Son who is the gift of God gives Himself to our humanity; unceasingly the eternal Father begets His Son in a new nature. . . .

The spirit of God by which this mystery has been brought about, the interior state of the exterior mystery, the power that makes this mystery living and operative in us, the merit by which Jesus has won us for His Father, even the actual desire and the living disposition by which He works this mystery—all these are forever actual and present to Him. This fact obliges us to treat the mysteries of Jesus and all that concerns Him, not as things past and done with, but as things living and present, even eternal, from which we are to gather fruit both present and eternal. . . .

Let us take note that the living Heart of Jesus is wounded enough by love, and that is why the lance-wound was kept for His dead Heart, as though, before His death, the steel could not have pierced it more, so torn was it by love. . . .

Thus His Heart is eternally open, eternally torn; His glory does not take away His wound, for it is the wound of love; this rent made by the lance is but a mark of the true interior rending of His Heart. This rent side is peculiarly His; it is not shared with others who bore the same torment, or who bore crucifixion; it is an eternal wounding. It is a pain and a wound unto death, but lasting unto eternity; a wound begun in death but to last on into life. This is not the way of other wounds, for they will not endure through the resurrection. Thanks be to the eternal Father who has left in His Son this wound, that we may dwell in His Heart forever. For as God in His glory is Himself our inheritance and our portion, so Jesus also, in His states and His mysteries, is Himself our portion, and by giving us a share with Himself, He wishes us to have part in His states, according to His choice of us, and His love for us.[8]

Members of the Oratory spread the influence of the "School of Bérulle" to directors of souls who caught its spirit. Among them was a Franciscan, Father Timothée de Raynier, who wrote:

We are all in the Heart of Jesus Christ, since He loves us all, for the way of love is for the lover to lodge the beloved in his heart. The perfect Christian is convinced of this truth; he thinks of himself always as in the Heart of Jesus Christ. He dwells there and never comes out; he there performs all his works, his actions, his acts of virtues, according to the dispositions of the divine Heart. What joy to be united to Jesus Christ in the Sacred Heart which is continually united to God, not only by the hypostatic union but by the union of acts of love! He of whom I speak lives in such recollection that I dare to say that he deserves to be called an interior soul, because he never leaves the depths of the Heart of Jesus Christ.

It is in this divine Heart that the interior soul is united to the Spirit of Jesus Christ, to honor the mysteries of His life and death with the holy dispositions of the same Heart. . . . It is there that the Holy Spirit keeps before his eyes the various states of the adorable mysteries of Jesus Christ. There he sees these divine mysteries in their true source. . . . Above all, that Spirit keeps before his eyes all that passes within, in the soul and the Heart of Jesus Christ, with regard to the accomplishment of those mysteries. The spirit and the inner sense of a mystery are its very substance; the exterior form is like the shell, the accidental being; the exterior of a mystery is passing, but the interior—its spirit and the graces that dwell there—is eternal.

From the exterior one passes to the interior, to share in the dispositions and inner sentiments with which Our Lord accomplished these mysteries, and to penetrate more deeply the splendor of His divinity. And thus he is filled not only with the general dispositions of the divine Heart of Jesus Christ, but also with the special dispositions which were His in the accomplishment of each mystery.

In this Divine Heart, as in the treasure house of God's marvels and the sanctuary of His adorable secrets, the interior soul prays. There he receives the sacraments; there he confesses his sins, receives Communion and practices all the virtues. The Heart of Jesus Christ is thus the true tribunal where the perfect Christian accuses himself of his sins, and when he is in the confessional he is there only in body, for his mind is in the Heart of Jesus Christ. There he is united to Christ's hatred of sin and to the contrition that He felt for the sins of the world.

It is surpassingly sweet to think how the interior man is united with the saints and to the divine dispositions of Jesus Christ when he goes to Holy Communion, for while he partakes of His precious body and sacred blood at the holy table, he partakes also of the inner life of Jesus Christ in His divine Heart. The appearances of bread and wine are the means by which Our Lord gives His body and blood, and the body and blood are the means by which He gives His spirit. In Holy

Communion the perfect Christian shares so deeply in the inner life of Jesus Christ and in His spirit that he enters not only into partnership but also into oneness of spirit with Him, to give to God all the adoration, praise and love that Christ Himself gives.[9]

The zeal of Cardinal Bérulle was caught and magnified by the founder of the Sulpician Seminary, the many-sided Monsieur Olier (1608–1657). The prodigious social and pastoral reform which he carried out in the Parish of Saint Sulpice did not keep him from writing, though he abandoned for its sake the path of brilliant scholarship that lay open to him. His books were the fruit of the hours of prayer that underlay his hard work:

In the Heart of Jesus you will enter into the enjoyment of all that He is; you will enter into the intercourse, the mutual give-and-take between Him and His Father. Here in the Heart of the Son of God is the dwelling-place of the elect; this is the jewel in the storehouse of Jesus; this is the treasury of God Himself, into which He pours all His gifts, to which He communicates all His graces. It is in the Sacred Heart, in its adorable depth, that all mysteries are first wrought; it is there that God gives to His Saints the most intimate communications and most perfectly expresses His divine mysteries.

What can be said of the glory that God's majesty receives from the Heart of Jesus alone, that Heart which gives more homage to God than all the saints? For saints and angels are made but to express the feelings and thoughts of the Heart of Jesus.

The praises of the Church and all the sentiments of love which she renders in heaven to her God, are nothing more than the very sentiments of Jesus Christ. From this it follows that all the praise and respect that the saints have ever rendered to God are drawn from the Heart of Jesus Christ, and from His fulness. "Of His fulness we have all received," as said Saint John. It is this great Heart that holds all that is poured out so lavishly in the Church: "The whole earth is full of His glory." All our sanctuaries resound only with the praises which are given to God in that beautiful Heart. Our hearts and our shrines are only echoes which re-tell and repeat the harmonies which rise to God from the Heart of Jesus. O magnificent Heart of Jesus, adorable source of our religion, source, too, and plenitude of our homage to God, since all in us is drawn from you!

So it is with the works of holiness which are done in the Church like praises which she offers to God. All the acts of virtue practiced by the whole Church, were practiced by the Heart of Jesus Christ alone, so much so that Our Lord alone practiced within Himself what the whole Church together, during the succeeding centuries, practiced throughout its duration. Saint Paul calls the Church "the fulness of Christ." That which Jesus Christ wrought in His Heart, spreading through the Church, has made its heart expand and grow great, according to Saint Paul again: "For from Him the whole body (being closely joined and knit together through every joint of the system according to the functioning in due measure of each single part) derives its increase to the building up of itself in love."[10]

Among the early members of the Oratory was Saint John Eudes (1601–1680), who later founded the Congregation of Jesus and Mary, known now as the Eudist Fathers, and the Refuges which later developed into the Order of the Good Shepherd. The Church herself, in the Decree of his Beatification, declared that:

Burning himself with singular love for the most Holy Hearts of Jesus and Mary, he was the first—and this was not without a kind of divine inspiration—who had the idea of a public cultus in their honor. He is therefore to be regarded as the creator of this sweet devotion, for from the beginning of the foundation of his Congregation of Priests, he caused the Feast of these Hearts to be celebrated among his spiritual sons; as its doctor, for he composed for these Hearts a Mass and Office; lastly as its apostle, for he devoted himself with his whole heart to spreading everywhere this salutary devotion.[11]

John Eudes was drawn both to the interior life and to a very active apostolate as a preacher of missions. His love of Mary revealed her heart to him, and it was she who led him to the Heart of her Son. At first he found these two hearts even grammatically inseparable: the phrase "Ave Cor Jesu et Mariae" held the key to his thought, though later he used the plural "hearts," in the interests of theological clarity. His personal life was a constant expression of his own form of the Magnificat:

My soul doth magnify the admirable Heart of Jesus and Mary, and my spirit rejoices in my great Heart. Jesus and Mary have given me their Heart, this immense Heart, in order that all in me may be performed in its love. Infinite thanks to them for their unspeakable gift.[12]

It is Saint John Eudes' effort to establish public worship and a liturgical cultus in honor of the hearts of both Mother and Son that gives him his special place in the history of the Devotion. In 1646 he instituted for his two Congregations the Feast of the Holy Heart of Mary, for which he composed a Mass and Office. Then, in 1672, he wrote a letter to his spiritual sons, announcing that Our Lady had "obtained from her beloved Son a most signal favor that He has bestowed upon His Church, granting to her the Feast of His royal Heart, which will be a fresh source of infinite blessings for those who dispose themselves to celebrate it in a holy manner."[13] This Feast, kept by the Eudists on October 20, with its proper Mass and Office, was approved by local ecclesiastical authority. Saint John further founded seven Confraternities, approved by the Holy See, which spread the Devotion widely among the laity of France.

Just before his death in 1680, the Saint published his greatest work: *The Admirable Heart of the Mother of God,* of which the twelfth and last Book was devoted to the Sacred Heart of Jesus. The work includes the theological ponderings of the Saint followed by passages drawn from his predecessors: Saint Gertrude, Saint Bonaventure, Lanspergius and anonymous writers, and ends with two series of meditations, pulsating with passionate love and, in spite of their rapturous wording, highly ascetic. The rich language of the whole clothes the Devotion in a tapestry of metaphor and apostrophe through which the outlines of its theology are firmly drawn. Yet the pattern differs in some respects from the traditional one, and the elaborate variations are due to the various senses in which Saint John Eudes employs the word "heart," and the breadth which he gives to its symbolism.

He bases these multiple interpretations squarely upon Scripture:

I beg of you to consider that this noun "heart" has several meanings in the Sacred Scripture:
1. It signifies that material and corporeal heart that we bear within our breasts—the seat of love, of hate, of joy and of sorrow, of anger, of fear, and all the other passions of the soul.
2. The word "heart" is used in Scripture to signify memory.
3. It denotes the understanding.
4. It expresses free will.
5. It means also that supreme part of the soul which theologians call "the point of the soul," through which it contemplates.
6. It sometimes stands for the whole interior of man.

7. It signifies the Holy Spirit who is the Heart of the Blessed Trinity.
8. The Son of God is called the Heart of the Eternal Father.
9. The word "heart" signifies any faculty or capacity for loving, whether in the superior or inferior part of the soul, whether natural or supernatural.[14]

Within this wide range of meaning, it is not easy to define precisely the elements of Saint John Eudes' Devotion to the Sacred Heart. In his view, the formal object is rather the loving and the lovable Person of the God-man, expressed in the many metaphorical implications of the word "heart," than His physical Heart taken as the symbol of His love. Yet, high and daring and poetic as his flights may be, they circle round that Heart of flesh in rainbows of rapturous meditation. His thought is complex, his language lavish, but his love is simple.

As in his study of the holy Heart of Mary, Saint John Eudes finds in Jesus "three hearts which are but one heart," and he writes of them in a meditation:

We have three Hearts to adore in our Savior which, nevertheless, are but one single Heart by virtue of the hypostatic union.

The first is His divine Heart existing from all eternity in the bosom of His Adorable Father, which is but one Heart and one love with the love and Heart of His Father, and which, with the Heart and love of His Father, is the source of the Holy Spirit. Therefore, when He gave us His Heart, He also gave us the Heart of His Father and of His Adorable Spirit; hence His marvelous words: *Sicut dilexit me Pater, et ego dilexi vos.* "I love you with the same Heart and the same love wherewith I love My Father." My Father loves me with an eternal boundless and infinite love; I love you also with a love that is eternal, boundless and infinite. My Father causes Me to be what I am, God like to Himself and Only Son of God; and I make you to be by grace and participation what I am by nature and essence, that is to say, Gods and children of God, seeing that you have but One and the Same Father as I, a Father who loves you with the same Heart and the same love wherewith He loves Me: *Dilexisti eos sicut et me dilexisti.* My Eternal Father has constituted Me universal heir of all His goods: *Constituit haeredem universorum;* and I make you My co-heirs: *Haeredes Dei et cohaeredes Christi;* I promise to give you possession of all My treasures: *Super omnia bona sua constituet eum.* My Father finds all His pleasure and delight in Me; and I take My delight and pleasure in you: *Deliciae meae esse cum filiis hominum.*

O goodness! O love! O God of love, how is it possible for the hearts of men to be so hard and cold towards Thee, who art all aflame with the fire of love towards them? Oh, let all my joy and delight be in thinking of Thee, in speaking of Thee, in serving and loving Thee! O my All, let me be wholly Thine, and do Thou alone possess all that is in me.

The second Heart of Jesus is His spiritual Heart, which is the will of His holy soul, a purely spiritual faculty, whose function is to love what is lovable and to hate what is hateful. But the divine Savior so perfectly sacrificed His human will to His divine Father that He never exercised it while on earth and will never exercise it even in heaven, but He sought uniquely and solely His Father's will, according to those words of His: "I seek not My own will, but the will of Him that sent Me." "I came down from heaven, not to do My own will but the will of Him that sent Me." Now, it is out of love for us that Our Lord renounced His own will, in order to perform the work of our salvation solely by the will of His Father, in particular when He prayed to Him in the Garden of Olives: *Pater, non mea voluntas, sed tua fiat,* "Father, not My will but Thine be done!"

O God of my heart, if for love of me Thou didst sacrifice Thy utterly holy and divine will, how much more should I renounce my own will for love of Thee, wholly depraved and corrupted as it is by sin! Ah, let me renounce it with all my heart forever, imploring Thee most humbly, O my adorable Redeemer, to crush it like a serpent full of venom and to establish in its place the rule of Thy divine will.

The third Heart of Jesus is the Sacred Heart of His deified body, a furnace of love divine and of incomparable love for us. Since the corporeal Heart is hypostatically united to the Person of the Word, It is enkindled with flames of infinite love for us. Its love is so intense that it constrains the Son of God to bear us continually in His Heart; to fix His eyes even upon us; to take such a great interest in the smallest things concerning us that He verily numbers all the hairs of our head, allowing not one of them to perish; to ask His Father that we might make our eternal abode within His bosom: *Pater, quos dedisti mihi, volo ut ubi sum ego, et illi sint mecum;* and to assure us that, if we vanquish the enemies of His glory and of our salvation, He will make us sit with Him on His own throne, and will let us enter into possession of the same kingdom and the same glory that His Eternal Father has given Him.

Oh, how abundant and rapturous is the love of Jesus for such faithless and ungrateful men as we! O Jesus, my love, either take away my life or let me live only to love Thee, to praise and glorify Thee un-

ceasingly. Let me die a thousand deaths rather than willingly do anything to grieve Thee! Thou hast three Hearts which are but one and
the same Heart, a Heart wholly devoted to loving me continually.
Would that I possessed all the hearts in the universe that I might consume them in Thy holy love! . . .[15]

Saint John Eudes, like his name-saint, is conscious of Christ as
"the Son," and thus essentially turned to His Father. In the following meditation God's adopted sons are likewise turned to their
Father:

"As the Father hath loved Me, I also have loved you." . . . But how
does this adorable Savior love us? Listen again to His sacred words:
"as the Father hath loved Me." I loved you with the same love as that
wherewith I am loved by My Father. Now what is that love wherewith the divine Father loves His Son? It is a love possessing four
great qualities, which are found in the love of the Heart of Jesus
for us.

First of all, the love of the Father for His Son is infinite, that is,
without bounds, limits or measure; a love incomprehensible and inexplicable; a love as great as the very nature of the Eternal Father.
Measure if you can the extent and magnitude of that divine nature,
and then you will measure the magnitude of that adorable Father's love
for His Son; at the same time you will measure the greatness and extent of the love of the Son of God for us, since He loves us with the
same love as that wherewith His Father loves Him.

Secondly, the Father's love for His Son is an everlasting love filling
all the spaces of eternity. The eternal Father has never been without that love for His Son; He loves Him continuously, without inter-
mission, and He will love Him eternally. O my Savior, how it fills
me with joy to see Thee loved as Thou dost deserve. The perfidious
Jews, the devils and the damned hate Thee, but Thou art no less
lovable, and the adorable Father loves Thee more in a single moment
than all those wretches could hate Thee in a thousand eternities, if
that were possible. . . .

As our third reflection, we must remember that the love of the Divine
Father for His Son is a tremendous love filling heaven and earth and
even hell; in heaven the Father loves this Son with the hearts of all
the angels and all the saints; on earth their mutual love embraces all
the hearts that belong to Him on earth; in hell the eternal Father loves
His cherished Son who, with the other divine Persons, is present there,
manifesting the same omnipotence as in heaven. . . .

In the fourth place, I could demonstrate to you further that, as the love of the eternal Father for His eternal Son is love in its essence, since He loves Him with His whole being, so also the love of the Son of God for us is love in its essence, since He is all heart and all love towards us and loves us with all His being. In other words, every-thing in Jesus, His divinity, His humanity, His soul, His body, His blood, and His thoughts, words, actions, privations, humiliations, suf-ferings, in short everything that He is, has, and all His potentiality, is bound up in loving us.[16]

In the following meditation the Heart of Jesus is seen in relation to the whole Trinity:

Consider that the Eternal Father is in the Sacred Heart of Jesus, bringing to birth His Well-beloved Son and causing Him to live there the same all-holy and divine life that He lives in His own adorable bosom from all eternity. He imprints there a perfect image of His own divine Fatherhood, so that this humanly divine and divinely human Heart shall be Father to all the hearts of the children of God. There-fore, we should look upon Him, love and honor Him as our Loving Father, and endeavor to imprint upon our own hearts a perfect likeness of His life and virtues. . . .

Consider that the Eternal Word is in that royal Heart, united with it in the most intimate union imaginable, the hypostatic union, which causes that Heart to be worshipped with the adoration that is due to God. He is there with a life that is somehow more helpful, if one may so speak, than His life in the Heart and bosom of His Father. The Word lives but does not rule in the Heart and bosom of the Heavenly Father; whereas He lives and rules in the Heart of the God-Man, ruling over all human passions which are centered in the heart so absolutely that they do not stir except by His order. . . .

Consider that the Holy Ghost lives and reigns ineffably in the Heart of Jesus, where He conceals the infinite treasures of the knowledge and the wisdom of God. He fills the Sacred Heart with all His gifts to a pre-eminent degree, according to His divine words: "The Spirit of the Lord shall rest upon Him, the Spirit of wisdom and of understanding, the Spirit of counsel and of fortitude, the Spirit of knowledge and of piety, and He shall be filled with the Spirit of the fear of the Lord."

Consider, finally, that these Three Divine Persons live and reign in the Heart of the Savior, as if they were seated on the most high throne of their love, in the primal heaven of their glory, in the paradise of their dearest delights. They there shed abroad, with inexplicable abun-dance and profusion, wonderful lights, and the burning fires and flames of their eternal love. O most Holy Trinity, infinite praise be to Thee forever for all the wonders of love that Thou dost work in the Heart of my Jesus![17]

While Saint John Eudes was thus writing, another manifestation was taking place in secret. His institution of a Feast of the Sacred Heart anticipated by three years Our Lord's request to Saint Margaret Mary, and the great Revelations of Paray were unknown to him. Yet if these two very different saints did not know each other, they each had been admitted to know the mind and heart of God, and were responsive instruments of His will. The active preacher and apostle was preparing the soil for the seed to be sown by the contemplative. The fruit for the future would grow from the Message given at Paray, but already, during the hours that Saint Margaret Mary spent kneeling in ecstasy behind her grille, the *Ecclesia Orans* was standing erect in public prayer as in each Eudist chapel a Mass was offered beginning "Gaudeamus omnes, festum celebrantes sub honore Sacratissimi Cordis Jesu" and priests chanted from their office books the new invitatory for Matins: "Come let us adore the most loving Heart of Jesus, who is our love and our life." It was the work of the Spirit of Love who, said Saint John Eudes, is "the Heart of the Father and of the Son, whom He desires to give us to be our spirit and our heart."

NOTES

1. I Cor. 12, 3.
2. "First Anniversary."
3. Bainvel, *op. cit.*, p. 224.
4. *Oeuvres de Saint François de Sales* (Annecy, 1908), Vol. XV, p. 63.
5. *Ibid.*, p. 47.
6. Studies of the numerous devotees of the seventeenth century may be found in Hamon, *op. cit.*, Vol. III, and in Bainvel, *op. cit.*, Ch. IV.
7. *Oeuvres Complètes de Bossuet* (Paris, 1862), Vol. VI, p. 277.
8. Quoted in Henri Bremond, *Histoire Littéraire du Sentiment Religieux en France* (Paris, 1929), Vol. III, pp. 65 ff. In the concluding chapter of this volume, Abbé Bremond makes a penetrating study of Bérullian spirituality, which he calls "the School of France" in contrast to "the School of Paray." He claims that Devotion to the Sacred Heart arose from the fusion of this spirituality with "devout humanism" (represented by Saint Francis de Sales) in the works of Saint John Eudes, and that the Revelations to Saint Margaret Mary need to

be complemented by this earlier theology. He concludes: "If the Devotion to the Heart of Love . . . is to bring forth all its fruits of grace, it must tend to become indistinguishable from the Devotion to the Heart as Person."

9. *L'Homme Intérieur ou l'Idée du Parfait Chrétien,* quoted in Bremond, *op. cit.,* p. 661.

10. Quoted in Bainvel, *op. cit.,* p. 200.

11. *Ibid.,* p. 259.

12. John Eudes, *The Sacred Heart of Jesus,* trans. by Dom Richard Flower (Kenedy, 1946), p. 175.

13. Hamon, *op. cit.,* Vol. III, p. 179.

14. *Ibid.,* p. 197.

15. John Eudes, *op. cit.,* p. 126.

16. *Ibid.,* p. 51.

17. *Ibid.,* p. 111.

CHAPTER IX

THROUGH THE LENS
1673–1690

*"I wish to use you
for My great work."*

The turning point in the history of the Devotion to the Sacred Heart came in the months following the profession of Sister Margaret Mary Alacoque in 1672, in "the house of Mary," the Visitandine Monastery at Paray-le-Monial. She was its chosen apostle, though she never left her cloister. The hours which the young contemplative spent in rapture behind her grille were God's chosen hours. He used them as a lens through which lines of light that had travelled from very far away in time were drawn together, and sharpened to a burning focal point which fell at last on Rome, on the heart of the Church. From there they would radiate in new directions, with a divine energy drawn from the divine authority of Christ's Vicar. Christ Himself, with a royal gesture, had pointed to His Heart of flesh, and re-expressed the message of love that holds the meaning of the Incarnation: "Behold this Heart that has so loved men."

The Holy Spirit had prepared the times; the world was ready though unaware. No one knew at the moment that an event of major importance for the life of the whole Church was taking place; it made no more stir in the world than had once been caused by the visit of the Angel Gabriel to a house in Nazareth. Margaret Mary Alacoque (1647–1690) had been born in a country house in the village of Lautecour, and her childhood, though marked by unusual conflicts caused by the evident handling of God, passed unnoticed by her intense and excitable generation. While the little girl was on her knees begging Our Lord Himself to teach her how to pray, Jansenism was troubling the theologians of the hour. The blackly narrow shadow of Luther's teaching had cut obliquely across the Catholic way of thought and chilled the prayer of the cloisters. Port-Royal was in the hands of Saint-Cyran; Holy Communion became the sacrament of fear, leading to distance rather than union. Mère Angélique Arnauld, who had walked in the way of self-willed fervor, died in fear of "a terrible eternity" in 1661, after refusing to sign the ineffectual Anti-Jansenist Formulary. A few years later Margaret Mary entered the cloister. Our Lord there fashioned her to condemn Jansenism with divine efficacy. During her noviceship He prepared her soul by bringing it to a purity far higher than the most ambitious dreams of Mère Angélique because, as He told her, "I have chosen you, an abyss of unworthiness, that all may be done by Me." She lived in such union with Him that her prayer was undistracted even while she was chasing a donkey through the vegetable garden. She was professed in 1672 and had not long to wait before the three Great Revelations came to her from the altar where the monstrance at first reflected only the quiet candlelight. It was the Feast of Saint John, 1673:

One day, being before the Blessed Sacrament, and enjoying a little more leisure than usual, I felt myself wrapped in that divine presence so strongly that I forgot myself and the place where I was, and abandoned myself to that divine spirit, yielding up my heart to the strength of that love. He made me rest for a long time upon His divine breast, where He opened to me the marvels of His love and the unspeakable secrets of His Sacred Heart which He had hidden from me until then, and which He opened to me for the first time in so effective and apprehensible a way that He left me no room for doubt, I who always fear to be misled.

And this is what seemed to me to happen. Our Lord said to me: "My Divine Heart is so passionately in love with men that it can no longer withhold the flames of that burning love; it must needs let them spread abroad by means of you, and reveal itself to men to enrich them with its profound treasures which hold the graces they need to be saved from eternal loss. I have chosen you, an abyss of unworthiness and of ignorance, to carry out so great a design, that all may be done by Me."

He then asked me for my heart, which I begged Him to take; He did so, and placed it within His own adorable Heart, in which He showed it to me like a tiny atom being consumed in that burning hearthfire. Then, drawing it out like a glowing flame in the form of a heart, He gave it back to me, saying, "See, My beloved, it is a precious pledge of My love. I will place within thy side a little spark of the mighty flame of My love, to serve you for a heart, and to consume you until your last moment."[1]

Again, in 1674, possibly on the Friday within the Octave of Corpus Christi, the divine call came. This time the visible presence of the Son of Man came before her eyes:

One day when the Blessed Sacrament was exposed and when I felt drawn within myself by extraordinary recollection, Jesus Christ, my sweet Master, appeared to me resplendent with glory, His five wounds shining like five suns; flames shone out from the whole of His sacred humanity, but above all from His adorable breast, which seemed like a hearthfire. It stood open, and through it He showed me his loving and lovable Heart, which was the living source of these flames.

It was then that He revealed to me the unspeakable marvels of His pure love; and He showed me to what lengths He had loved men, from whom He received only ingratitude. He said: "I feel it more deeply than all that I suffered in My passion. If they would only love Me in return, I would think little of all that I have done for them, and would wish, if I could, to do still more. But they meet My longings with coldness and contempt. You, at least, give Me joy by supplying, as far as you can, for their ingratitude."

I declared my insufficiency, and He said: "Here is what will supply for all that is lacking to you." And then there came from His open Heart so glowing a flame that I thought that I would be consumed. "Do not fear," He said, "I will be your strength. Only listen to what I desire of you, to be ready to carry out My designs." Our Lord then asked for two things: A Communion of reparation on the First Friday of every month, and a weekly holy hour every Thursday between eleven and twelve, in expiation for the sins of men.[2]

Then came the most significant and definite of the Great Revelations, on June 16, 1675, the one that would give to the Devotion to the Sacred Heart an integral place in the official life of the Church:

After pouring out overwhelming graces of His love, Our Lord appeared. He revealed His Heart, and said: "Behold this Heart that has so loved men that it has spared nothing even to exhausting and consuming itself in order to show them its love. And in return I receive from most men only ingratitude, by their irreverences and sacrileges, and by the coldness and contempt which they show to Me in this Sacrament of love. But what wounds Me yet more deeply is that this is done by souls who are consecrated to Me. That is why I ask that the first Friday after the octave of Corpus Christi shall be kept as a special Feast in honor of My Heart, that on that day Communion shall be offered as a special act of reparation for the indignities committed. And I promise that My Heart will pour out abundantly the power of its love upon those who pay it, or who cause others to pay it, honor."[3]

The divine intent was clear; the means of carrying it out were not. Saint Margaret Mary had to turn from the ecstasy of her contemplation to face the practical and trying human circumstances under which the Devotion in its new form slowly made its way. She had much to suffer still from the testing of doubt and antagonism, but gradually she saw her vision translated into the simple actualities of daily life. She was Mistress of Novices when, on June 20, 1685, her White Veils rashly rose before dawn to prepare a surprise for her, a private but intense celebration of a Feast of the Sacred Heart on the day for which Our Lord had asked. In the early morning light they read with her an act of consecration before the picture, crudely drawn by herself, of the thorn-ringed Heart with its legend "Charitas." A year later the Community that had so opposed her found itself kneeling before a chair transformed into an altar next to the grille where the saint had received the divine messages. The new practices of the Devotion then spread like ripples from one Visitation monastery to another; Communions were many on the First Fridays, pamphlets with prayers and litanies were printed, and even a High Mass was sung at Dijon, with the permission of Bishop de Langres. Sister Margaret Mary left her obscurity long enough to go to the parlor grille or to write letters like the following, with the aim of seeing the love of Our Lord's Heart carried into practice in the daily lives of souls. This was her apostolate:

I think the Sacred Heart asks three things of you: First, that you love Him with a love of preference, which will enable you to overcome your repugnances, and trample on your human respect, which says: "What will they say if I do so-and-so?" All such thoughts must be despised when there is a question of pleasing this Divine Heart. Then you must look down upon, judge, and condemn no one but yourself.

By doing this you will practice humility and charity, and will avoid the judgment and condemnation of your Judge. Thirdly, Our Lord desires to be the one object of your affections; you must delight in no other, so that you may be worthy for Him to take delight in you. Model your heart on the virtues of His. If you only knew how you sadden Him when you fail in charity or humility, or when you neglect the inspirations He gives you to withdraw from dissipation and thoughts of self-love. All this prevents Him from giving you His abundant graces. I think I have said all this to you before, but I want to remind you of it again, for it seems to me that He does not ask anything new of you just now, but that you will please Him very much if you are faithful to these practices He has given you. Try, then, to correspond with His love. Give Him all yours by an exact fidelity to all our holy observances, banishing all vain curiosity, and all surprise and discouragement at difficulties. Keep your soul in peace without complaining of anything, trying to find your delight in self-abnegation. If you love, nothing will seem difficult to you. . . .

The Sacred Heart will take especial care of you in proportion to the inviolable fidelity with which you confide in Him and abandon yourself to Him on those occasions in which you have an opportunity of showing Him your love, which, it seems to me, should consist particularly in that perfect forgetfulness of self and love of contempt which can endure everything in silence. . . . If you can do nothing at prayer, content yourself by offering that which Our Savior makes for us in the most Blessed Sacrament of the Altar, offering His fervor in reparation for all your coldness. In each of your actions say: "My God, I wish to do or suffer this in the Sacred Heart of Thy Divine Son, and according to His holy intentions, which I offer Thee in reparation of whatever is impure and imperfect in mine"; and so of all the rest. When any pain, affliction or mortification befalls you, say to yourself: "My soul, take what the Heart of Jesus sends thee to unite thee to Himself." Try especially to preserve peace of heart, which is better than all imaginable treasures. The means of preserving it is to have no longer any will of our own, but to put that of the Divine Heart in its place, so that It may will for us what ever is wanting on your part, for It will love God for you, and you will love in Him and through Him.[4]

In the last years of her life Saint Margaret Mary lived in a deep peace, confident that God would carry out in His own way the realization of His plans. She knew that after her death a new force would be released in the Church and would spread from land to land. The Devotion which had been the treasure of special souls would be entrusted to the many in forms easy to grasp, in acts easy to practice. The love of the God-man was to be set before the eyes of the world in a symbol through which sinners would find the source of the infinite ocean of mercy, tepid souls would become fervent, and fervent souls advance rapidly to perfection. God's blessing would fall where that image would be exposed and honored; it would bring peace to families, console the troubled, bless the undertakings of its apostles, give assurance through life and above all in death. Priests, through it, would find grace to touch the most hardened hearts and those who spread this Devotion would have their names written in the divine Heart itself, never to be effaced. Margaret Mary could not see the future Holy Hours on Thursday evenings, or the crowded altar rails on every First Friday in churches all over the globe, but she knew of the "Great Promise" made to those who communicate on nine First Fridays. They would not die in God's displeasure.[5]

Once in a letter to Father Claude la Colombière, she had described that Heart of flesh as it had been shown to her, and as it has been pictured ever since: burning, wounded, cross-crowned, and circled with thorns. Then, in one rushing, headlong sentence she poured out the purpose of this revelation:

And He made me see that the ardent desire which He had to be loved by men and to withdraw them from the way of perdition into which Satan was casting them in crowds had caused Him to form this plan of showing His Heart to men with all the treasures of love, of mercy, of grace, of sanctification, of salvation which it contained; so that all those who wished to give Him and win for Him all the love, honor and glory in their power He would enrich with an abundant outpouring of the divine treasures of the Heart of God which was their source, and which must be honored under the figure of the Heart of flesh, the image of which was to be exposed, and worn on my person and on my heart, to impress upon it all the gifts with which His Heart was filled, and to destroy all its unruly movements; and that wherever this holy image would be exposed for honor He would pour out His graces and blessings; and that this Devotion was like a final effort of His love which willed to favor men in these last centuries with such a loving redemption to draw them from the rule of Satan which He aims to overthrow, and to place us in the sweet liberty of the rule of His love, which He wills to establish in the hearts of all those who will make this Devotion their own.[6]

The Saint died in 1690. For the next six years the "new" Devotion made its way. Its forms and terms were those of Paray; the spirit that animated them was as old as contemplation. The force that guided their impetuous spread was a simple, supernatural enthusiasm kindled by the action of grace; the Holy Spirit moved over the faithful. Authorities took alarm at "novelty"; Jansenism had stiffened many, Quietism had shaken others. Confraternities were approved in some places and discouraged in others; enthusiasts went too fast in their manner of celebrating the Friday after the Octave of Corpus Christi. Finally both sides looked to the Holy See. Only when Devotion to the Sacred Heart could speak with the voice of Rome would the Work of Love have full play. In 1696 the first appeal was sent to the Sacred Congregation of Rites. A great struggle began in which the Devotion passed through the refiner's fire.

NOTES

1. Quoted in Hamon, *op. cit.*, Vol. I, p. 140.

2. *Ibid.*, p. 150.

3. *Ibid.*, p. 173.

4. Sister Mary Philip, *Life of Blessed Margaret Mary Alacoque* (Herder, 1919), pp. 171, 207.

5. The widely known Twelve Promises in their familiar form have been compiled from the letters of Saint Margaret Mary, where some of them are found repeated in varied wording more than once. They are not usually given as a direct statement in the actual words of Our Lord, as are the texts of the Great Revelations. However, they gain greatly in force and clarity when studied in the context of the letters. For instance, it is evident that the promise to "touch the most hardened hearts" extends to all those who teach as well as to priests if they practice Devotion to the Sacred Heart. The text of the Great Promise is incorporated into the Bull for the Canonization of Saint Margaret Mary, thus receiving the highest degree of approval that can be accorded by the Church to a private revelation.

6. Quoted in Hamon, *op. cit.*, Vol. I, p. 148.

CHAPTER X

TRIAL BY FIRE
1690–1794

"My Kingdom will come."

During the century which followed the death of Saint Margaret Mary, Devotion to the Sacred Heart passed through its trial by fire. In the course of its public examination before the bar of divine authority at Rome it entered into the conflict of human affairs at their most tumultuous. It was tested from above and below. It had come from heaven to cast fire upon earth; it met the flames of irreligious hate and of revolution, which tried its spirit. Life through death is the paradox of the supernatural order; the Redemption is triumph through defeat. In the eighteenth century the Devotion underwent its martyrdom, while the deliberate and unerring voice of the Apostolic See uttered the proclamations which made it an integral part of the undying Church.

The Reformation was completing its work of disintegration, while those who clung to the Church clung only too often to her external forms. An ambiguous liberalism and petty dynastic wars tried to maintain balance in the political order. And "by an unfortunate coincidence, during this period of transition from absolutism to the beginnings of modern democracy, the rising demand for equality and liberty was most loudly voiced by irreligious men; whereas churchmen were chiefly concerned with the defense of ancient institutions, class privileges or vested interests."[1] It was an age of scandal and luxury in high places, of starvation in attics and stony fields. The saints of the age were perforce austere and lonely souls whose lives were a contradiction to their times; Alphonsus Liguori, a moralist and preacher to the neglected; Paul of the Cross, founder of the Passionists, with the sign of the Crucified over his heart; Benedict Joseph Labre, a tramp. It was the "Age of

Enlightenment," of the rationalism that led to atheism, the age whose thinking was led by Locke, Kant, Wulff, Rousseau, Voltaire and the Encyclopedists, the age that ignored the underprivileged, that lived by the head and forgot the heart.

Through such heartless society the Devotion to the Sacred Heart burned its way; rationalism called for Love, and the Work of Love went on along the obscure and suffering road of Christian paradox. The history of this period of struggle for the Devotion centers in France, the country chosen by Providence as the scene of the chief events of its history. The struggle spread to Italy, Austria and Germany, while in other parts of the world the Devotion was growing normally. But it was in the offices of the Sacred Congregation of Rites in Rome that the Spirit was at work most manifestly, and the series of documents issued with papal approval throughout the eighteenth century record the divine purpose in plainly official language.

Saint Margaret Mary had known well enough that her mission would require recourse to the Holy See, and that she was powerless to make such a move. But in 1688 Our Lord revealed the providential role of the Society of Jesus in the spread of the Devotion. He appeared to her "in a very high place, spacious and extraordinarily beautiful," showing His Heart with its deep wound. The Mother of God was there, and Father la Colombière. To the Visitandines first Our Lady entrusted the treasure of the Devotion, and then to the Jesuits she gave the Mission of "making known its profit and value." In another vision there was promised to their preaching "the unction of an ardent charity" with graces "strong as two-edged swords to penetrate the most hardened hearts." When Our Lord gave to her His most explicit command concerning the Feast of His Heart, she protested that in her poverty and weakness she could do nothing to carry it out. But "give me, Lord," she prayed, "the means to do as Thou wilt." "Go to My servant, Claude la Colombière," came the answer, "and tell him from Me to do all in his power to establish this devotion."[2]

Blessed Claude la Colombière (1641–1682) was the first Jesuit apostle of the Devotion in its developed form; the keynote of his spirituality was confidence in the divine love. The brilliant young scholar who had served as tutor to the sons of Colbert and who could have had the cultured world at his feet, had already been disciplined by the Holy Spirit to keen sanctity, so much so that he was called "my faithful servant and perfect friend" by Our Lord Himself in an apparition to Saint Margaret Mary. He confirmed the latter in her way, he sanctioned her visions, and then their paths parted. He was sent in 1676 to London as chaplain to the eighteen-year-old Duchess of York, Mary Beatrice of Modena, who in the stormy days of Charles II kept a hidden shrine of prayer in the midst of the English court. He lived in constant danger of the Penal Laws, the atmosphere around him was brewing suspicions and mad terrors soon to break out in the Popish Plot. He was finally thrown into prison, from which he was sent home in ignominy to die soon after, broken by his labors for the glory of the Sacred Heart. For at the Court of Saint James he had won souls to fervor by means of it, and had preached a Heart-centered spirituality in sermons like the following:

Let us enter into the Heart of the Son of God and consider how it is disposed as regards His enemies. Consider its meekness and humility. Nothing that He endures from His persecutors prevents His doing justice—to say the least—to them; He recognizes that they are acting in extreme ignorance; and, though in truth envy, human respect, self-interest, hatred, pride, injustice mingle in the motives that urge them on, still the kindliness of His Heart causes Him to dwell on everything that diminishes the gravity of their sin rather than on what may render them more guilty. How often have we occasion to behave in the same manner toward those who offend or injure us! We ought to see how much more of thoughtlessness, of ignorance, than of malice there is in the conduct that annoys us; we ought to make allowances in some for a naturally hasty disposition, in others for the annoyances and embitterments they have themselves to endure, in others for mistakes and various natural defects. But alas, instead of thus excusing our neighbor, we do the contrary; we exaggerate small matters into crimes and gross injustices. We make much of injuries which, if it were the case of some other person, we should treat as nothing. When there are many grounds for justifying, or at least excusing, the words or deeds of our neighbor, we seek out the least favourable interpretation and prefer to dwell on that. We are gratified by the misfortunes of those whom we regard as our persecutors; we view with regret their success and prosperity. What weakness of soul all this shows! What reason to feel ashamed of ourselves when we give way to such unworthy and miserable thoughts and actions. Is not this to behave like unreasoning animals? Truly, my God, if You were to judge us in such a spirit, we should be lost.

But, as for our divine Lord, not only is He just to all those who are unjust or cruel to Him, but He regards them with a profound pity; He deplores their blindness and the evils they are bringing on themselves; He laments with tears: "Oh, that thou hadst known the things that are for thy peace!—but now they are all hidden from thee." He asks them to weep over their own misfortunes rather than His: "Weep not for Me, but for yourselves and your children." He prays for His enemies, suffers for them, offers His blood to save them; and His prayer and sacrifice bear fruit. For amongst those who were converted by the first preaching of the Apostles were those guilty ones. "This man," said Saint Peter in his sermon on the day of Pentecost, "you have crucified and slain by the hands of sinners, You have rejected the just and holy one; you have asked that a murderer should be given over to you; but the Author of life you have slain." "And that day there were added to the Church three thousand souls." . . .

Such are the lessons given to us by the Sacred Heart of our suffering Lord. "Learn of Me," He says, "not to create the world, not to bring into being all things visible and invisible, but that I am meek and humble of heart." (So Saint Augustine expands for us certain memorable words of the Gospel.) To learn that great lesson let us go to school to that divine Heart, especially during the holy time of Lent and the Passion; let us strive to enter into it, abide there, study its movement, and learn to conform the movements of our own hearts to its example.

Yes, divine Lord, I wish to dwell in Your Heart, and there to lose whatever of gall and bitterness there is in mine; for in the love and sweetness of Yours all that will be quickly consumed. I will study perfect patience in that retreat, there I will exercise myself in silence, resignation to Your divine will, and invincible constancy. I will learn how to thank You for the crosses You send me, and to ask Your blessings on any person that annoys or injures me.

To acquire Your spirit of patience and meekness, Your forgiving love, is not the work of one day; but with Your help it can be gained at last. You prayed for Your persecutors. O most loving Jesus, You will not refuse Your help to a soul that desires to love You; I desire ever to love the cross, to love my enemies for love of You. Amen.[3]

After the death of Father la Colombière, Saint Margaret Mary turned confidently for help to other young Jesuits. She asked Father Croiset, "her very dear brother in the Heart of Our Lord," to write a little book. She died before its completion, so that when it appeared, it contained a sketch of her own life. In the pages of *The Devotion to the Sacred Heart of Our Lord Jesus Christ* the outlines of the cultus as shaped by the Revelations of Paray are drawn with firm clarity:

The special object of this devotion is the immense love of the Son of God which led Him to deliver Himself for us today, and to give Himself completely to us in the Blessed Sacrament of the Altar. . . . . The end placed before us is first of all to acknowledge and to honor as far as in us lies all the dispositions of love and tenderness which Jesus Christ has for us in the Adorable Eucharist, by our frequent adoration, by a return of love, by our thankfulness and by all possible homage; secondly, to repair in every possible way for the indignity and the outrages to which love has exposed Him during the course of His mortal life, and to which the same love exposes Him every day in the Holy Sacrament of the Altar. Thus, this devotion consists in nothing less than an ardent love for Jesus Christ whom we have with us unceasingly in the Adorable Eucharist, in the expression of that ardent love by the regret we have at seeing Him so little loved and so little honored by men, and by the means which we take to repair for this contempt and lack of love. But since we need for the exercise of even the most spiritual of devotions objects which are in some way material and sensible, which striking us more forcibly, stir our memories and encourage our practical efforts, so the Sacred Heart of Jesus has been chosen as the sensible object most worthy of our respect and the best fitted for the end proposed by this devotion.[4]

Father Croiset's book appeared in 1691, and the life of its author was a shining illustration of the doctrine contained in it; he spent his nights and days spreading what was then called, with considerable suspicion, "the new devotion." His eagerness was unmeasured, and was checked by his superiors. And then, in 1704, his book, which had already reached far abroad in many translations, was placed on the Index, where it remained for nearly two centuries. When finally removed from the Index, it was not changed in any way from the original.

This fantastic fact had no other cause than the one ascribed to it at the time by another champion of the Devotion, Father Gallifet: "some malice on the part of men, and much on the part of the devil." It was another proof that a turning point had come, a crisis in the battle between good and evil; the Sacred Heart was to be, throughout the eighteenth century, "a sign of contradiction."

Undoubtedly, it had always been sweet and profitable to speak of the Divine Heart; the devotion which rises to it finds both its reason for being and its beauty in the truths of faith, for the Revelations of Paray-le-Monial added nothing to Catholic doctrine. But, because God willed it so, the hour struck, at the close of the seventeenth century, for manifesting to all souls the devotion reserved until then for a chosen few, and to make of it a universal devotion. The divine thought became known through the Revelations made to Sister Alacoque. They alone created a movement which many failed at first to understand.[5]

The incredible persecution which the new cultus underwent was more than a matter of misunderstanding; it was the crucible through which the Work of Love had to pass in its change from private prayer to a public cult. The storm was roused against the visions of Paray, and against the forms and practices there demanded; it was roused especially against the Feast which would make the Devotion liturgical. In the struggle, those truths of faith which are "its reason for being and its beauty," stood out in their unanswerable splendor and in their full authority, until the quiet sentence that stills storms could be heard: "Rome has spoken."

Rome had to be approached many times before she spoke favorably. During the years from 1690 to 1765, the history of the Devotion is interwoven with complex strands of secular and religious history. The forces of rationalism and ignorant prejudice were rampant, allied with a fear of novelty and of illuminism justified by notorious events of the day. They all fell upon the "new devotion," finding leaders in Jansenistic bishops and borrowing weapons from the fanatical hatred of the Jesuits which was then troubling international relations. Paradoxically, these attacks fell into line with the strongly reasoned opposition of a great and enlightened churchman, Cardinal Lambertini, the future Pope Benedict XIV, through whose prudence the slow wisdom of the Church came into play.

The exiled queen of James II of England, the Mary Beatrice who had learned to love the Divine Heart under the guidance of Father la Colombière, was the first to voice the appeal of thousands of souls. She wrote in 1696 to the Holy Father, Innocent XII, requesting permission for the Visitation Order to celebrate the Feast of the Sacred Heart on the Friday after the Octave of Corpus Christi. The question was referred to the Sacred Congregation of Rites, and the Postulator of the cause pleaded as follows:

Just as the supreme and all-perfect God, who could have made all things at once in a single moment, willed to create the world successively through a space of six days, so His ineffable goodness and mercy have disposed His plans and times with marvelous wisdom. Thus He has roused the minds of the faithful to His worship and to that of the Saints by various cycles and seasons, so that many and diverse Feast days have been instituted by Holy Church. That this is fitting was made clear by Saint John Evangelist in a vision to Saint Gertrude; for when she asked him why he had not, for the greater good of the Church, revealed to all those heart-beats of divine sweetness which He drank from the fountain of the Lord's breast, he answered as follows: "The message of the sweetness of those heart-beats was kept for later times, that by hearing it the ageing world in which the love of God was growing cold might be re-kindled." This is apparent especially in that most religious cultus which is due by every right to the most Sacred Heart of Our Lord Jesus Christ, for it is well known that since the beginning of the church many saints have been drawn to it; in our times, however, when the love of men is growing cold, there are scarcely any who turn the affection of their heart towards it. . . . [Many examples follow, drawn from the lives of early saints.]
    The institution of this Feast involves a matter that is weighty, true, useful and conducive to good living, since by it the hearts of the faithful are stirred up to the love of Christ Our Lord; it is in accord with Sacred Scripture in which this devotion is adumbrated; it is in accord with the doctrine and example of the Fathers, as we have admirably shown in our memorial. From all that we have said, since it is just to render to the Sacred Heart of Jesus, seat and source of love, a privileged cult in memory of its innumerable benefits, as the greatest saints have rightly done, it seems that the desire of her most serene Highness, Queen of England, should be granted.[6]

The answer to this request was a compromise. Without mentioning the Sacred Heart, the Sacred Congregation gave permission for the Mass of the Five Wounds to be said on the day named, in Visitation chapels. To a similar request from another Order came a clear *Non expedit*.

It was, however, expedient to pray, publicly as well as privately, and in 1720 the whole of France was swept by a wave of confidence when Marseilles was delivered from the plague and its attendant horrors in answer to the official consecration of the city, made by its Bishop and civil rulers together, to the Sacred Heart. The Venerable Madeleine Rémuzat, a Visitation nun, had inspired this municipal act, while in her cloister she collected current invocations to the Sacred Heart into the Litany that we know today. This litany was a response to popular demand; a supernatural current of enthusiasm was sweeping over the country. The Devotion had, *de facto,* spread far and wide; it was time for a new appeal to Rome.

Father Joseph Gallifet (1643–1747), Assistant General of the Jesuits, was its champion. In his youth, he had been recalled from the point of death to active health by a vow made for him by Father Croiset, by which his whole life was to be consecrated to the spread of the Devotion. The petition which he sponsored came again from royal pens, those of the Kings of Spain and Portugal. In order to prepare the way by enlightening minds, Father Gallifet, as Postulator of the cause, gathered his material into a book, the first systematic study of the Devotion from the points of view of theology, of philosophy, of history, and (less happily for the results) of physiology. In his work, *De Cultu Sacrosancti Cordis Dei ac Domini nostri Jesu Christi,* he penetrated into the central question of the relation of the Heart of flesh to the Divinity of Christ, and of His divine to His human love:

We must first consider this Heart as intimately and indissolubly united to the soul and adorable Person of Jesus Christ, elevated by this union to a position absolutely divine, full of life, of feeling, of intelligence. We must consider it in the second place as the principal and most noble organ of the sensible affections of our Lord, of His Love, His zeal, His obedience, His wishes, His griefs, His joy, His sadness, as the source and the seat of these same affections and of all the virtues of the Man-God. In the third place we must consider it as the center of all the interior sufferings which our salvation cost Him, and besides, as cruelly wounded by the blow from the lance which He received when on the Cross. Finally, we must consider it as sanctified by the most precious gifts of the Holy Spirit, and by the infusion of all the treasures of grace of which it is capable. All these

belong, in truth, to this Divine Heart; all are its characteristics; from
them it derives its dignity, its price, its excellence, and consequently
all enter into the aim of the devotion to the Heart of Jesus. It is this
Heart, thus moved, thus on fire, thus afflicted, thus wounded, which
is the real object of the devotion of which we treat. . . .

We may also form an estimate of the Heart of Jesus by the holiness
which belongs to it. It is of faith that the Heart of Jesus is holy with
the holiness of the Eternal Word, Who is united to it, and therefore
it is holy with an infinite holiness. But as this holiness is common to
all the component parts of the Body of Jesus, it is not this that we
have in this instance specially in view. There is a holiness which belongs
peculiarly to His Heart, for the human body participates in the holiness of the soul that gives it life, and of all parts of the body that
which participates most intimately in the holiness of the soul is the
heart. . . .

Moreover, it is constantly evident from the testimony and experience of the saints, that the heart is the seat in which the Holy Spirit
dwells in a sensible manner, and where Jesus Christ makes His presence felt by His spouses in a special way. It is there that He dwells
as upon His throne, and as in His garden of delights. It is thus
that the saints speak. All that is so sure, from the experience of pure
souls raised to divine union, that no one who knows anything of such
matters can question it.

From this, it is easy to understand how wonderfully the heart
must be sanctified by the infusion of these heavenly gifts, by all
these impressions of joy, sorrow, delight, grief, which belong to the
heart and have no relation to other parts of the body. Now it is evident that the more excellent are these supernatural graces, the more
they will give to the heart that sanctity of which it is capable. From
this follows what we wish to establish by these reflections: the ineffable holiness of the Heart of Jesus Christ. For all the graces of this
kind which have been communicated to the hearts of the saints, even
if united together, would be as nothing compared to the riches of the
Divine Heart.[7]

This book was dedicated to Pope Benedict XIII, and received
the full and gracious approval of Cardinal Lambertini before
Father Gallifet's Petition of 1726 was presented to the Sacred Congregation. This document was urgent in its wording, and its author was confident of success:

It should finally be clear and certain that the intrinsic qualities of the
Heart of Jesus are such as to make it most worthy of a special cultus.

As was said above, if the matter is attentively considered, it is evident that there exists no corporeal or sensible thing in the whole world, whether in heaven or on earth, which could be more fitting, just, proper and fruitful as the object of the devotion of the faithful than this most holy, loving and afflicted Heart. There is nothing, moreover, which contains and represents sublimer mysteries; nothing of which the sight and consideration can arouse holier affections in the hearts of the faithful; nothing more apt to recall to the minds of men all the kindnesses of our loving Redeemer; nothing which shows more vividly the bitter interior sorrows which Christ bore for our sakes. All these things are not only contained and represented in that most Sacred Heart, but are, as it were, drawn and engraved in it. From this it follows that no object holier, sweeter and more lovable could be placed before the faithful, and what is more, none more apt to powerfully stir up the gratitude of souls towards our most loving Redeemer, to inflame their love, to increase their holy desires, and finally to strongly arouse their most sacred affections. Let other sensible objects already venerated in the Church—the cross, the wounds, the name of Jesus, the instruments of the Passion—be compared with this most divine and holy Heart, and from this comparison, let any man with a heart decide what should be felt concerning the Heart of Jesus.[8]

The document opened a series of burning discussions: this cultus is not only new but unnecessary in the Church; it is dangerous, as it leads men to "divide Christ," thus opening the door to a return of Nestorianism; it is unsound, as the physical heart is not, in fact, the "seat" of love.[9] So grave were the difficulties felt to be that the theologians returned an answer: *non proposita,* thus advising that the matter should be dropped, unanswered. But Father Gallifet could not drop the zeal that consumed him; he re-appealed and, in 1729, drew the answer: *negative.* He did not live to see the triumph of the cause which he knew to be divine.

Nearly fifty years of struggling cross-purposes followed. In France the conflict was sharp. The Bishop of Soissons, Monseigneur Languet, wrote the first full life of Sister Margaret Mary Alacoque, which he dedicated to the Queen, Marie Leczinska. It drew down upon him the petty attacks of a host of minor Jansenists, "philosophers" and Gallicans, bracketed in a common hatred of the Devotion to the Sacred Heart. An odious weekly magazine, the *Nouvelles Ecclesiastiques,* organ of the less reputable Jansenists, began to appear from a secret press in 1727, and soon spent its

wit in mockery of the *Cordicoles,* or the *Alacoquistes.* Far more
serious in its effects on the practice of the Devotion, and on the
spiritual life of many religious communities, was the attitude of
several bishops and priests who sided with the *Appelants,* or ec-
clesiastics who had appealed against the Papal Bull *Unigenitus*
which, in 1713, had re-enforced the condemnation of Jansenism,
and who thus incurred excommunication. Support of the Devotion to the Sacred Heart became practically a badge of loyalty to
the Holy See; conflict with "the heresy of fear" gave new life to
the Devotion of Love.

Among its supporters the Jesuits were the most eminent and the
most active; and this complicated the situation, as a network of in-
trigue, largely political, was beginning to close around the Society
of Jesus. Some scandalous cases of false visionaries drew further
discredit on the Devotion, expressed by noisy religious journalists,
but the body of the faithful remained untroubled. They said their
prayers earnestly from the many manuals of the Sacred Heart that
came from less noisy presses, and by the middle of "the century of
enlightenment" the Holy See had approved of more than seven
thousand Confraternities in honor of the Heart of Christ.

Meanwhile, the Devotion was passing the frontiers unquestioned
and unhindered. Throughout Europe the Benedictines, Dominicans and Franciscans were making of their monasteries tranquil
centers for its spread. In Spain, the enthusiasm was most ardent,
kindled by the saintly Father Hoyos and his fellow Jesuits, many of
whom carried it overseas through the Spanish Americas. In Syria,
the life of Saint Margaret Mary was read in Arabic; in Pekin, new
converts prayed to the "Heart of Jesus, temple of the adorable
Trinity," while in Hang Tcheon there was a parish church dedicated to it when as yet there was none in Europe. A businessman
in Constantinople, brother of Sister Madeleine Rémuzat, said the
Litany of the Sacred Heart among the Turks; in California, Friar
Junipero Serra, apostle to the Indians, wrote on the adobe walls of
his beloved mission at Carmel-by-the-Sea a single exclamation:
"O Sagrado Corazon!"

In the meantime the unhappy Queen, Marie Leczinska, was
spreading through the royal circles of France and Poland her own
warm trust in the Heart of Christ. Letters from Kings and princes

reached Pope Clement XIII, urging that the difficult times through which the Kingdoms of Europe were passing called for a solemn and public cultus in its honor. Finally a *Memoriale* drawn up by the Bishops of Poland asked that a proper Feast and Office, for that country, might be granted. The Devotion could no longer be called "new"; it was an integral part of the worship of the faithful, and the Petition went deep into the underlying theology of this fact which a century of turbulent history had brought about:

In order to meet all objections, let this be observed, and kept well before our eyes: in this devotion the Heart of Jesus is never considered as an inanimate object, devoid of sensation, but as living and feeling, always intimately united to the soul and person of Jesus. Thus the Heart of Jesus is not to be considered as an isolated thing; but it is as forming one thing with His soul and with His person that it constitutes the object of this devotion. It is this single entity formed by the union of the Heart of Jesus, and of His soul and of the Person of the Son of God, together with all the graces and the treasures of heavenly gifts and the virtues proper to this most Sacred Heart, and finally the wound received on the cross by which His last remaining blood was poured out after His death for our sakes, which is proposed for the veneration of this devotion. From which it necessarily follows: (1) that whatever honor is offered to the Heart of Jesus is referred wholly to the Person of Christ; (2) that it may truly and properly be said of the Heart so understood, that it may love and suffer injuries, and grieve, and so with all other feelings; (3) that to that same Heart speech may be fittingly addressed and prayer offered, and the whole cult of honor paid which the Divine Person is capable of receiving, since whatever is referred to the Heart is necessarily referred to the Person who lives in that same Heart. . . .

The objection might be raised that the human heart, as such, has nothing to do with producing spiritual love; nevertheless it is the instrumental cause, and the seat of that sensible affection which leads naturally to the spiritual, as Saint Thomas, in explaining the precept to love God with the whole heart, says: "As it is natural for fire to give heat, so it is natural for the heart to burn with love. The life of the heart is love; and it is impossible for a heart that desires to live to be without love."[10]

When the Promotor of the Faith mechanically repeated the old objections of 1726, the Postulator replied:

We must consider that

(1) the Heart of Jesus forms one thing with the soul of Jesus and with His Divine Person because of their intimate union;

(2) it is the symbol or natural seat of all the virtues and all the interior sentiments of the Lord Christ, above all of the immense love which He has for His Father and for mankind;

(3) further, it is the center of all the sorrows of the most loving Redeemer, sorrows suffered throughout His whole life, and especially during His Passion, for the salvation of men;

(4) the wound received upon the cross must not be forgotten, a wound made not so much by the lance of the soldier as by the love of Jesus which directed the lance towards the Heart.

All these things belong to the Heart of Jesus; united in Him, all these constitute with Him the proper object of this Feast. Hence it follows—and this point is of great weight—that this object so understood embraces, truly and really, the whole of the interior life of Christ the Lord. That this is a divine thing, and full of the deepest mystery, is plainly seen.[11]

At last on January 26, 1765, Rome annulled its earlier cautious pronouncements, and spoke in favor:

Requests having been urged for the granting of a Mass and Office of the Sacred Heart of Jesus by most of the Bishops of Poland and by the Archconfraternity of Rome erected under that title, the Sacred Congregation of Rites, in its session of January 26, 1765, recognizing that the cultus of the Heart of Jesus is already spread through almost all parts of the Catholic world, favored by Bishops, enriched by the Holy See with thousands of briefs of indulgences, and with innumerable confraternities canonically erected under the title of the Heart of Jesus, understanding moreover that the granting of this Mass and Office has no other end than to develop a cultus already existing, and to renew symbolically the memory of that divine love by which the only-begotten Son of God took human nature and, obedient unto death, willed to show men by His example that He was meek and humble as He had said; for these reasons, according to the report of his Eminence the Cardinal Bishop of Sabino, after having heard the Reverend Cajetan Fortis, Promotor of the Faith, annulling the former decision of July 30, 1729, it has seemed best to grant the request of the Bishops of the Kingdom of Poland and the Roman Archconfraternity. The Mass and the Office will be drawn up. When this decision of the Congregation was reported by me, as secretary, to our lord Pope Clement XIII, his Holiness fully approved.[12]

The Feast so long desired had been officially granted to those who asked for it; soon more and more groups were asking and none were refused. Priests at the altar began their sacrifice with the Introit *Miserebitur* of the new Mass. The next few years were a brief era of triumph.

Then the Devotion to the Sacred Heart passed, with Europe, through the Revolution. Admitted by the Church to a place in her public worship, it endured the Church's own trial by fire; sanctioned as a part of the devotional life of the people, it shared in their social and political vicissitudes. It first became a rallying sign for religion against irreligion, then a stable center about which the revolutionary forces were to sway up and down for many years, and finally, in the next century, a symbol for the reconstruction of a new order. The crisis was one of more than human intensity; satanic violence, blood-drenched and black, beat against the white serenity of Providence.

The strongest bulwark of the Devotion disappeared before the coming of the actual Revolution when, in 1773, Pope Clement XIV suppressed the Society of Jesus, reluctantly but "inspired by the Holy Spirit," as he declared in the Brief *Dominus ac Redemptor*. It was to be but one more instance of the repeated death and resurrection which is the rhythm of Christian life inspired indeed by the Holy Spirit. With the learned defenders of the Devotion thus silenced, the last and bitterest attack against its doctrinal content was raised when Jansenism made a final effort to revive its moribund tenets. Scipio de Ricci, Bishop of Pistoia, hated the "new" Devotion with a blind and petty hatred, and had scandalous pictures painted on the walls of his country house in mockery of it. He admitted that Rome had approved, but maintained that "one risks, when practicing it, falling into the error of the greater number of the Cordicoles who, through malice or ignorance, abuse the permission that they have wrested, and adore what they know not or should not adore."[13] As a Jansenist professor wrote: "It is not Christ whole and entire but a divided Christ that is offered to our adoration. . . . To adore the Heart of flesh separated from the Person of Christ, is to be in the proximate occasion of idolatry." It was, then, the old charge of Nestorianism that Ricci raised when he summoned two hundred and thirty-four priests to his Synod of Pistoia in 1781. The charge was incorporated, together with the most radical propositions of Jansenism, into the decrees of the Synod which were speedily promulgated, and added fuel to the outbreak of Josephism that was troubling the Austrian Empire, thus involving the Devotion to the Sacred Heart in another Church-and-State controversy.

Years passed before the Decrees of this heretical council could draw from Rome the most luminous of its doctrinal pronouncements concerning the Devotion, and in the meantime the Terror washed over France. There was something diabolical in the virulence with which the Devotion was attacked not only as a theory but as a way of life. Never had it been practiced with more fervor than in the days when the forces of atheism were putting men to death for its sake, and its first martyrs entered heaven.

No one at the time knew what took place during the summer of 1792 in the prison cell where Louis XVI was awaiting death. He wrote his testimony of faith in the Heart of Jesus, and, knowingly or unknowingly, fulfilled the request that the Divine Heart itself had made, through Saint Margaret Mary, to Louis XIV in 1689. In a document only made public years later, the unthroned king acknowledged to God that the calamities fallen upon his nation were perhaps due to his own failure to repress vice and irreligion, and then prayed: "O Jesus Christ, divine Redeemer from all iniquities, it is in Your adorable Heart that I lay the outpourings of my afflicted soul. I call to my help the tender heart of Mary, my august protectress and my mother." Then followed the terms of the formal vow by which he promised to solemnly consecrate the kingdom of France to the Sacred Heart, to keep its Feast, and to give it public honor upon his release from prison, and he ended: "O adorable Heart of my Savior, may I forget my right hand, may I forget myself, if ever I forget Your benefits and my promises, or cease to love You and place in You my confidence and all my consolation. Amen."[14]

But it was not to be Louis XVI who would build a national shrine to the Sacred Heart. His private testimony to the tardily recognized rights of the King of Love passed unnoticed for the time, while others publicly witnessed to the living flame of love by their death. It was easy to pick out those devoted to the Sacred Heart, because from Visitation Convents all over France, as in lands beyond, little embroidered badges, *sauve-gardes* against the perils of the hour, were scattered by millions among the faithful. They became the badges of "anti-revolutionaries"; they were found on the blouses of peasants left dead on the field after the fearful uprising in the Vendée in 1793. The Devotion became a political menace to those in power, something to be cut off, with the heads of priests, religious and aristocrats, by the guillotine. Mademoiselle Victoire de Saint Luc, young, beautiful and high-spirited, was arrested for having given a Sacred Heart badge to a friend; both were put to death for the Heart of the King of Martyrs.

A diabolical scene of consummate blackness and blasphemy took place in that same year. Marat was murdered by Charlotte Corday; at his funeral his body was worshipped with incense as the people cried: "He died for us." An altar was then set up in the Luxembourg Gardens where the heart of Marat was exposed for veneration, while a sacrilegious invocation coupled the heart of the atheist with the Heart of the God-man. A cry of agonized reparation rose from the lovers of the Heart of Jesus. Father Cormeaux offered his life in atonement; God accepted his offer, and he went to the guillotine.

Then, while the Terror was still raging, Pius VI gave the Church's answer to the charges of Pistoia, and vindicated the blood shed for the Heart of Christ. In 1794, the quiet tones of the Bull *Auctorem Fidei,* unheard for the moment in the uproar, turned the Christological truths defined in the early Councils of the Church to shine upon the Devotion now in its agony. This Bull is of the first importance not only as a theological vindication of the Devotion, but also as an exposition of its ultimate object. In the solemn language of formal Papal pronouncements it clarified the very basis of the cultus paid to the Heart of the Word made flesh, which is indeed the object of latria, of adoration in the fullest sense. From then on, in the words of an adversary brought to his knees, this Devotion is "so founded, both in itself and in its adorable object, that according to the doctrinal and definite judgment of the Holy Apostolic See, no one henceforth may think, teach or preach anything to the contrary."[15] This has remained true throughout the wide amplification of the scope of the Devotion in recent times. The *Auctorem Fidei* first expresses the mind of the Church on the adoration given to the flesh of Christ, then applies this statement to His Heart:

The proposition which asserts that to directly adore the humanity of Christ, and above all a part of that humanity, is always to render a creature the honor due to the divinity—in as much as by the word "directly" it is intended to blame the cult of adoration which the faithful render to the humanity of Christ, as if the adoration given to the humanity and the living flesh of Christ, not considered simply as flesh but as united to the Divinity, were a divine honor paid to a creature and not rather the same unique adoration which adores the word Incarnate and the flesh which is His own—this proposition is false, captious, prejudicial and injurious to the pious cult of the humanity of Christ which the faithful have rendered and must render to it.

The teaching which rejects the Devotion to the Sacred Heart of Jesus as among those devotions described as new, erroneous or at least dangerous—if understood of this Devotion such as the Apostolic See has approved it—is false, rash, pernicious and injurious to the Apostolic See.

In the same way, the proposition which censures the worshippers of the Heart of Jesus (even by that name) for not perceiving that the sacred flesh of Christ, or even the whole humanity when separated and divided from the divinity, cannot be adored with the worship of latria—as if they were adoring the Heart of Jesus separated and divided from the divinity, whereas in reality they adore it as it is: the Heart of Jesus, the Heart, that is, of the Person of the Word, to Whom it is inseparably united in the same way as the bloodless body of Christ in the three days of death was adorable in the sepulchre without separation from the divinity—this proposition is captious, and injurious to the faithful who worship the Heart of Christ.[16]

By the time this Bull was promulgated the fires of the Revolution had begun to burn down. When the smoke had settled it was found that under the pressure of suffering the first Religious Orders devoted to the Heart of Christ had come into being. The Work of Love could now take on the lines of the *Corpus Mysticum* as its stature grew through a new century of social unity. It is the work of the Spirit of Love to make one of many.

NOTES

1. J. McSorley, *Outline History of the Church by Centuries* (St. Louis, Herder, 1943), p. 700.

2. Bainvel, *op. cit.*, pp. 26 ff.

3. G. O'Neill, *The Servant of the Sacred Heart* (St. Louis, Herder,

1933), p. 82. An excellent biography of Blessed Claude is *Perfect Friend,* by Georges Guitton, S.J., trans. by William J. Young, S.J. (St. Louis, Herder, 1956).

4. Jean Croiset, *La Dévotion au Sacré Coeur* (France, 1895).

5. Hamon, *op. cit.,* Vol. III, p. 316.

6. N. Nilles, *De rationibus festorum Sacratissimi Cordis Jesu* (Oeniponte, 1875), p. 18.

7. J. Gallifet, *The Adorable Heart of Jesus* (Philadelphia, 1890), p. 58.

8. Nilles, *op. cit.,* p. 73.

9. Father Gallifet, in his insistance on this point, went so far as to say that "as the soul sees through the eyes, so it loves through the heart." Cardinal Lambertini censured this dubious physiology, and later, as Pope Benedict XIV, clarified the matter in his Bull, "On the Canonization of the Saints" (Bk. IV, 2, Ch. XXXI). However, in the same Bull, he admitted the soundness of the doctrinal basis of the Devotion when he wrote that it "does not consist in the Heart by itself, considered alone, but in the Heart of Jesus united to His sacrosanct humanity and His divine body and consequently forming one entity with the soul and divine Person."

10. Nilles, *op. cit.,* p. 121.

11. Quoted in Hamon, *op. cit.,* Vol. II, xiv.

12. Nilles, *op. cit.,* p. 163.

13. Hamon, *op. cit.,* Vol IV, p. 270.

14. *Ibid.,* Vol. IV, pp. 302–304. It is not known with historical certainty whether Louis XVI had knowledge of the message which Our Lord sent to Louis XIV through Saint Margaret Mary in 1689, requesting that a shrine to the Sacred Heart be erected at Versailles, but it is highly probable that he did. A tradition concerning that request seems to have been handed down in the royal family.

15. Hamon, *op. cit.,* Vol. IV, p. 277, note.

16. Denziger, *Enchiridion Symbolorum,* 1561–1562–1563.

CHAPTER XI

ONE WORLD
1794–1870

*"My whole desire is to
set the world on fire."*

In the nineteenth century frontiers expanded and interlaced, as science drew all the lands of the globe into swift intercourse with each other and formed new tensions of give-and-take; the patterns grew more intricate as the peoples one after the other took over their own governments, and new levels of society became articulate. The world became conscious of itself as one world, and the Church more than ever before asserted her mark of catholicity in unity. She rode on the crest of the waves of opposition that tossed her over former barriers. The Devotion to the Sacred Heart, now inseparable from her in daily life, expanded with her growth and reached into the complicated pattern of progress, an element of unity and of social regeneration through the Spirit of Love.

For the first fifty years popular revolutions shook Europe and the Americas till Democracy was dominant and Liberalism passed Acts of Toleration and allowed Catholic Parties to form. But Liberalism also grew into the bitter anti-clericalism that set Freemasonry to work and, coupled with a godless spirit of nationalism, wrested from the Papacy its temporal power. Then the spirit of Empire reached out into the older civilizations of Africa and Asia; missionaries went through the opened doors, carrying the freedom of the Gospel. The Industrial Revolution set machines in motion, and men were split into the orders of capital and labor till the *Communist Manifesto* pointed to the struggle of the future, and was met by the *Rerum Novarum*. Astounded at their own power, scientists released the forces of indefinite progress or destruction. Darwinism turned these forces against the very existence of the supernatural order; philosophy took the same tone, and Higher Criticism attacked Revelation. God answered with the miracles of Lourdes and placed Our Lady in a rocky niche to be freely visited; the Papacy answered with the *Syllabus of Errors* and a recall to the *philosophia perennis* of Saint Thomas. Literature first emphasized self-expression and the primacy of sentiment in Romanticism, then hardened, overshadowed by fear of blind mechanism. In the long afternoon of the century, surfaced with self-complacent optimism but breeding fear and war within, prayerful thinkers became aware that romantic passion and cold scientism called for the same remedy: divine Love. In 1875 an anonymous article appeared in the *Dublin Review* which, in an acute analysis of the times, declared that:

The eyes of faith can discern that all these changes were long ago present to the mind of God; and that He has devised, if we may use the expression, a counter-scheme, a further unfolding of the hidden strength of the Incarnation, in which, by the merciful blending of tenderness with suffering, and of suffering with love, the restlessness of His sinful creatures may find a respite, and come to a perfect peace. This fresh instance of God's Providence over men is the spread of Devotion to the Sacred Heart.[1]

The writer then brought the theology of the Devotion and the time-spirit of the nineteenth century face to face, and found that the one was the salvation of the other.

The first of the new forms in which the Work of Love adapted itself to the new century stood revealed as the air cleared in the streets of Paris after the Revolution. In the core of the Terror several new Religious Orders had taken shape, the very reason for whose existence was the glory of the Sacred Heart of Jesus. The Devotion which in the first ages had lain hidden in monastic cloisters from which it had emerged into the lay world until the Church was compelled, so to speak, to acknowledge it as part of herself, now found corporate expression in new Religious Rules for both men and women, founded in most cases upon the spirit of the Counter-Reformation Rule of Saint Ignatius. They gave to the Devotion one of the most powerful forms possible for radiation and vivifying influence: organized bodies of apostles of the Sacred Heart whose prayer-rooted lives were to be molded upon its virtues, who would do throughout the world in contemplation, charity and self-sacrifice all that the Heart of the God-man had done during the short space of His mortal life, all that it does continually in the unending life of the Mystical Body.

The earliest Order to bear the name of Sacred Heart appears to be the Congrégation du Sacré Coeur d'Ernemont, founded in 1669, and several others were formed in the eighteenth century, and shared in its perils. On Christmas Eve, 1800, Father Joseph Marie Coudrin vowed to devote his life "To the Sacred Hearts of Jesus and Mary, in whose service I will to live and to die." The result was the foundation of the Congregation of the Sacred Hearts of Jesus and Mary, who became known as the Picpus Fathers. Today, together with the Picpus Nuns, they do missionary work in the South Sea Islands. Since 1800 the number of societies, of both men and women, who bear the name of Sacred Heart is amazing, and many who do not bear the name draw their spirit from it.[2] Every form of contemplative and active life is represented, ranging from the Adorers of the Sacred Heart, founded by Mother Peter on Montmartre for pure prayer, to the Missionary Sisters of the Sacred Heart founded by Saint Frances Xavier Cabrini to circle the globe with good works. Thus each Order by its work or influence impresses upon the body of the faithful some special likeness to the divine Heart.

The founding of one of these Orders at the dawn of the nineteenth century will illustrate this phase of spiritual re-creation as the Spirit moved once more over chaos. Father Léonor de Tournély, just ordained, had fled from the Revolution into the Low Countries where, praying one day before a crucifix, he entered, like the contemplatives of old, into the wounded side of Christ; and there he sounded "the thoughts of His Heart." He saw that a Religious Order essentially founded upon the interior life and devoted to the apostolate of education as a means of spreading the love of the Heart of Christ was part of God's plan for rebuilding the shattered social order. He died before he could complete his dream, but his friend, Father Joseph Varin, met one day in Paris a young Burgundian girl named Madeleine Sophie who longed to become a Carmelite. He opened her heart to the call of the Heart of Christ, and on November 21, 1800, she and a few companions consecrated themselves to its glory.

The new Society of the Sacred Heart opened its first school in Amiens, and for sixty-four years Saint Madeleine Sophie governed its spread through Europe and into America and continents beyond.[3] Its growth kept pace with the growth of the Devotion that was its life as the latter, freed finally from persecution, sent its healing, unifying power through the recurring social revolutions of the nineteenth century. The Saint knew what it was doing for her own times, and what it would do for times to come. She wrote:

Devotion to the Sacred Heart of Jesus goes back to the first centuries of the Church, the Holy Fathers spoke of it in several of their writings; it is probable too that Saint John at the moment when the soldier pierced the side of Our Lord to draw from it the last remaining drops of blood, understood from then on the mysteries of love held in that adorable Heart, and that it was from this source that he drew the divine secrets which he has handed on to us in his wonderful Apocalypse. Moreover, the worship of the Heart of Jesus must have begun at the same time as the worship of the sacred humanity of our Savior, that is, immediately after His death; but it is during these latter centuries that this Heart was to receive a more special honor, an honor more intimate, more universal, more widespread. . . .

The promises which He made to his privileged soul [Saint Margaret Mary] of pouring out abundant graces upon those who should honor His Heart, are fulfilled continuously, as idolatrous nations open their eyes to the light of faith. The Heart of Jesus is made known to them, and it is by this very means that these nations come to throw themselves into the arms of the Church. Now, under what circumstances and for what reason should Our Lord manifest His Divine Heart? It is in this very hearth-fire of love that we must seek to fathom the mystery. What then was the state of the world? Profanations, crimes, abominations of all sorts were afflicting the Church of Jesus Christ. Scarcely had America been discovered than heresy planted its banner on these shores. As we see continually in the history of the Church, in every war against religion the enemy begins by attacking the most Blessed Sacrament; altars were overturned, sacred vessels profaned, and crimes of every kind committed, not only in France but in Germany and even in England, then so Catholic.

And after heresy had somewhat spent its rage against the sacred humanity of Jesus Christ, there arose a sect of philosophers like those whom Saint John in his Apocalypse has well described as locusts who come from the depths of the abyss, and which spread over the face of the earth with a power like to that of scorpions. In fact, they did more

evil than the heretics; the latter still admitted a God, but the philosophers denied even the existence of the divinity, and it is to them that
we may attribute in part the miseries of the French Revolution; their
children sucked the milk of atheism, and thus there arose a new generation of philosophers.

Finally, these evils reached their climax. The anger of God, too long
provoked, was ready to strike. It seemed as though the earth must
perish, but at this moment the Heart of Jesus was revealed in a clear
and evident manner. . . . What then was the purpose of Our Lord in
revealing to us devotion to His Heart? It is to give us a means of
adoration, of reparation, and of love. We see that He asked of Margaret Mary special prayers and acts of reparation. He wishes one day
of each month to be consecrated to the honor of His Heart; He asks
for further penance, and well she understood her mission! With what
generosity, what eagerness, what love she fulfilled it till the end of
her life. Thus the Heart of Jesus appeased the anger of God. It was
made manifest at a time when unheard-of crimes were being committed throughout the world; things reached such a point that new
theological solutions had to be found for the cases presented; such
were the crimes which the Heart of Jesus willed to repair.

Child of the French Revolution as she was, Saint Madeleine
Sophie had experienced in her own person the stress of human
history as it is unwittingly shaped to a plan. Turning from the outer
to the inner world she saw the silent forces of divine history being
shaped in the souls of God's instruments, above all by the two
virtues for which she herself would later be canonized, for, as the
collect for her Feast Day says, the Sacred Heart "wonderfully
graced Saint Madeleine Sophie with humility and love."

Again she wrote:

We have been chosen by God in these unhappy times to rekindle
Devotion to the Divine Heart of Jesus. This Devotion must be the mainspring of souls who truly love God at a moment when faith is weakening in many hearts. This Devotion is not concerned with a heart of flesh
only. As the heart is the center in which all the affections of the soul
meet, it follows that the Divine Heart of Jesus is all-worthy of our
adoration and of our love, since the ardor with which He was consumed for God the Father, for His glory, and for the salvation of men,
would have brought His life to an end before the time appointed Him
to suffer, if His almighty power had not worked a continuous miracle.
Our whole merit and our whole security thus lie in uniting ourselves

to this Divine Heart, since through it we can truly glorify God, love Him as He deserves to be loved, and draw as from their fountainhead all the virtues, especially humility, since Our Lord has said to us: "Learn of Me that I am meek and humble of Heart." Let us love the Divine Jesus! Let us enter deeply into His Divine Heart as into a shelter unassailable by the attacks of our enemies, and let us draw from it His own Divine Love. We must make up our minds to suffer, to love sufferings and humiliations, all those things which Our Lord has loved; it is only by uniting ourselves to His Divine Heart that we will draw from it these determinations. . . .

All the mysteries of love spring from the Sacred Heart of Jesus. As soon as the Sacred Humanity of our Savior was united to the Divinity in the womb of Mary, His little Heart consecrated its first affections to us. He offered Himself to His Father to expiate and to save us. . . . Devotion to the Sacred Heart is the devotion of love. If we understood it, how we would love it! What a burning desire we would have to see it spread abroad; what holy pride we would feel in belonging to this Sacred Heart, in bearing its name, in being persecuted for its love. . . . Humility and meekness must become our special virtues; they must be deeply implanted in our souls, and pass, so to speak, into our veins. We shall never be united to Him with plenitude and to that degree which He desires if we have not deeply within our hearts the love, the attraction and the practice of humility. I would like to see it graven there with a stylus of iron, made white-hot in the fire. . . .

This Sacred Heart began to be busied with us, and it has never ceased to be so busied. From this Heart came forth those sublime virtues which we can never thoroughly understand. In this Heart arose all those mysteries of love and grief which overwhelm us: God, born in a stable, fleeing from the persecution of a cruel king, passing thirty years in a life most humble and most hidden, and finally dying in the most appalling pain upon the Cross. He allowed that after His death His Divine Heart should be opened to show all the treasures hidden in this Heart. Thus, Devotion to the Sacred Heart is the union of all things; it is the Devotion of love.[4]

Pius VII, in 1814, reconstructed the Company of Jesus, calling again into the field the militia of the Church that had been disbanded. It had been kept alive in White Russia during the years of suppression by the providential obstinacy of Catherine the Great, and now it stepped back with its old vitality into the front ranks. Jesuit schools were once more opened in national capitals and in desolate mission fields, and when fresh anti-clerical uprisings occurred in France and Piedmont the whole Society was once more under persecution.

The first General after the restoration was Father John Roothaan (1785–1853), who had made his noviceship in Russia. In 1848 he wrote a letter to his suffering sons in which he entrusted the future of the Company to the Sacred Heart of Jesus. He began by relating memories of the time when the Society existed in the Russian Empire alone, when the Fathers had so often said to each other: "The fact that this Society has been so marvelously preserved, and has even begun, little by little, to make new increase, is due to the Sacred Heart of Jesus, and furthermore, what we hope for in the way of future restoration is also to be sought for from that same most Sacred Heart." Their earnest prayers and practices went on for ten years, until the longed-for restoration was granted. And so later he wrote:

in the midst of catastrophes, beneath the weight of which almost half the Society lies prostrate (and how much more of it will so lie in the future he alone knows who knows all things), I feel that the comfort and the help which we seek lies in that refuge which is open to all in need, the most Sacred Heart of Jesus, who once spoke and will always speak those appealing words: "Come to Me all you who labor and are heavy-burdened."

Then, with that strong serenity which builds a future from a ruined present, he recalled to his sons the grace that was theirs:

If we consider this special aim which the Lord has placed before us by introducing the cultus of the Sacred Heart among the faithful, we shall understand still more clearly the peculiar and special interest which our Society must have in it. Evidently Jesus willed that in these latter ages, when the charity of many is growing cold, in the time of falling away which we see coming to pass in our own days almost everywhere, He should raise up faithful souls by this new means of healing, that is, a loving Devotion to His Sacred Heart, lest even the elect should fall into snares and error. What indeed could be more evident than that our Society should find in this cultus a most powerful weapon, since it is called to be a new army, instituted by divine power to this end, that it should strengthen and aid the Church Militant by holding off and beating back, or at least checking, the attacks of enemies who rush in upon it from all sides? And who does not know how efficacious the Devotion to the Sacred Heart will be in preserving and encouraging numbers of the faithful, and saving them from well-nigh universal apostasy? For when impiety was let loose and blasphemously attacked Jesus and His holy religion and when armies of conspirators broke out ready to overturn everything sacred, what a great protection it was to the faithful to recall with special zeal the benefits of our loving Savior, His Passion and Death, and the institution of the most Holy Eucharist; and when the faithful further realize that they are entrusted with the duty of repairing the injuries which are committed against the mysteries of the love of Jesus by apostates, by false Christians, by wicked Catholics and even by not a few priests, they will devote themselves to this holy work with a new ardor, especially by instituting sodalities which will stand as a wall before the house of God, and thus oppose impious fellowships with religious ones.

The General then led his militia away from the battlefield back to the place of refreshment, the source of new zeal: contemplation. They must meet their leader in prayer; then only will they be strong to fight and to endure:

It will help us greatly, dear Fathers and Brothers, if we apply to ourselves the words of the Apostle: "But we all, beholding the glory of the Lord with open face, are transformed into the same image, from glory to glory, as by the Spirit of the Lord." We who call ourselves the companions of Jesus, and who wish to be so in truth, behold the glory of His open face, not as in the Old Law, in symbols and figures, but as afterwards, "when He was seen on earth and spoke with men," beholding as with our own eyes Jesus the Savior, "beautiful above the sons of men," from whose lips grace is poured abroad; we, I say, gazing face to face upon the glory of the Lord (whose whole glory, like that of the King's daughter, is from within, that is, from the Heart, as when He moved among men), gazing upon the very Heart of our Lord, are transformed into the same image by imitation, from glory to glory, from virtue to virtue, from good to better, from perfect to more perfect, to humility ever deeper, to patience ever stronger, to meekness ever more gentle, to obedience ever more generous, to charity ever more ardent, to zeal ever more fervent and more kind, to the perfect man, perfect in all his acts, not by his own virtues or efforts but by the Spirit of the Lord. And indeed, if no one can say "the Lord Jesus" but by the Holy Ghost, how much more is the grace of that same Holy Ghost necessary for penetrating the inner life of Jesus, and contemplating His most Sacred Heart. Trusting thus in the grace of the Spirit, dear Fathers and Brothers, I beseech you to enter this door of safety, this sanctuary of the divinity, as Jesus Himself invites, since His side was not merely struck or wounded upon the cross, but opened, according to the Gospel, as Saint Augustine says; take thence for yourselves an infinite treasure of virtues and graces, by gazing, contemplating, meditating; take all that is needful for your own salvation and perfection, and for that of others. . . .

Therefore, most dear Fathers and Brothers, contemplating this great love hidden in the Heart of Jesus, yet shown outwardly by such wonderful and such magnificent proofs, shall we not try to repay it, burning as we should be with a sincere and ardent love, a love ever more ardent, ever more burning? The love of His Heart was to Jesus a never failing stimulus to do and to suffer for us. And should not our love, not content with words or with empty feelings, stir us powerfully to do and to suffer for Him, without ever saying that it is enough? If we contemplate the Heart of Jesus as an infinite sea of sorrow and of love, we shall understand that these two sentiments of sorrow and of love should be as the two poles about which our lives must turn, so that love tempers grief and grief perfects love. Would that the image of that Sacred Heart might be ever before our eyes. There we see the thorns, the cross, the open wound with flames coming from it on every side. These are the symbols both of the love and of the sorrow of Jesus. And truly these rays with which we see His Heart surrounded represent not only its glory but also the flood of spiritual light, of the help which we need, a flood which is poured out from this Heart to all who venerate it, to enlighten and enflame them. See—not only come and see, but taste and see. . . .

I shall end my letter with the words with which Saint Peter closed his second Epistle: "Grow in grace and in the knowledge of Our Lord and Savior Jesus Christ. Devotion to the Sacred Heart will bring this to pass, that Devotion which I have explained and put before you, though my words sound cold and weak. But the Heart of Jesus will enlighten those who come to Him, and they will come. Growing in knowledge of Him you will grow also in His love; imitation will follow upon love, and in its turn imitation will cause both love and knowledge to grow ever more strong, and in time will make us fit instruments for enkindling in the souls of our neighbor, according to our vocation, that knowledge of Our Lord and Savior Jesus Christ. To Him be glory now and throughout eternity. Amen.

I earnestly ask a remembrance in your prayers and in your Holy Sacrifices.

John Roothaan

Octave of the Ascension of Our Lord, 1848[5]

In the meantime, outside the Religious Orders, constructive movements, inspired by the Devotion and often led by the laity, were carrying its influence into many phases of secular life. In 1818 Pauline Jaricot, a young girl living in her comfortable home in Lyons, laid aside her silks and went in and out among the factory workers to collect pennies to help the Missions. The plans that she organized later developed into the Society for the Propagation of the Faith, but in the beginning her little group of workers were moved to give of their poverty because they were called "Reparatrices of the Heart of Jesus." In 1833 a child named Angèle de Sainte Croix, in the convent school of Les Oiseaux in Paris, wondered one day after Holy Communion "why there is not a month of the Sacred Heart, as there is a month of Mary." She spoke of her inspiration to the Bishop, and June was not long in becoming the world-wide month of the Sacred Heart. And on December 3, 1844 Father Gautrelet, realizing that his Jesuit students were restless for a more active apostolate, preached a sermon in which he urged them to transform their hours of study into an Apostolate of Prayer. The idea caught fire; it was organized and spread on the basis of daily offering and impetration. In 1860 it was given official form by Father de Ramière, who fused it with his League of the Sacred Heart, of which the *Messenger* soon became the organ in many languages. The thousands who then began their day with the morning offering soon grew to millions. It was the fulfillment of a wish of Saint Margaret Mary: "If there could be instituted an association in honor of this Devotion, one in which the members could be sharers in each other's spiritual good, I think it would be most acceptable to the Divine Heart."

Keeping pace with these movements was the authoritative advancement of the cultus by the Church. Saint Margaret Mary was beatified in 1864. In 1856 Pius IX had completed the great act of 1765 by extending the Feast of the Sacred Heart to the universal Church, with the rank of Double Major. It is this act that Pius XII signalized so gloriously when he celebrated its centenary by the publication of the Encyclical *Haurietis Aquas*. Leo XIII raised the Feast to a Double of the First Class in 1889. Most important, perhaps, for its effect upon the faithful at that time was the permission given in 1875 for every bishop in the world to consecrate his diocese to the Sacred Heart for, as the Decree of the

Sacred Congregation of Rites declared, all "will find in this Divine Heart an unassailable refuge from the spiritual dangers that surround them, strength of soul in the present troubles of the Church, and finally consolation and unshakable hope in the midst of their trials." As the unknown author of the article already quoted wrote: "Catholics . . . seeing the importance of such an act in itself, will judge that it must be important, too, as happening at this time. . . . They will discover tokens of God's presence in the unnoticed origin, the secret yet steady growth, the final acceptance on all hands of a Devotion which brings the Incarnation into the center of our hearts and Christ into the midst of modern life."[6]

Nowhere was this promise more clearly verified at that date than in England. There the mediaeval form of the Devotion, profusely cut into the stones and captured in the stained glass of parish churches, and brightly sung in the lyrics of wandering minstrels, had all but vanished with the Reformation. Even when the Penal Laws ceased to operate actively, they continued to chill Catholic life through the eighteenth and into the nineteenth centuries; until gradually the Work of Love awoke to play its part in England's "Second Spring." At the time when the Devotion was at its most violent crisis in France it crossed the Channel and helped to keep the revival of "the Old Faith" free from the dangers of the Gallicanism, ultra-Liberalism and Jansenism rampant on the Continent. It is possible to see more clearly, in the calmer atmosphere of England during the Revolution, that Devotion to the Sacred Heart had more than a devotional influence during those stormy years. By its stress upon the limitless love of Christ for all men it was a dogmatic safeguard against the Calvinistic and Jansenistic denial of the universality of Redemption; and the acceptance of its practices, following the Bull *Auctorem Fidei,* became a hall-mark of loyalty to the Apostolic See in England.

The man who saw these truths most clearly was Bishop John Milner, Vicar Apostolic of the Midland District (1803–1826). He had drawn Devotion to the Sacred Heart from a manual of prayers in his student days at Old Oscott; as Bishop he saw that the Jansenistic tendencies of the time were dividing English Catholics at the very moment when the Church was emerging again into national life. A spirit of obedience to Rome, free and fervent devotional life, a grasp of the full scope of the doctrine of the Incarnation, were what he tried to inculcate. In Devotion to the Sacred Heart he found a single means to this triple end. He placed a window to the Sacred Heart over the altar in the college chapel, and in 1820 issued a pastoral letter outlining the dogma of the Devotion, and instituting definite practices to make it living.[7]

Soon greater pens than his gave literary expression to these movements. John Henry Newman preached his sermon "The Second Spring" in honor of the restoration of the Hierarchy. By that time the Oxford Movement had brought Catholicism back to its place in the intellectual life of the land, and the minds of great converts were open to his words. So were their hearts, and many of them recognized, wrote about, and practiced Devotion to the Sacred Heart. When Newman himself became a Cardinal, he took for his motto "Cor ad cor loquitur," and among his papers were found the following meditations:

1. O Sacred Heart of Jesus, I adore Thee in the oneness of the Personality of the Second Person of the Holy Trinity. Whatever belongs to the Person of Jesus, belongs therefore to God, and is to be worshipped with that one and the same worship which we pay to Jesus. He did not take on Him His human nature, as something distinct and separate from Himself, but as simply, absolutely, eternally His, so as to be included by us in the very thought of Him. I worship Thee, O Heart of Jesus, as being Jesus Himself, as being that Eternal Word in human nature which He took wholly and lives in wholly, and therefore in Thee. Thou art the Heart of the Most High made man. In worshipping Thee, I worship my Incarnate God, Emmanuel. I worship Thee, as bearing a part in that passion which is my life, for Thou didst burst and break, through agony, in the garden of Gethsemani, and Thy precious contents trickled out, through the veins and pores of the skin, upon the earth. And again, Thou hadst been drained all but dry upon the Cross; and then, after death, Thou wast pierced by the lance, and gavest out the small remains of that inestimable treasure, which is our redemption.

2. My God, my Savior, I adore Thy Sacred Heart, for that heart is the seat and source of all Thy tenderest human affections for us sinners. It is the instrument and organ of Thy love. It did beat for us. It yearned over us. It ached for us, and for our salvation. It was on fire through zeal, that the glory of God might be manifested in and by us. It is the channel through which has come to us all Thy overflowing human affection, all Thy Divine Charity towards us. All Thy incom-

prehensible compassion for us, as God and Man, as our Creator and our Redeemer and Judge, has come to us, and comes, in one inseparably mingled stream, through that Sacred Heart. O most Sacred Symbol and Sacrament of Love, divine and human, in its fulness, Thou didst save me by Thy divine strength, and Thy human affection, and then at length by that wonder-working blood, wherewith Thou didst overflow.

3. O most Sacred, most loving Heart of Jesus, Thou art concealed in the Holy Eucharist, and Thou beatest for us still. Now as then Thou sayest, *Desiderio desideravi*—"With desire have I desired." I worship Thee then with all my best love and awe, with my fervent affection, with my most subdued, most resolved will. O my God, when Thou dost condescend to suffer me to receive Thee, to eat and drink Thee, and Thou for a while takest up Thy abode within me, O make my heart beat with Thy Heart. Purify it of all that is earthly, all that is proud and sensual, all that is hard and cruel, of all perversity, of all disorder, of all deadness. So fill it with Thee, that neither the events of the day nor the circumstances of the time may have power to ruffle it; but that in Thy love and Thy fear it may have peace.[8]

Cardinal Manning (1808–1892) dared to stand on the London docks during the terrifying strike of 1889, and lived in the hearts of Englishmen after his death as the champion of social justice. Yet he too was a thinker, not along abstruse lines but along those of history-in-the-making. His central idea was that of the abiding and active presence of the Holy Ghost in the Church, and for this his dearest ideal was the training of a holy priesthood. In 1876 he published a book called *The Glories of the Sacred Heart of Jesus*.[9] It was dedicated "to the students of the Seminary of Saint Thomas of Canterbury, with an earnest prayer that all who go forth from its threshold may be apostles and evangelists of the Sacred Heart of Jesus." Priests enlightened by the profound doctrine there unfolded, and fired by the radiance of its language of love, would indeed be fit instruments for the spreading of the Devotion on the level of high intelligence and purposeful dedication:

As the doctrine of the Incarnation is the true test of the disciples of Jesus Christ, so the divine glory of the Sacred Heart is the true test of the doctrine of the Incarnation. . . .

There were in Jesus two distinct and perfect natures—neither changed nor confounded. It is impossible that the divine nature should become human, or that the human should become the divine: for eternity and infinity cannot be communicated to the creature; neither can eternity or infinity be put off or circumscribed to the outline and stature of the creature. The two natures were perfectly distinct, without diminution or confusion. They were so united that in Christ there were two intelligences. There was the divine intelligence of the Son of God, which adequately contemplates Himself and all things possible to His almighty power. There was also a human intelligence, in which was all knowledge of which the finite intelligence of man is capable. And as there were two intelligences, so I may say there were also two hearts; for the Holy Ghost, writing of the perfections of God, has used the language of man. In the book of Genesis we read that: "when the Lord beheld the wickedness of man upon earth He was touched with sorrow of Heart," and when the Holy Ghost would describe the perfections of David, and the love that God had for him, He described him as "a man after God's own heart." The love and sanctity of God are here spoken of under the symbol of a heart. And this, I may say, is the eternal heart of God. But the heart of Jesus is a heart of flesh—a heart taken from that substance of His Blessed Mother— a symbol, indeed, because it best symbolizes and manifests the eternal love of God; but it is more than this, it is also a reality. And that human heart of Jesus was, in the hypostatic union, united with the eternal charity and sanctity of God—all the ardor of the eternal love was there, and all the fervor and all the tenderness of our humanity was there. And as He had two hearts, He had also two wills. There was in Him from all eternity the divine will, which is the love and wisdom of God acting in the absolute harmony of their perfections. And there was also a human will like our own—the spring and origin of all our actions. And these two wills were so perfectly conformed to each other—like two notes in harmony—so indentical and yet so distinct that there never was, and never could be, a variation or shadow of conflict between them. . . .[10]

To sum all up in a word. As the Incarnation is God's Book of Life, and the knowledge of His Sacred Heart is the interpretation and the unfolding of that Book, the whole mystery of God and of man, and the relations of God and man in grace and glory, are all written in the Sacred Heart. They that know the Sacred Heart know God; they that love the Sacred Heart love God; and they that are made like to the Sacred Heart are made like to God. It is the compendium of the whole Science of God, of the whole way of salvation, of the whole gospel of eternal life. . . .[11]

The Sacred Heart is the key of the Incarnation; the Incarnation is the treasure-house in which are all the truths of the Father, Son and

Holy Ghost. . . . Any one who knows the Sacred Heart aright will know, as I said in the beginning, the whole science of God and the whole science of man, and the relations between God and man and between man and man. These truths are the dogma of dogmas, the treasure hid in the Sacred Heart, the tabernacle of God. . . .

Love, then, the Sacred Heart, and that love will pass into the Beatific Vision; for charity is eternal, and the love of the Sacred Heart is the union of our faint weak charity with the fervent charity, divine and human, of Jesus Christ, our Lord. Adore the Sacred Heart, and it will pass into the worship of the eternal throne, where there will be prayer no longer and reparation no more; but praise for ever and thanksgiving to all eternity. . . .[12]

The second glory of the Sacred Heart is in its relation to the Ever-blessed Trinity. It is the eternal bond between the uncreated and the creature. God has many kingdoms; but of all, the highest and the amplest is the Sacred Heart. From all eternity, God dwelt in His own immensity. He inhabited His own glory; and He rested in His own bliss. The mutual knowledge and love of the Father, Son and Holy Ghost constitute the divine glory and the divine beatitude. But the charity of God willed not to be contained within the limits of His own bliss. He, of His own free will and out of His own divine love, called into existence all orders of created things, that there might be out of Himself an object of His complacency; a friend whom He might love, and by whom He might be loved again. Therefore, He created man to His own likeness for His own glory and for our bliss. But even this did not suffice; it was not enough that we should exist and that He should have, out of Himself, the love of His creatures; He willed to identify Himself with them; He therefore took upon Him a created nature. God the Son assumed a created manhood into the unity of His Person: and the created and the uncreated were joined together by a personal and eternal bond. The immensity of the divine nature and glory met the highest perfection of human nature in the unity of the Person of the Incarnate Word. The whole divine and uncreated glory was in contact with, and more than in contact with the whole world of created existence in only one point; and that point of contact is the Sacred Heart of Jesus. It became, therefore, the most glorious of the kingdoms of the eternal Father. . . .

Cardinal Manning was here writing primarily for priests, and for secular priests. He was, in fact, a vigorous champion of the secular clergy in every case where he could promote their interests and importance, declaring that this "Order of the Gospel" was prior in every sense to all other Orders of priests. Throughout its history the Devotion to the Sacred Heart had been promoted by many Religious Orders of men, each in a way accordant with its own spirit. Now the Cardinal emphasized its accordance with the fundamental and all-pervading spirit of those priests in whose care was placed the greatest number of the parishes of the Church, the diocesan clergy. He could not fail, when writing of the Heart of Christ, to see it as the Heart of the great High-priest, the Priest who, as Head of the Mystical Body, offers perpetual sacrifice in the very glory of the Trinity. He would have been glad to know, could he have seen the future, that in the following century, the votive Mass of Christ the High-priest would be offered by many priests on the eve of every First Friday. To the priests of his own diocese he wrote:

But it is more than the Kingdom of the Father. It [the Heart of Christ] is the special sanctuary in which the great High-priest has redeemed the world. In it, He for ever glorified God by a worship of infinite humility and fervor. In the moment of the Incarnation a human heart loved God with all its strength and saw God with all the intensity of the Beatific Vision. When by the will of the Father, and the co-operation of the Holy Ghost, the Son assumed the vestments of His Priesthood, they assisted in vesting the great High-Priest for His eternal sacrifice. He put on our humanity as the alb and the stole of his sacerdotal office. And in that sacerdotal vesture, He will stand before God forever, assisted by those whom He has made a kingdom of priests unto the Father. But the Sacred Heart is the victim as well as the priest. He is the spotless lamb, the Lamb that will lie to all eternity as slain upon the altar. And that altar is also the Sacred Heart, in which He is for ever saying "Not My will but Thine be done." It is likewise the golden censer in the hands of our great High-Priest, from which the frankincense in a cloud of praise and thanksgiving goes up for ever before the eternal throne. Though, when all is fulfilled, He will no more offer sacrifice nor exercise the priestly office, nevertheless He will be for ever the eternal High-Priest reigning in the glory of the new creation redeemed with His Divine Blood.

But once more, the Sacred Heart will be to all eternity the most perfect creation and the most glorious temple of the Holy Ghost. It was "conceived by the Holy Ghost," and from that instant it was inhabited and sanctified by the Third Person of the Holy Trinity, who not only replenished it with all created grace, but united Himself to it by a substantial union. As in all the just the Holy Ghost dwells not as the fragrance only of the ointment, but as the very substance, so He dwells in fulness in the Head of the Mystical Body, and in the Heart from which its eternal life is derived. The Sacred Heart was always in the Beatific Vision in right of the Eternal Son; but the soul of Jesus has also the light of glory from the Holy Ghost, with which it beholds the uncreated nature and threefold personality of God.[13]

The soaring and peaceful exultation of such passages as these belongs to the realm of prayer under the rule of theology. But it must coexist, in this unfinished world where the Body of Christ struggles to grow to its full stature, with conflicts like those which broke out with menacing prophecy in the latter part of the century of progress.

NOTES

1. *Dublin Review,* LXXVII, 3.

2. More than forty such Orders are listed by Hamon (*op. cit.,* Vol. V, pp. 230 ff.) and many others have been founded since he wrote.

3. The Society of the Sacred Heart now numbers 182 houses, with its Mother House in Rome. The purpose of its existence is "the greater glory of the Sacred Hearts of Jesus and Mary"; it is fundamentally based on prayer and the interior life, and reaches souls principally through the apostolate of education.

4. These passages are taken from privately printed sources, and from: *L'Esprit et les Vertus de Madeleine Sophie Barat* (Paris) and A. Brou, *Travail et Prière* (Paris).

5. *Opera Spiritualia,* Vol. I (Rome, 1936), p. 413.

6. *Dublin Review,* LXXVII, p. 30.

7. See: G. E. Price, *England and the Sacred Heart* (Washbourne, 1913), p. 83.

8. *Meditations and Devotions* (Longmans, 1893), p. 412.

9. Cardinal Manning's book is included in the present chapter although by date it belongs in the next, in order to round out the study of the Devotion in England.

10. Henry Cardinal Manning, *Glories of the Sacred Heart* (Sadlier, 1885), p. 11.

11. *Ibid.,* p. 70.

12. *Ibid.,* p. 97.

13. *Ibid.,* p. 283.

CHAPTER XII

ONE RACE
1870–1899

*"I wish to reign over souls, over
nations, over the whole world."*

The outbreak of the war of 1870 released new forces of irreligion
but also brought about the fulfillment of another wish of Our Lord
expressed to Saint Margaret Mary: the sign of His Heart appeared
upon banners. Love sometimes brings "not peace but the sword,"
and through conflict the Devotion was woven into national histories. A saintly invalid, Monsieur de Montagu, grieving for the
fall of Paris, was inspired to have a flag embroidered in letters of
gold "Coeur de Jésus, sauvez la France." It was made by the
Religious of Paray and given to Colonel de Charette, leader of the
Papal Zouaves, who carried it into the smoke of the battle of
Loigny. At the sight of it a wave of courage swept the regiment
into combat, where many "fell in the Heart of Jesus."

Then after the bitter days of the Commune, as by a wide-reaching inspiration of the Holy Spirit, groups of laymen who were
loyal to their fatherland brought about the forming of "the national vow": to build a basilica in honor of the Heart of Christ.
The vow was approved by the National Assembly on July 23, 1873.
The intention in the minds of thousands of people who had peti-
tioned for it was the deliverance of the Sovereign Pontiff, then
lately deprived of the Papal States, and the well-being of France.
The cornerstone of the basilica of Montmartre was laid two years
later, on the day named by Pius IX for the universal consecration
of the Church to the Sacred Heart, June 16, 1875. The magnificent
shrine rose rapidly on the ancient Hill of Martyrs. What Louis XIV
would not and Louis XVI could not do, the people of France had
done.[1] They wrote their national consecration in large letters

over the door of the cathedral which soon became a center of the Devotion for the whole world: "Christo ejusque sacratissimo Cordi Gallia poenitens et grata et devota."

The consecration of other nations preceded and followed that of France, each a step in the spiritual unification of Christendom: the Tyrol, Ecuador, Portugal, Belgium, Ireland, Spain.[2] It was the expression in larger units of the tendency towards group consecration of which the formation of the "Society for the Social Reign of Jesus Christ" was indicative, and which became the theme of the first Eucharistic Congresses.[3] Factories, communes, employment groups, cells of Catholic Action invoked the Divine Heart in their titles and in their programs. It was the era of "Cor Jesu, Rex et Centrum Omnium Cordium."

It was fitting that the Pope of social justice, Leo XIII, should bring these unifying themes of the Devotion to a climax at the end of the century of social developments. He himself called his action of June 12, 1899, "the greatest act of my pontificate." This act was the completion of that of Pius IX. Signs that it was inspired by the Spirit who is the soul of the Church were widespread throughout the faithful at the time. One of these signs was manifested at a Good Shepherd Convent in Portugal, whose superior was Maria zu Droste Vischering (1863–1899). She was a niece of the heroic Bishop Ketteler, champion of the Church in Germany during the Kulturkampf, who had entered the Good Shepherd Order as Mother Mary of the Divine Heart and been sent to Oporto in Portugal. Neither illness nor the pressure of trying work could keep her contemplative soul from constant awareness of the love of the Divine Heart and of its desires for the love of the whole human race. These desires became overwhelmingly powerful in her own soul, and then very explicit, till she knew that she must appeal to the Head of the Church. From her sickbed she wrote, on January 6, 1899:

Most Holy Father,
　　　　I come to the feet of Your Holiness, in deep confusion, to ask you very humbly to permit me to speak to you again on the subject on which I wrote to Your Holiness last June. . . .
　　　　Last summer, when Your Holiness was suffering from an indisposition which, taking into consideration your great age, filled the hearts of your children with anxiety, it was a great consolation to me to

know from Our Lord that He would prolong the life of Your Holiness, in order to bring about the consecration of the whole world to His Sacred Heart. Later, on the first Friday of the month of December, He told me that in order to grant you this great grace, He had prolonged the life of Your Holiness, and He left me under the impression that, after making the consecration, Your Holiness would soon finish your earthly pilgrimage.

On the eve of the Immaculate Conception Our Lord made me understand that, by this fresh development of the cultus of His Divine Heart, He will illuminate the entire world with fresh light, and these words of the third Mass of Christmas penetrated my heart: "Quia hodie descendit Lux magna super terram." I seemed to behold rays descending from this light, the Heart of Jesus, that adorable sun, and shedding its rays upon the earth in a faint manner at first, then brighter and brighter, till the world was illuminated. And He said: "People and all nations shall be enlightened with the brightness of this light, and warmed by the intense heat of its rays." I understood the ardent desire He has that His adorable Heart may be glorified more and more, and be better known, and spread Its gifts and blessings over the entire world. And He has chosen Your Holiness, prolonging your days in order that you might give Him this honor, console His outraged Heart, and draw down on your own soul those choice graces which flow from this Divine Heart, the source of all grace, the abode of peace and happiness. I feel unworthy to communicate all this to Your Holiness; but Our Lord, after impressing my misery on me more and more, and making me renew the sacrifice of myself as victim and spouse of His Heart, accepting willingly all kinds of sufferings, humiliations and contempt, gave me a strict order to write again to Your Holiness on this subject.

It may seem strange that Our Lord should ask for the consecration of the whole world, and not be satisfied with the consecration of the Catholic Church. But His desire to reign, to be loved and glorified and to inflame all hearts with His love and mercy, is so intense that He wills that Your Holiness should offer Him the hearts of all those who, by holy baptism, belong to Him, in order to facilitate their return to the true Church, as well as to hasten the spiritual birth of those unbaptized ones who have not yet been made partakers of the spiritual life, and yet for whom He has given His life and shed His Blood, and therefore has equally called them to be one day children of Holy Church.

In my letter of June, I explained the graces which Our Lord wished to grant in consequence of this consecration, and the manner in which He wished it to be carried out; but considering the recent earnest entreaties made by Our Lord, with the most filial submission, I earnestly beseech Your Holiness to grant Our Lord the consolations He asks for, and to add still greater splendor to the worship of His Divine Heart, according to the inspirations He will give you. Our Lord not only spoke to me, directly, of the consecration, but on different occasions He has shown me the burning desire He has that His Heart might be more glorified and loved for the good of nations. It appears to me that it would please Him greatly if Your Holiness, by an exhortation to the clergy and faithful, and by granting new indulgences, were to increase the devotion of the first Fridays of the month. When Our Lord spoke of the consecration, He did not say this expressly, but without being able to affirm this positively I thought I discerned the ardent desire of His Heart.[4]

Leo XIII may have been impressed by this letter, but he did not wish to act on a private revelation alone; his response must rest upon the principles of theology and of Catholic tradition. He consulted his theologians. Could he, even though Vicar of Christ, speak in the name of those outside the Mystical Body of Christ? Could he consecrate to the Heart of Christ those non-believing members of the human race who would repudiate such a consecration? The answer came in the clear tones of Saint Thomas:

We must therefore consider the members of the Mystical Body not only as they are in act but as they are in potentiality. Nevertheless some are in potentiality who will never be reduced to act, and some are reduced at some time to act; and this according to the triple class, of which the first is by faith, the second by the charity of this life, the third by the fruition of the life to come. Hence we must say that if we take the whole time of the world in general, Christ is the Head of all men, but diversely. For first and principally He is the Head of those who are united to Him by glory; secondly of those who are actually united to Him by charity; thirdly, of those who are actually united to Him by faith; fourthly, of those who are united to Him merely in potentiality which is not yet reduced to act, yet will be reduced to act according to divine predestination; fifthly, of those who are united to Him in potentiality which will never be reduced to act, such are those men in the world who are not predestined, who, however, on their departure from this world, wholly cease to be members of Christ, as being no longer in potentiality to be united to Christ.[5]

And so Leo XIII, as head of the actual and potential members of Christ's Body on earth, decreed that on the Feast of the Sacred Heart, in 1899, the whole human race should be consecrated—knowingly or not, willingly or not—to the Heart of Christ. Day-laborers and millionaires, the sin-sick and those vibrant with holiness, peoples of white, black, yellow and red skins, old men who had seen the first railroad and little children who would see the first atom bomb, nomads in primitive backlands and workers hanging from subway straps, all were sealed with the sign of the all-possessive Love, the Heart "in whom all hope is to be placed." The Encyclical *Annum Sacrum* told the world the reasons for this mighty act:

But a short time ago, as you well know, We, by letters apostolic, and following the customs and ordinances of Our predecessors, commanded the celebration in this city, at no distant date, of a Holy Year. And now today, in the hope and with the object that this religious celebration shall be more devoutly performed, we have traced and recommended a striking design from which, if all shall follow it out with hearty good will, We not unreasonably expect extraordinary and lasting benefits for Christendom in the first place, and also for the whole human race.

After tracing the historic growth of the idea of consecrating the world to the Sacred Heart, the Holy Father continues:

We consider that the plan is ripe for fulfilment. This worldwide and solemn testimony of allegiance and piety is especially appropriate to Jesus Christ, who is the Head and Supreme Lord of the race. His empire extends not only over Catholic nations and those who, having been duly washed in the waters of Baptism, belong of right to the Church, although erroneous opinions keep them astray, or dissent from her teaching cuts them off from her care; it comprises also all those who are deprived of the Christian faith, so that the whole human race is most truly under the power of Jesus Christ. For He who is the only-begotten Son of the Father, having the same substance with Him and being the brightness of His glory and the figure of His substance necessarily has everything in common with the Father, and therefore sovereign power over all things. This is why the Son of God thus speaks of Himself through the Prophet: "But I am appointed King by Him over Sion, His holy mountain. . . . The Lord said to Me, Thou art My Son, this day have I begotten Thee. Ask of Me and I will give Thee the Gentiles for Thy inheritance and the utter-most parts of the earth for Thy possession."[6] By these words He declares that He has power from God over the whole Church, which is signified by Mount Sion, and also over the rest of the earth to its uttermost ends. . . .

But this is not all. Christ reigns not only by natural rights as the Son of God but also by a right that He has acquired. For it was He who snatched us from the powers of darkness and "gave Himself for a redemption for all."[7] Therefore not only Catholics, and those who have duly received Christian Baptism, but also all men, individually and collectively, have become to Him a "purchased people. . . ."[8]

To this twofold ground of His power and domination He graciously allows us, if we think fit, to add voluntary consecration. Jesus Christ, our God and our Redeemer, is rich in the fullest and most perfect possession of all things; we, on the other hand, are so poor and needy that we have nothing of our own to offer Him as a gift. But yet, in His infinite goodness and love, He in no way objects to our giving and consecrating to Him what is already His, as if it were really our own; nay, far from refusing such an offering, He positively asks for it and desires: "My Son, give Me thy heart." . . .

And since there is in the Sacred Heart a symbol and a sensible image of the infinite Love of Jesus Christ which moves us to love one another, therefore it is fit and proper that we should consecrate ourselves to His most Sacred Heart—an act which is nothing else than an offering and a binding of oneself to Jesus Christ, seeing that whatever honor, veneration, and love is given to this divine Heart is really and truly given to Christ Himself.

For this reason We urge and exhort all who know and love this divine Heart willingly to undertake this act of piety; and it is Our earnest desire that all should make it on the same day, so that the aspirations of many thousands who are performing this act of consecration may be borne to the temple of heaven on the same day.

The vision of Leo XIII here ranged once more over the face of the globe, and he enumerated all who sit in the shadow of death or of ignorance, finding hope for all:

Such an act of consecration, since it can establish or draw tighter the bonds which naturally connect public affairs with God, gives to States a hope of better things. . . . When the Church, in the days immediately succeeding her institution, was oppressed beneath the yoke of the Caesars, a young Emperor saw in the heavens a cross, which became at once the happy omen and cause of the glorious victory that soon followed. And now, today, behold, another blessed and heavenly token is offered to our sight, the most Sacred Heart of Jesus, splendid amidst flames of love. In that Sacred Heart all our hopes should be placed, and from it the salvation of men is to be confidently sought. . . .

Given in Rome, at Saint Peter's, on the 25th day of May, 1899, the twenty-second year of our Pontificate.

Leo XIII, Pope[9]

In answer to this Encyclical bishops and pastors the world over read the now familiar "Act of Consecration of the Human Race to the Sacred Heart of Jesus" composed by Leo XIII for the Feast Day in 1899. Mother Mary of the Divine Heart died while the bells were ringing for First Vespers, to share from heaven in the outpouring of graces promised by the Pope as a result of this "greatest act" of his pontificate.

Some years after, the first synthetic study of the Devotion combined with its history appeared. Father Jean Bainvel, S.J., closed his work with a chapter entitled "Harmonies Found in the Devotion," in which he recognized, from the vantage point of the turn of the century, "the harmony and concord of the historical development of the Devotion." He first asks why a Devotion which sums up Christianity so well should have taken so long to develop, since we have in it "an excellent formula in which the very essence and spirit of Christianity are admirably expressed." He answers that "even when an intuition of a genuine formula has been found, it can only be propagated in a society prepared to understand it." After a rapid survey of the growth of the Devotion in earlier centuries, he shows that it is both the providential expression of the best in the spirit of an age and a "divine antidote" for the virus of its heresies. It is, at every stage, a blending of complementary tendencies in the life of the Church. He then illustrates this profound concept by a study of "some points in the Devotion relative to the conception, the worship, or the omission of love in the course of the nineteenth century":

The nineteenth century has deified love, even human love, even sinful love. In practice such has always been the tendency; love, like all the passions, has received man's idolatrous homage. But to maintain in theory the absolute rights of love, to justify it even in its most monstrous excesses, to insist that all laws, human and divine, should give way before it, to make it the supreme god, this task was reserved for the literature of the nineteenth century. This is what the masters of the greatest repute in poetry, in fiction, in dramatic art, have done.

And they have found only too many disciples prompt to accept their teachings. To this idolatrous worship of human love, of selfish love, the Devotion to the Sacred Heart opposed the worship of the true God who willed that He should be described as love (*Deus caritas est*); of the divine love that gave us Jesus, and became incarnate in Jesus; of love supremely noble and well-ordered; of love divinely pure and disinterested; of the love that sacrifices itself to teach us how to love Him whom we should love, and how we should love; which gives us as our model, our rule, as an incentive to our love, even the love of God, the love of Jesus, that thus by deifying our love we may labor to divinize, if I may so speak, our lives.

Together with this idolatry of love, the nineteenth century, under cover of science, has preached a conception of the world in which love should no longer have any place except as a blind instinct and as an unconscious force. All would be ruled by fatal laws. Everything would be reduced to the evolutions of an impersonal nature, without soul or heart, in which man would be but one of the countless wheels of the immense machine, carried away himself in the universal movement with phosphorescent gleams on the surface of the waves, then to be lost forever in the fathomless abyss. Such for a half century was the self-styled scientific conception of the universe. Such was the conception to which many *savants* steeped in philosophy, many philosophers steeped in science, have lent the seductiveness and prestige of their learning or of their style. In face of this fatalistic conception doomed to end in gloomy pessimism, stoically resigned (like that of Taine), or in false, mocking laughter (like that of Renan), Christian philosophy, apologetics and theology have valiantly maintained the unshaken truths of reason and of faith, the Christian and judicially optimistic conception of the world. But for souls something more was necessary than abstract naked truth. Devotion to the Sacred Heart, by offering them the Heart of Jesus, reminds them of the supremacy of love in the government of the world, makes them see and experience in everything the loving and fatherly providence of God, see and prove the love of Jesus, who has become our brother to make us children of God and to draw down upon us, guilty, miserable children as we are, the divine favors that, from the well-beloved Son in whom they abide, flow down upon us.

The author then turns his thought towards the coming century:

These reflections and many others of the same kind that could be made, will help us to understand the attraction by means of which divine grace draws so many souls, the most religious, most fervent souls, to the Sacred Heart. For these souls, Devotion to the Sacred Heart is, in these days of ours, the natural form of devotion to Jesus; they know that in laboring to increase it in themselves and in those around them, they are laboring that Jesus may reign within themselves and in others. And as the cause of God and the cause of Jesus are but one and the same, we can understand how it is that so many chosen souls who desire to live but for God and for others, for His love, in complete self-forgetfulness and sacrifice of themselves, turn to the Sacred Heart of Jesus, addressing Him in the terms, or their equivalent, of the beautiful prayer addressed to Him by one of those souls, a prayer which sums up so well both the perfection of the Devotion to the Sacred Heart and the perfection of the Christian life: "Sacred Heart of Jesus, my light, my love and my life, grant that I may know but Thee, that I may live only in Thee, through Thee and for Thee."[10]

As the Devotion thus became more public and more far-reaching in society, it followed the inevitable rhythm of the spiritual life; as it grew outward its life reached deeper into the roots of contemplation. In the closing years of the century, Sister Theresa of the Child Jesus, in the Carmel of Lisieux, was learning from the Spirit of Love in her own heart a "way" for souls to follow: "We must approach Him through His Heart; on that side He is defenseless," and "Perfection . . . means taking Jesus captive through the Heart" . . . by "the smallest actions done through love." And: "Since I have been given to understand the love of the Heart of Jesus I confess that all fear has been driven from me. . . . How little is known of the merciful love of the Heart of Jesus! It is true that to enjoy that treasure we must humble ourselves, must confess our nothingness . . . and here is where many a soul draws back." And so in prayer she turned to Him for others: "O my God, must Thy love, which is forgotten, lie hidden in Thy Heart? It seems to me that if Thou shouldst find souls offering themselves as victims of holocaust to Thy love, Thou wouldst consume them swiftly. Thou wouldst be glad to let escape the flames of infinite tenderness that are imprisoned in Thy Heart." Then, gazing over the world from the sublimely simple heights to which her Divine Eagle had carried her, she saw the Heart in the Body Mystical:

As I meditated on the Mystical Body of Holy Church I could not recognize myself among any of its members described by Saint Paul; or rather was it not that I wished to recognize myself in all? Charity gave me the key to my vocation. I understand that since the Church is a body composed of different members, she should not lack the most necessary and most nobly endowed of all the bodily organs. I understood therefore that the Church has a heart, and a heart on fire with love. I saw too that love imparts life to all the members, so that should love ever fail, apostles would no longer preach the Gospel, and martyrs would refuse to shed their blood. Finally, I realized that love includes every vocation, that love is all things, that love is eternal, reaching down through the ages and stretching to the uttermost limits of earth."[11]

What Saint Theresa saw in this luminous flash of understanding she left for the twentieth century to explore after her; it would find that the love animating the Church's members was that of the Heart of the *totus Christus*.

NOTES

1. The message given to Margaret Mary for Louis XIV was thus fulfilled unknowingly, nearly two centuries later. See the history of the building of Montmartre in Hamon, *op. cit.,* Vol. V.

2. These were all cases of consecration made by representatives of civil authority, such as can only be made in Catholic countries. In countries in which the faith is not recognized by the government, consecrations can be made by ecclesiastical authorities.

3. The movement for Eucharistic Congresses was initiated by Mlle. Marie-Marthe Tamisier (1834–1910), who had a profound devotion to the Sacred Heart which she found living in the Blessed Sacrament. She was educated at the Sacred Heart Convent at Marmoutier, and later devoted much time to the care of the shrine of Our Lady of the Sacred Heart at Issoudun.

4. L. Chasle, *Sister Mary of the Divine Heart* (New York, Benziger, 1906), p. 352.

5. *Summa Theologica,* III, q. 8, a. 3.

6. Ps. 2, 6.

7. I Tim. 2, 9.

8. I Pet. 2, 9.

9. *American Catholic Quarterly Review,* July, 1899.

10. Bainvel, *op. cit.,* p. 345. The prayer quoted is that of Saint Madeleine Sophie.

11. *Soeur Thérèse of Lisieux* (Kenedy, 1924), p. 203. The other short quotations are taken from scattered passages in the Saint's letters, etc.

CHAPTER XIII

THE HEART AND THE BODY
1900–1928

"My work is love."

As the twentieth century gained speed, cities tapered up into sky-scrapers and the highest reaches of the air hummed with the wings of planes; the pilots saw time and distance shrink into negligibility beneath them. Intellectual as well as political frontiers were over-lapping into complex patterns. Yet the first Pope of the century was an unhurried saint, a quiet codifier of law, a firm hater of heresy, whose life moved in serene Gregorian cadences. Pius X met the tensions of the age by reminding his children to eat their daily Bread, the Eucharist that holds the love of Christ, and he added to the prayers after Mass the triple invocation to the Sacred Heart. But the nations massed against each other, as the interdependencies binding the globe in one snapped apart into global war. Benedict XV held his many-nationed flock together with supranational charity, saying that the Sacred Heart had been offered by God to the world as the object of a special Devotion in the very form that it most needed. In the uneasy stretch of peace jarred by depression before the coming of another war, Pius XI recognized the Kingship of Christ and thus made the Heart of Christ "King and Center of all hearts." Under such leaders the Church, thinking and acting with the nations along global lines, was ready for a new realization of the mystery of her own nature as the Body of Christ, the key doctrine of the twentieth century, and, turning within herself for the love with which to meet hate, found that her own heart was the Heart of Christ.[1]

Although the primary doctrinal foundations of the Devotion were by now unassailable by controversy, several secondary points were under lively discussion at the opening of the twentieth century.[2] One concerned the light thrown on the Devotion by modern physiological discoveries, a light which seemed to strengthen the formidable objections first offered by Pope Benedict XIV when, as Cardinal Lambertini, he had returned a *non expedit* to the petition for a Feast. Can it be said, in fact, that the human heart is the seat or the organ of emotion? As early as 1880 the controversy on this point had been so sharp that Pius IX had silenced it for a time. But as it became evident that the heart is not the source of emotions, a deeper fact emerged all the more clearly: while not their source it is their register. It manifests them by its physical reactions, or in the words of Gerard Manley Hopkins, the poet-priest: "the heart is of all the members of the body the one which most strongly and of its own accord sympathizes with and expresses in itself what goes on in the soul. . . . The beating of the heart is the truth of nature."[3] Hence the symbolism, current from primeval times, which sees love in the shape of a heart. The psychological basis of the Devotion remained unchanged by science.

A second controversy concerned the question as to whether the Devotion has for its exclusive object the created human love of the God-man, or whether it also includes the eternal, uncreated love of the Word.[4] The point was keenly debated, but theological searching into the matter has resulted in a deeper harmony, and new lines have been opened up. The Encyclical *Haurietis Aquas* now leaves no doubt that divine love is of the essence of the Devotion. From all the give-and-take in periodicals came several admirable books synthesizing the many aspects of the Devotion revealed by this enriching study. The following is the thought of Father Vermeersch:

The love which Christ has for us in His human nature is not a purely human love; it is divine, because of the Person who loves. It is the love of one who is God; its value is infinite. We should call it theandric rather than human; it is the love of God in the nature which He has taken to Himself.

Seen as a work of love, the redemptive Incarnation is attributed to the love of the Father who sends and hands over to us His own Son, to the love of the Word who offers Himself to the Father and wills to come to earth for our salvation, and to the love of the Holy Ghost who creates the soul of the Word and consummates the Incarnation by forming the body in the womb of the most pure Virgin. And so this work of grace, of love and of sanctification which, as such, is attributed to the Holy Ghost, implies under one aspect or another the loving participation of each of the three divine Persons, in accordance with their personal character. So we have a right to speak of a love which moved the Father to give or to send His Son, of a love which makes the Son take human nature, of a love which leads the Holy Ghost to form the body of the Savior, by making the most blessed Virgin to be the Mother of God.

While bending our minds before this mystery, we shall form a better idea of it if we understand well that since the Incarnation human nature is not something exterior to the Person of the Word, like a mantle in which He is clothed. Far from being a mere juxtaposition, the union of the Word with His human nature is as close as that of our nature with our own personality. The Person and the nature form a single subsistent being. The nature receives from the person that completion without which it cannot be conceived as existing. It is impossible to address oneself to the nature without doing so to the person. One might as well honor a thought aside from the thinking mind. To bring out this idea let us recall the Thomistic doctrine which makes us understand this intimacy. This doctrine finds two principles in every being: one, the essence by which a thing is this thing rather than that; the other its existence, by which it is. These two principles form a single concrete reality. Now the human nature of the Word is not completed by a created existence; without any change in itself the Person of the Word supplies for this act in the human nature of Christ; it is that by which this nature exists. Seen thus, the dignity of the Word is necessarily shared by its human nature; the latter can in no wise be the object of an homage proportioned only to its finite essence. It is co-adorable with the Person of the Word, as a single humano-theandric reality. To the question, is there in Christ a complete and purely divine reality, we must answer: yes. But to the question, is there in Him a reality purely human, we must answer: no. There is a divine reality and a humano-divine reality. O marvel of almighty power and bounty, that God should give us in the Heart of the Incarnate Word, a love which has been deified! . . .

And the goodness of God has given us the man-God, who can love both as man and as God. As man, His is a love which, taken in itself, stands at the summit of all creation. Think of it. A divine Person, infinitely happy and with no human ego, Christ has for us, in His human nature, an affection which is unselfish and complete, as no merely human affection could be. None is more pure in its intention,

more long-lasting, more magnificent in its gifts, more unspeakably
tender in its expression.

As the charity of Christ, who is the new Adam, this affection
dwells in a will rich unto plenitude with graces and gifts, which becomes
for us an inexhaustible fountain; it is at the disposal of all. As the
charity of Christ, who is the Son of God, it shares in the substantial
holiness of the Word; as the charity of Christ who is a divine Person,
it has literally infinite value.

Besides this created love, Christ, as God, possesses a charity which
is uncreated, eternal, immutable, common to the whole Trinity. A
perfect harmony reigns between these two forms of love, but their
harmony implies no absorption, for such harmony cannot have a
complete coincidence of object. It is true that the Heart of Jesus was
formed by an inspiration of divine love for us; but the created affections of the Savior cannot be taken for simple repercussions of
uncreated love, analogous to the sensible effects produced in us by
our higher sentiments. It is true that all the love of Christ tends to
please the divine will sovereignly, but to say that the Heart of Christ
always beats under the influence of both His created love and His
uncreated love, is not true. These two forms of love are not in the
immediate relation of subordination. The created acts of the love of
Christ were called into being by the lovableness of those things proposed to it by the human intelligence of Christ, as seen to be acceptable
according to the divine plan, and we know that all the knowledge of
Christ was not drawn from the infinite knowledge of the divinity.
We may thus draw the following conclusion: the created love of
Christ, together with His physical Heart, forms the primary object of
Devotion to the Sacred Heart.

But the author does not rest in this conclusion; he rises from
the thought of the created love of Christ to its necessary complement in His divine love, and in so doing borrows the words of the
zealous promoter of the Apostleship of Prayer who, fifty years
earlier, had shown that activity draws its supernatural value from
contemplation. Here he shows that the finite draws its value from
the infinite.

It is through His Heart, and through the human love of His Heart,
that "Our Lord reveals to us with the greatest splendor the infinite
love of God for man. Love has three supreme desires: to give, to be
united, to sacrifice. The Incarnation of the Word of God is the sovereign triumph of love precisely because in this mystery God gives Himself completely to us, is united perfectly with us, is entirely sacrificed

for us. But if in the Person of the Word Incarnate we seek that point where the donation has been most complete, the union closest, the sacrifice most generous, that culminating point of the mystery, the meeting point of divine union, the chosen scene of the great sacrifice, the luminous center, the burning hearthfire of all light and of all love, it is the lovable Heart of Jesus. What reveals to us more than all the rest the unspeakable mystery of the love of God, is the fact that He took a Heart like to ours, a Heart passionately in love with our happiness, compassionate with our miseries, and infinitely desirous of sharing with us all Its riches" (Père Ramière).

It is, further, through the Heart of Jesus and through the human love of that Heart that we receive most abundantly the outpourings of uncreated love. Divine life in us results from the union of the Holy Ghost with the soul, but "if this divine Spirit is given to us, it is by means of the communication which the Heart of Jesus makes to us of divine life. Since the humanity of our Savior is, with regard to the just, what the head is for its members and the sap for the branches, there can be no doubt that the communication which His humanity makes to us of its life and of its sap is, on His part, an act of love, the result of the impulse of His Heart. . . . This continual outpouring of grace which, according to the Council of Trent, vivifies the souls of the just, comes from the Heart of Jesus. They are the beatings of the Heart of Jesus, the overflowing of His human love which causes a flood of grace to flow through the veins of the Church, just as the beating of our hearts causes vivifying blood to flow through our members" (Père Ramière). Thus can the symbolism of the Heart of Jesus be enlarged. For, on account of the unity of His Person, any love, human or divine, which can be called the love of Jesus Christ can be naturally represented by His Heart. Sublime are the manifestations of this made upon the cross, and in the Holy Eucharist; still more sublime is the love which inspires them. And when this love is conceived in human fashion, and yet is found to be divinized by the Person who holds its source within Himself, these created outpourings of God have an irresistible attraction which carries us even to God and to His infinite love. The Heart of Christ is the supreme pledge of the eternal love of God.[5]

The reasons why "there is perhaps no Devotion which has so profound and immediate an effect upon the spiritual life" of the many are revealed in the gracious writings of Mother Janet Stuart.[6] This English convert from Protestantism and Superior General of the Society of the Sacred Heart from 1911 to 1914 was an instinctive educator, combining a profound interest in psychology with personal charm and a winning style. Her natural greatness of mind and heart became transfused with supernatural power as she followed the call of prayer into depths beyond speech, then wrote of what she had experienced in a way easy for others to follow because so simple, attractive and real. She writes with the beauty of expression of a Christian humanist whose intellectual cultivation had deepened her personal holiness, and the earnestness of an educator to whom character training meant the forming of Christ in the souls of the young. She integrated into her educational teaching that Devotion to the Sacred Heart to which her life was vowed, even when composing simple meditations:

It is said in the Mass of Saint Gertrude: "Thou hast prepared a home for Thyself in her heart"; one idea of a home is a place where everyone loves, everyone trusts, where there are no dark secrets, no rooms shut off. In a home we may leave our things about, we may come and go as we please. If our hearts are a home for our Lord, He is a guest who comes, not to go again. He can go in and out, every place is His own; He can, so to speak, leave His things there—leave His intentions, His joys and sorrows there; He knows they will be taken care of.

Had we but the generous heart of Gertrude! She trusted our Lord, she took Him literally. Aubrey de Vere has said of her: "What we profess, she believed, what we believe, she saw." It is in our power, at any rate, to take our Lord's words literally, by thinking of them and by passing them over and over in our minds. Someone has said that the only thing necessary for sanctity is to take Our Lord's words literally. . . .

Devotion to the Sacred Heart has more than one aspect. In one sense it has as many aspects as there are souls to understand and practice it; for not all the millions of worshippers in the Church or the thousands of consecrated members could absorb those "unsearchable riches" of the love of God which is in Christ Jesus our Lord. Nor could they exhaust the points of view from which this central object of their devotion may be studied. It has been said that devotion to the Sacred Heart is all devotions under one aspect; but whether it be one under many, or many under one, it is true to say that there is no end to it except the capacity of each one's understanding and power of love.

The form of the devotion by far the most widely spread is that of which Saint Margaret Mary was so faithful a disciple, into which she entered with such a gift of intimacy, enhanced by the continuous sufferings of her own life, which seemed to give her right of entrance into that sanctuary of pain, and to carry her deeper into its mysteries than most would dare or be able to follow.

The devotion to the Sacred Heart in the Passion, rich with its hidden gifts to souls such as hers, has also its gracious side of appeal to the many. "Behold this Heart which has so loved men!" Anyone can stop and listen to that great cry, and make some sort of response in the language of his own heart and mind. It can give new hope to the despairing and awaken the indifferent; it can win a return from the simple hearts of children, and carry comfort to souls in every trouble.

But by the side of this great and world-wide devotion another line is visible, and, perhaps, tending to make progress as the knowledge of it extends. It is the love of Christ as manifested in His whole life on earth; the inward life of the Sacred Heart, with all Its expressions of Itself, with Its tenderness, Its splendors, and the glow of Its sanctuary fire. It is a form of the devotion that lends itself to endless meditation and study, and in its joys and sorrows makes appeal to every attentive worshipper. . . . No season of the year and no disposition of soul lie outside it, since the mysteries of the Holy Infancy and Hidden Life, of the Public Life, and Passion, of the Resurrection and Ascension, and those of the sacramental life of our Lord, all come within its scope, and all may be studied in the light of His Sacred Heart. The expression of His love in every mystery is what this devotion feeds upon, giving in return love and worship. This meditative, imitative, penetrating, inward manner of devotion which imposes no set form, and admits of endless diversity of assimilation, was what Saint Madeleine Sophie sought; and it is rooted in the society which she founded.

Knowledge and imitation, zeal and devotedness for the glory of the Sacred Heart—these are the practical manifestations and the essential points of teaching which give a tone to the devotion; and it will easily be seen what variety and scope are given for their working out according to the gifts and dispositions of each one. The mind of Christ, His teaching, and even, so far as they can be gathered, His tastes and inclinations, are given as the pattern according to which any virtue should be practiced, and even the common actions of daily life accomplished. "Learn of Me" is the expression of the invitation that draws the soul inwards to study and contemplation. "I am come to cast fire on the earth, and what will I but that it be kindled," this is the call to spend and to be spent for the same end, and having freely received, to give freely.[7]

Mother Stuart anticipated, by the instincts of a born reader of character, the integration of psychology and supernatural asceticism which is the Christian view of psychiatry. Grace building on nature was of absorbing interest to her, and in the following sketch she unconsciously reveals what Devotion to the Sacred Heart had done to one human character—her own:

It is not to be wondered at that the devotion to the Sacred Heart produces in its disciples a maturity, a spiritual virility of mind and heart difficult for some within the Church to understand, and inexplicable to those without. For it presupposes an advanced religious sense which is nothing else than a divinely implanted instinct for the realities of life, and a calm insusceptibility towards the false realities which are ever being taken for the true. It is an instinct towards that pain which few love—but which Love itself chose for love—for the rough and royal road of the Holy Cross which those hate to tread who will not remember that it is enough for the servant to be as the Master—a calm insusceptibility to pleasure which so many mistake for happiness, to the countless confusions and distractions of this little porch of life which men so love and cling to that they dread to enter the unseen palaces; of the beginning which timorous souls mistake for the end. "It is true," says the lover of the Sacred Heart, "that there is all eternity for loving and enjoying God, but only this little bridge of time for proving that love and for determining the extent of that enjoyment." "He has loved me and delivered Himself for me." *Quid retribuam?* And the divine instinct within answers: "Not an ordinary Faith and Hope and Love, not a paid service." Oh no; the lover of the Sacred Heart knows that he has not yet believed until he has said his Credo in the midst of doubts, or hoped until he has hoped against all hope when all seemed lost, or loved until he has given all the substance of his house and counted it as nothing, or served until he has served in the midst of overwhelming difficulties, or sung to Him until he has sung in the night. "Not mere goodness, but sanctity," he cries: "not mere fidelity but activity; not mere worship but supreme adoration." And this is supreme adoration, to return to Him as far as we can, His own trust. For as He loved us first, so He trusts us first.[8]

The principles underlying this work of Christian education—a work as old as the Church—were reaffirmed by Pope Pius XI, who wished to see the same principles carried into adult activities in the form of Catholic Action, which he defined as "the participation and collaboration of the laity with the apostolic hierarchy."[9]

As the lay apostolate (a most evident result of a movement of the Holy Spirit in modern times) grows in importance and in extent, an understanding of the role of the Devotion to the Sacred Heart in Catholic Action is also growing. This role can be best grasped by considering its integration with the key-doctrine of the twentieth century: that of the Mystical Body. A penetrating study of this question has been made in an article entitled "The Mystical Body and the Devotion to the Sacred Heart."

The author shows that there are today "three grand concepts inspiring the spiritual life of the faithful: the Mystical Body, the Sacred Heart, and Christ the King." The steady historical growth of these vital concepts is outlined, and the intimate relations between them are brought out in the light of dogmatic theology. Then: "Devotion to the Sacred Heart, precisely because it is a devotion, admirably complements the doctrine of the Mystical Body. For any doctrine is reinforced by a devotion." Turning to Saint Paul's teaching on the Mystical Body, we find that he emphasizes love as the bond between the members and the Head:

Hence we clearly see the importance of Devotion to the Sacred Heart in the life of the Mystical Body; it is the great means of our age, provided by Christ Himself and fostered by His Vicars, to bring the members to perform, out of love for Christ, those actions which produce growth in their own spiritual life, and through which they reap benefits which membership in the Mystical Body can bring to themselves, to the whole body and to society at large.

However, it seems that power of the Devotion to bring to the Mystical Body solidarity of social action is "most apparent through its part in gradually evolving the modern devotion to Christ the King." The author gives a detailed account of how groups and individuals most devoted to the Sacred Heart finally obtained the official recognition of this devotion by the Church, and concludes:

The wheel set moving by the preaching of Christ has now come full turn back to its starting point, and those three great concepts of modern Catholicism which to some have seemed to be rivals—the Mystical Body, devotion to the Sacred Heart and devotion to Christ the King—can now be seen aptly complementing one another in a synthesis which is dogmatically sound.

Christ came as a King and founded a Kingdom which Saint Paul called Christ's body. In His providential solicitude for the welfare of this Mystical Body Jesus established devotion to His Sacred Heart. He did this to unite its members more closely to Himself by love, and more intimately among themselves through charity, into solidarity of action in the practice of Christian virtue. Largely as the upshot of this devotion His entire Mystical Body now honors Him as its all-wise King who rules by love. . . .

To sum up, the doctrine of the Mystical Body is aptly complemented by that ensemble of thoughts, emotions and practices which is devotion to the Sacred Heart. For this devotion is a great means of these latter days, inaugurated by Christ Himself and fostered by His Vicars, to bring the members of the Mystical Body to a strong personal love of Christ, so as to make them perform the actions whereby they realize those benefits which their membership in the Mystical Body can bring to themselves and to society. If we, by following the lead of our modern Popes, intelligently practice devotion to the Sacred Heart of Christ, the King who is the head of that supernatural society which is His Mystical Body, we shall be active, enthusiastic members of that body, and the body itself will exert tremendous force in the field of social action.[10]

The passing of dogma into action so penetratingly studied above is actually made along the hidden road of prayer. A cross section of the history of the Church at any age reveals this truth; and the fact that contemplation is the source and condition of supernatural efficacy is perhaps most evident in an age of high-geared activity such as the twentieth century, when the members of the Catholic Evidence Guild learn to spend an hour in the presence of the Blessed Sacrament before mounting the soapbox for an hour of heckling in Hyde Park; when the meetings of the Legion of Mary are interrupted for the recitation of the rosary; when lay men and women give up their week-ends to make retreats; and when the making of a daily meditation trains time-pressed students to pause and look to God as part of the day's work. Along all these lines Devotion to the Sacred Heart gives motivation, form and fire to the basic practices of the spirituality of the rank and file of the Church Militant. And out of the rank and file a few become special recipients of a message for the many.

The speeding, practical twentieth century has not been lacking in those mystical phenomena of an extraordinary nature which have attended the growth of the Devotion to the Sacred Heart since its first clear emergence in mediaeval times, those signs of a charismatic nature by which the finger of God underlines in each age some aspect of His Providence for the world. The canonization of Saint Margaret Mary in 1925 once more showed the validity of private revelations so abundantly proved to be in accord with the unchanging Divine Revelation. As Liturgy and Catholic Action tended to develop ever more fully the public and practical aspects of the Devotion, still further private revelations were calling souls to "come within." "From time to time I thirst to make heard a new call to Love."[11] These words were spoken to a modern "messenger" of the Sacred Heart.

Sister Josefa Menendez (1890–1923) grew up in Madrid, the child of an artisan whose death left her responsible for the support of her mother and sisters. She became a dressmaker, working day and night while the call of the Divine Heart grew clearer in her soul, a call to give herself to Him for the salvation of souls. But when the time came to enter the Society of the Sacred Heart, in Madrid, she hesitated, through a too human fear for those she loved, and when she again applied for admission she was sent, as a test of the reality of her vocation, to a convent in Poitiers, France. Here she found herself in the old cloister that had been the first noviciate of the Society in the days of Saint Madeleine Sophie. From the very beginning of her short religious life of three years she was drawn, in spite of herself and of her overwhelming attraction for the common path, into a way of direct communication with the supernatural in which the things of faith became manifest to her senses. She had constant, at times daily, visions of Our Lord and of Our Lady, sometimes of Saint Madeleine Sophie and of Saint John, who had throughout the centuries so shown himself as the guardian saint, so to speak, of the Devotion of Love. She had other and very terrifying visions of the devil, who did his utmost, in his hate, to turn her from love by fear. But if he often dragged her through an experience of hell, Our Lord sometimes held her in the heaven of His Heart, and taught her "to come and go in love," and to be co-redeemer with Him by the offering of each moment of her life for the salvation of souls in need. The Community with whom she lived and worked knew nothing of these miraculous happenings; they were aware only of the refreshing presence of God in a humble and unselfish Sister. Only her Superiors, whom she obeyed like an unquestioning child, knew that

Josefa was being fashioned into sanctity in this powerful way, not for her own sake but for the sake of the new-old Message that Our Lord's Heart willed to speak through her to the world. This was the Work of Love for which the Holy Spirit had chosen the hour and the instrument. The book entitled *Un Appel à l'Amour*[12] is compiled from the pages which Sister Josefa wrote so laboriously at Our Lord's command and often at His dictation. Its author, one who had intimate knowledge of Josefa, sets her life and work against the doctrinal background of Revelation, and of the life of the Church in tradition and in our own twentieth century, in the following passages:

What at once stands out in Our Lord's teaching, as in His action on Josefa, is its doctrinal character which sets in relief the guiding principles of our faith. He seems to have wished to remind souls of these principles by a divine object lesson.

The Sovereign Dominion of the Creator over His Creature and what this implies of dependence on the Divine Will and surrender to His guidance appears in the first place as the solid foundation of true love. "Do not forget," Our Lord said to Josefa, "that I have all rights over you." "Let Me do what I like with you." And these words: "Let Me work . . . Let Me act . . . Let Me dispose of you . . . Leave Me free in you . . ." constantly recur, insisting on the completeness of His rights.

At the same time the whole history of Josefa is indeed that of Divine Providence which makes no mistakes in its ways. "As you are very small," Our Lord said to her one day, "you must let yourself be controlled and guided by My fatherly hand which is powerful and infinitely strong." "I will mould you as is best for My glory and for souls." "Do not fear, for I am looking after you with jealous care, such care as the tenderest of mothers takes of her little child." Magnificent definition of divine fidelity, which can say to us at the turning-point of life, as He said to Josefa: "I never fail My word!"

We are constantly reminded of the Presence of Grace giving life to the soul, the foundation of its incorporation with Christ. "I am in her," He said. "I live in her; I delight in making but one thing with her." But in return He asks her never to leave Him alone . . . to consult Him about everything . . . to ask Him for everything . . . to clothe herself with Him and disappear beneath His life: "The more you disappear, the more shall I be your life." Is not this a commentary on the words of Saint Paul: "I live, now not I but Christ liveth in me"?

Then light is thrown on the value of this life-giving union with Him, transforming the least activities by gilding them with the supernatural. More than once and in tangible ways Our Lord showed Josefa what love can make of the most insignificant actions when they are united to Him. So, He wished to revive in souls the joy of believing in the wealth at our disposal. "How many souls would regain courage," He said, "if they realized the results of their efforts." "And how great is the value of a day of divine life."

Here we reach the dogma which seems central in this wonderful teaching, participation in the infinite merits of Jesus Christ. Our Lord constantly reminds Josefa of this power over the treasures of His redemption given to the baptized soul. If He asks her to complete in herself what is wanting in His passion, to repair for the world and to satisfy the Father's justice, it is always with Him, through Him, in Him. "My Heart is yours, take it and repair with it." Then He makes those offerings all powerful over the Heart of the Father, which Josefa heard and passed on to us: "Good Father, Holy Father, Merciful Father! Accept the Blood of Your Son . . . His Wounds . . . His Heart! Look upon His Head pierced with thorns . . . do not allow His Blood to be once more useless." "Do not forget that the time for justice has not yet come, but that now is the hour of mercy."

Lastly the great reality of the Communion of Saints runs through the warp and weft of Josefa's vocation and forms the background of the picture of her life. Our Blessed Lady, Mediatrix of all Grace and Mother of Mercy, has her special place in the centre of this wonderful exchange of graces and merits, between the saints in heaven, the souls in purgatory and the church militant on earth. . . . Only hell is excluded. Josefa, a tiny member of the Mystical Body of Christ, learns from Him the repercussions in the world of souls of fidelity, sacrifice, suffering, and prayer.

But beyond these doctrinal lessons which seem already very valuable, the Direct Message which the Heart of Jesus will entrust to her to pass on to the world is an appeal of Love and Mercy. One day she said to her Master: "Lord, I do not understand what this work is that you are always telling me about." "You do not know what My work is?" He answered. "It is love . . . I want to use you to reveal more than ever before the mercy and love of My Heart. The words or desires that I give to the world through you will rouse zeal in many souls and will prevent the loss of many others, and they will gain an even fuller realization that the mercy of My Heart is inexhaustible."[13]

The following passages contain the words of Our Lord Himself to His messenger to whom He said: "This will be our work, Josefa, from the heights of heaven: to teach souls to live united to Me and not as though I were far away, for by My grace I live in them":

The soul who constantly unites her life with Mine glorifies Me and does a great work for souls. Thus, if engaged on work of no value in itself . . . if she bathes it in My Blood or unites it to the work I Myself did during My mortal life, it will greatly profit souls . . . more perhaps, than if she had preached to the whole world . . . and that, whether she studies, speaks or writes . . . whether she sews, sweeps or rests . . . provided first that the act is sanctioned by obedience or duty and not done from mere caprice; secondly, that it is done in intimate union with Me, with great purity of intention and covered with My Blood. . . .

My love goes so far that My souls can draw great treasure out of mere nothing. When as soon as they wake they unite themselves to Me and offer their whole day with a burning desire that My Heart may use it for the profit of souls . . . when with love they perform their duties, hour by hour and moment by moment . . . how great is the treasure they amass in one day! I will reveal My love to them more and more. It is inexhaustible, and how easy it is for a loving soul to let itself be guided by love. . . .[14]

I am Love! My Heart can no longer contain its devouring flames. I love souls so dearly that I have sacrificed My life for them. . . . I have revealed My Heart to them. This devotion has been as light cast over the whole earth, and today is a powerful means of gaining souls, and so of extending My kingdom.

Now, I want something more, for if I long for love in response to My own, this is not the only return I desire from souls: I want them all to have confidence in My mercy, to expect all from My clemency, and never to doubt My readiness to forgive.

I am God, but a God of love! I am a Father, but a Father full of compassion and never harsh. My Heart is infinitely holy but also infinitely wise, and knowing human frailty and infirmity stoops to poor sinners with infinite mercy. . . .

Never shall I weary of repentant sinners, nor cease from hoping for their return, and the greater their distress, the greater My welcome. . . . This is what I wish all to know. I will teach sinners that the mercy of My Heart is inexhaustible. Let the callous and indifferent know that My Heart is a fire which will enkindle them, because I love them. To devout and saintly souls I would be the way, that making great strides in perfection, they may safely reach the harbour of eternal beatitude. Lastly, of consecrated souls, priests and religious, My elect and chosen ones, I ask, once more, all their love and that they should not doubt Mine, but above all that they should trust Me and never doubt My mercy. It is so easy to trust completely in My Heart! . . .

Write for the world:

I want to forgive. I want to reign over souls and pardon all nations. I want to rule souls, nations, the whole world. My peace must be extended over the entire universe. . . .[15]

Man was not created to live for ever here below. He was made for eternity. . . . If then he is immortal, he should live, not for the passing things of time, but for that which will never die. Youth, wealth, wisdom, human glory, all that is nothing, it will all end with this life; God only will endure for ever.

The world is full of hate, races are in perpetual conflict with one another, so are nations, and even individuals, and all this is due to the decay of faith. Only let faith reign once more over the world and peace and charity will return to it.

Faith in no way impedes civilization and progress. The more it is rooted in individuals and peoples, the more wisdom and learning increase, for God is infinite in wisdom and knowledge. But whenever faith is completely lacking, peace, civilization and true progress likewise vanish, for God is not in war, and in their place come enmities, clash of opinions, class wars, and within man himself, rebellion of passions against duty. All that is noble in humanity is exchanged for revolt, insubordination and warfare. . . . Let yourselves be convinced by faith and you will be great. Let yourselves be ruled by faith, and you will be free; live by faith, and you will escape eternal death. . . .[16]

I ask three things of My consecrated souls:

Reparation, that is a life of union with Him who makes Divine Reparation: to work for Him, with Him, in Him, in a spirit of reparation, in close union with His feelings and desires.

Love, that is intimacy with Him who is all Love, and who humbles Himself to ask His creatures not to leave Him alone, but to give Him their love.

Confidence, that is trust in Him who is Goodness and Mercy . . . in Him with whom I live day and night . . . who knows Me and whom I know . . . who loves Me and whom I love . . . in Him who calls His chosen souls in a special way to live with Him, to know His Heart and so to trust Him for everything.[17]

Thus, in the time between wars, forestalling the fission of the atom and heralding a new consciousness, on the part of the *Corpus*

Mysticum, of the Heart that rhythms her life, the message of Love was expressed again. The day when the last lines of the message were written has been called: "A new opening in time upon 'the unsearchable riches of Christ'; a turning point in the road of redemption; a hidden spring from which will soon rise a torrent of mercy to submerge the wickedness of the earth, a volcano from which will spring tomorrow a flame for the warming of the world; the dawn-point of a great 'day of the Divine King.' "[18]

That this would in time be carried out in practical reality is evidenced by the fact that outside the cloister tides of popular sentiment, set in motion by the living practice of the Devotion, were rising in the world-wide body of the Faithful. An awakened sense of the love of Christ working to draw all men under its sway led to a consciousness of the reality of the social reign of Christ. A petition for a Feast which would embody this idea had been sent to the Sacred Congregation of Rites as early as 1899. A lay organization, "The Society for the Social Reign of Christ," carried on a long campaign, headed by George and Marthe de Noaillat, who consecrated their married life to this apostolate.[19] The *Messenger* sponsored the cause in all languages. Petitions poured into Rome from the Americas and the Orient as well as from Europe, and in 1924 Pope Pius XI, in *Quas Primas,* proclaimed the new Feast of the Kingship of Christ. He himself sang its Mass for the first time on December 31. Four years later the heavenly King returned the compliment, so to speak, when the lost kingdom of the Papal States was returned to its rightful sovereign, Pius XI. In the meantime the Pope had recognized in the Heart of the King the center of His reign of love over the human race. In 1928 he completed the act of consecration called for in *Annum Sacrum* by stressing the note of reparation. The second Papal Encyclical on the Sacred Heart, *Miserentissimus Redemptor,* called upon the whole world "to repair the rights that have been violated of Christ the King of Kings and our most loving Master," it stirred the Church into realizing its own power to "fill up what is wanting in the passion of Christ."

Our most merciful Redeemer, having assured the salvation of the human race by His death on the cross, before He ascended to His heavenly Father, said these consoling words to His sorrowing Apostles: "Behold, I am with you all days, even to the consummation of the world."[20] These happy words are also our own source of hope and salvation, words which, Venerable Brothers, come readily to mind every time when, from this high watchtower, as it were, we look down upon the human family afflicted by so many grievous ills, and upon the Church, assailed without respite by attacks and plots. . . .

From among all the proofs of the infinite goodness of Our Savior none stands out more prominently than the fact that, as the love of the Faithful grew cold, He, Divine Love Itself, gave Himself to us to be honored by a very special devotion, and that the rich treasury of the Church was thrown wide open in the interests of that devotion by which we honor the Most Sacred Heart of Jesus "in whom are hid all the treasures of wisdom and knowledge."[21] . . .

Are we not to see, Venerable Brothers, in that blessed sign and in the devotion which flows from it, the very substance of our holy religion, as well as the rules to guide us toward a more perfect form of life, since the Sacred Heart is the road which will most surely lead us to know intimately Jesus Christ and will cause our heart to love more tenderly and imitate Him more generously than we have heretofore done? . . .

Among the different practices which directly accompany devotion to the Sacred Heart, assuredly the foremost is the act of consecration by which we offer to the Heart of Jesus both ourselves and all that belongs to us, recognizing that all we have comes to us from the infinite charity of God. . . .

Moreover, to all these expressions of veneration, and especially to that most fruitful one, the act of consecration, which by means of the institution of the Feast of Christ the King has been, as it were, again confirmed, it is expedient that another be added, and of this last, Venerable Brothers, we wish to speak now somewhat at length. We refer to the act of expiation or of reparation as it is called, to be made to the Sacred Heart of Jesus.

If in the act of consecration the intention to offer in return, as it were, for the love of the Creator the love of us creatures, stands out most prominently, there follows almost naturally from this another fact, namely, that if this same Uncreated Love has either been passed over through forgetfulness or saddened by reason of our sins, then we should repair such outrages, no matter in what manner they have occurred. Ordinarily, we call this duty, reparation. . . .

As the act of consecration proclaims and confirms our union with Christ, so that act of expiation, by purifying us from our sins, is the beginning of such union; our participation in the sufferings of Christ perfects it, the offering we make to Him of our sacrifices for the welfare of our brethren brings such union to its final consummation. This was precisely the design of the mercy of Jesus when He unveiled to our gaze His Sacred Heart, surrounded by the emblems of His Passion, and aflame with the fire of love, that we, on the one hand, perceiving the infinite malice of sin, and on the other, filled with a knowledge of the Infinite Love of Our Redeemer, might detest sin more cordially and substitute for it an ardent love for Him. . . .

But how can we, one may ask, believe that Christ reigns happily in Heaven if it is possible to console Him by such acts as those of reparation? We answer in the language of Saint Augustine, words quite apposite to our subject: "The soul which truly loves will comprehend what I say."[22]

Every soul which burns with love of God, if it but turns its thoughts to the past, sees in meditation and can contemplate Jesus suffering for mankind, afflicted by grief in the midst of sorrows suffered "for us men and for our salvation," weighed down by agony and reproaches, "bruised for our sins,"[23] in the very act of healing us by His bruises. With so much the more understanding can pious souls meditate upon these mysteries if they appreciate that the sins and crimes of men, no matter when committed, were the real reason why the Son of God was condemned to death, and that even sins committed now would be able of themselves to cause Christ to die a death accompanied by the same sufferings and agonies as His death on the cross, since every sin must be said to renew in a certain way the Passion of Our Lord, "crucifying again to themselves the Son of God and making Him a mockery."[24] And if, in view of our own future sins, foreseen by Him, the soul of Jesus becomes sad even unto death, there can be no doubt that by His prevision at the same time of our acts of reparation He was in some way comforted when "there appeared an angel from Heaven"[25] to console that Heart of His bowed down with sorrow and anguish.

At the present time, we too, in a marvelous but no less true manner, may and ought to console that Sacred Heart which is being wounded continually by the sins of thoughtless men, since—and we read this also in the sacred liturgy—Christ Himself grieved over the fact that He was abandoned by His friends. For He said, in the words of the Psalmist, "My heart hath expected reproach and misery. And I looked for one that would grieve together with Me, but there was none: and for one that would comfort Me, and I found none."[26]

To the above we may add that the expiatory passion of Jesus Christ is renewed and in a certain manner continued in His mystic body, the Church. To use again the words of Saint Augustine, "Christ suffered all that He had to suffer: nothing at all is lacking to the number of His sufferings. Therefore His sufferings are complete, but in Him

as in the Head; there remain even now the sufferings of Christ to be
endured in the body. . . ."[27]

Given at Rome, at Saint Peter's, the ninth of May, 1928, the
seventh year of Our Pontificate.

Pius XI[28]

Strengthened by the voice of the Vicar of Christ, calling for an
inseparability of prayer and action in the unity of the Spirit of
Love, the Church moved firmly on into contemporary times.

NOTES

1. In referring to the Sacred Heart as the heart of the Mystical
Body, care must be taken not to mix metaphors to the point of theological confusion. A true approach to this concept will be found in the
article by the Reverend George Ganss, S.J., quoted later in this chapter.

2. See Hamon, *op. cit.,* Vol. V, Ch. 4, for an account of the controversy carried on in periodicals, largely in France, in the late nineteenth and early twentieth centuries.

3. See sermon on the Sacred Heart in *The Note-Books and Papers
of Gerard Manley Hopkins* (New York, Oxford, 1937), p. 295.

4. An excellent summary of the pros and cons of this point may be
found in Bainvel, *op. cit.,* pp. 92 ff.

5. A. Vermeersch, S.J., *Pratique et Doctrine de la Dévotion au
Sacré Coeur de Jésus* (Tournai, Desclée, 1906), Vol. II.

6. See Maud Monahan, *Life and Letters of Janet Erskine Stuart*
(New York, Longmans, 1922).

7. *Prayer in Faith* (New York, Longmans, 1936), Vol. II, p. 57.

8. From an unpublished compilation.

9. *Non Abiamo Bisogno,* ed. National Catholic Welfare Conference, 1931, p. 5.

10. George Ganss, S.J., "The Mystical Body and Devotion to the
Sacred Heart," in *Ecclesiastical Review,* XCVII: 321, 471.

11. *Appel à l'Amour* (Toulouse, 1944), p. 294. The quotations
under the chapter headings of the present work are all taken from
Sister Josefa.

12. The English version is entitled *The Way of Divine Love* (Westminster, Newman, 1949).

13. *The Way of Divine Love,* p. 202.

14. *Ibid.,* p. 236.

15. *Ibid.,* pp. 376–378.

16. *Ibid.,* p. 396.

17. *Ibid.*, p. 453.

18. *Ibid.*

19. These fervent lay-apostles dedicated their married life to furthering the recognition of the Kingship of Christ by obtaining signatures and petitions requesting the establishment of the Feast of Christ the King. Marthe was inspired to undertake the work while praying in the Sacred Heart shrine at Paray-le-Monial.

20. Matt. 28, 20.

21. Col. 2, 3.

22. *Tractatus in Joannem,* XXVI, 4.

23. Is. 53, 5.

24. Heb. 6, 6.

25. Luke 22, 43.

26. Ps. 68, 21.

27. *On Psalm LXXXVI.*

28. *Catholic Mind,* XXVI, 221.

CHAPTER XIV

THE HEART AND THE SPIRIT
1928–1956

*"Love transforms and
divinizes all."*

Cardinal Pacelli, the "peace-bringer," began his reign as Pope
Pius XII in the year of renewed strife. Not long afterward he
could write:

We have had the great consolation of witnessing something that has
made the image of the Mystical Body stand out most clearly before
the whole world. Though a long and deadly war has pitilessly broken
the bond of brotherly union between nations, We have seen our children in Christ, in whatever part of the world they happened to be,
with one heart and one affection lift up their souls to the common Father, who, carrying in his own heart the cares and fears of all, is guiding
the bark of the Catholic Church in the teeth of a raging tempest.[1]

The children of God the world over have continued to recognize
their Father in his efforts for peace even from a bomb-beleaguered
Vatican; in his prodigious charity signalized by the impulsive visit
to the victims of the first air-raid on Rome in which the white
papal cassock was stained red; in his wide-armed welcome to the
tumultuous audiences of the Holy Year. The spirit of his heart is
none other than that of the Heart of Christ, revelation of the Spirit
of Love, the Holy Spirit, bond of the Trinity Itself, of whose nature
as bond of the Church the Holy Father has written:

If we examine closely this divine principle of life and power given by
Christ, in so far as it constitutes the very source of every gift and
created grace, we easily see that it is nothing else than the Holy Spirit,
the Paraclete who proceeds from the Father and the Son, and who is
called in a special way the "Spirit of Christ" or the "Spirit of the Son."
. . . And while Christ alone received this Spirit without measure, to
the members of the Mystical Body He is imparted according to the

measure of the giving of Christ, from Christ's own fulness. But after Christ's glorification on the cross, His Spirit is communicated to the Church in an abundant outpouring, so that she and her single members, may become daily more and more like to Our Savior. . . .

To this Spirit of Christ, too, as to an invisible principle, is to be ascribed the fact that all the parts of the Body are joined one with the other and with their exalted Head. . . . It is He who through His heavenly grace is the principle of every supernatural act in all parts of the Body. . . . This presence and activity of the Spirit of Jesus Christ is tersely and vigorously described by our predecessor of immortal memory, Leo XIII, in his Encyclical Letter *Divinum Illud* in these words: "Let it suffice to say that as Christ is the Head of the Church, so is the Holy Spirit her soul."[2]

Once, in speaking over the radio, Pius XII referred to the microphone that he was using as "a symbol of the Mystical Body."[3] There is nothing in the age of progress which cannot, so to speak, furnish God's house on earth, be at home there for His use. The Devotion to the Sacred Heart in modern times is characterized by this same at-homeness on all continents and in all languages. Thus the "Sacred Heart Hour" over the radio[4] reminds housewives of the morning offering while they prepare early breakfast, or it brings a final religious consolation when noisier programs have died into the night. "First Friday Clubs" draw businessmen[5] together at the lunch hour to remind them that Christ is not absent from the professional world unless someone has closed the office-door to Him. Grammar-school children, as "Tarcisians,"[6] collect golden pennies of acts of love to be spent for souls, and in their homes the older members of the family rise in turn through the night for an hour of reparative prayer, keeping watch under the olive trees with a Heart in agony.[7]

This at-homeness of Christ in the Christian family, the fundamental unit of the Mystical Body, has been brought about largely through the efforts of a twentieth-century apostle. Father Mateo Crawley-Boevey of the Picpus Fathers, when a young priest, paid a visit to the shrine of Paray-le-Monial in order to make a last offering of his life to the Sacred Heart, as he was incurably ill. While praying there he was simultaneously cured and inspired to dedicate what was to be in fact a very long life to the enthronement of the Sacred Heart in families. Pope Pius X, when asked for his approval of the work, answered: "I not only approve, I command," and called Father Mateo's mission the "work of social salvation." The movement was first spread through the letters of school children in South America, and was then taken up around the world. In city slums Religious engaged in social work made the enthronement of an image of the Sacred Heart in a home the crowning act of their efforts to rectify marriages and recall stray sheep. In mission lands the image was placed in the niche once filled by statues of pagan gods. In his book, *Jesus King of Love,* Father Mateo gives an insight into the now widespread practice of family consecration:

What is the work of the Enthronement? It can be defined as the official and social acknowledgment of the sovereignty of the Heart of Jesus over a Christian family, an acknowledgment made tangible and permanent by the solemn installation of the picture of the Divine Heart in a place of honor, and by an act of consecration.

The God of mercy has said that, "being the source of all blessings, He will pour them out abundantly upon the places where an image of His Heart shall be loved and honored." And again: "I shall reign in spite of My enemies and of all those who would oppose Me."

The Enthronement, then, is nothing less than the complete fulfillment of all the requests made by the Sacred Heart at Paray-le-Monial, and of the magnificent promises that accompanied these requests. I say *all,* because the family to be sanctified is the final end of this apostolate; as a social cell, it must be the first living throne of the King of Love.[8]

In emphasizing family life Father Mateo had also emphasized that true democracy of the spirit that cuts across all social levels, creating the only true "classless society" that can, perhaps, exist on earth. Nazareth was a workingman's home (as the Feast of Saint Joseph the Worker was soon to recall to the world), but its members were of the royal house of David and of the aristocracy of grace. Nazareth is the universal home, and in these days of the shifting and merging of social levels, the King of Love finds His home again in the abiding Nazareths of Christian homes, rich or poor:

The great evil of our society is that it has lost the sense of the divine. What can be done to remedy this evil? Come back to Nazareth. It was at Nazareth, with the founding of the Holy Family, that the Word of God began the redemption of the world. Society must come back there to be redeemed. Terrible pictures have been placed before our eyes of the devastation of churches in invaded countries; as Catholics, you have been horrified. But the ruin of the Christian family is a still greater evil. The family is the shrine of shrines. It is not splendid churches, stone churches, that will save the world. It is Christian families; it is Nazareth.

That is understandable. The family is the source of life, the child's first school. If the source of national life is poisoned, the nation will perish. What we long to do is to plant faith deep in families, and love for the Sacred Heart. If Jesus Christ is in the roots, the whole tree will be Jesus Christ.

Now the Enthronement is Our Lord coming to reclaim His place at the fireside, as when of old, in the evenings of His apostolic journeying, He asked hospitality at Bethany. He claims a place of honor, for He is King and—we repeat—He must reign over each family if He is to reign soon over society; He claims an intimate and familiar place, for He is a friend, and it is by His Heart and by His love that He would reign. . . .[9]

The great work to be done, then, is the reconstruction of Nazareth, the home of the Holy Family, and of Bethany, the home of the friends of Jesus.

I say Bethany, because Nazareth is unique throughout the centuries with an inimitable sublimity, while Bethany is a household like our own, and as such is, in every way, perfectly imitable. At Nazareth, there were no moral miseries, never an ailing, agonizing heart. But how many homes, like Bethany, have their Magdalene and their Lazarus, their prodigal and their dead. Let Jesus enter there, as a member of the family, and He will work marvels; there will be spiritual resurrections like that of Lazarus, and returns as touching as that of Magdalene.

Yes, our whole being has need of God. There is no moment of our days, of our lives, when we can do without Him. You do not struggle, you do not live in church; you do not suffer and you do not die in church. If you need a God to pray to in a church, you also need a God to pray to in your dwelling. The pagans had in their homes statues of their household gods; the first Christians brought the Blessed Sacrament to their homes, and kept It there. The Sacred Heart, enthroned in the family, will take Its place for Christians of a later day. Not that a picture of the Sacred Heart is to be likened to a consecrated Host, but the Enthronement, well understood, will bring with it special graces of God's presence, and of a Christian life with Jesus, through Jesus, under the eyes of Jesus.

We can never emphasize enough the closeness of the relationship between the devotion to the Sacred Heart of Jesus and that to the Eucharist, between two tabernacles, that of the altar and that of the home. All our efforts tend to form, by the Enthronement lived in actuality, families truly eucharistic. There are two tabernacles, and a single, only Jesus, King and friend. Then is He truly Master, and when Jesus is truly the King of a household, when He is at home, then He shows what He can do.[10]

Pope Pius XII himself ratified this practice of family consecration in a radio address, June 7, 1945, to the families of France:

We are with you in heart, families of France who have just renewed your consecration to the Heart of Jesus. A million families consecrated to the Heart of Christ Who loves your people—what splendor! what strength! What responsibility also! For the destinies of your country are in your hands, but on the double condition that, proud of your dependence upon Christ and conscious of the strength that He imparts, you will prove to be unshakably faithful to that dependence and will courageously make use of that strength.

The worth and the prosperity of a family rest not on the blind action of an indeterminate multitude but on numerous healthy-minded families normally organized under the revered authority of the father, under the wise and vigilant guardianship of the mother, in the close, mutually faithful union of the children. Each family reaches out and extends itself through relationships formed by ties of blood. Further alliances between families are then formed, and by their harmonious interweaving they constitute link by link that great network, the suppleness and the strength of which assures the vital unity of a nation, that one great family around a single hearth which we call the fatherland. This network is so perfect and so delicate that any link which is broken or weakened is a danger to the integrity of the whole net, to the whole social organism. Now this breaking or weakening, this lowering or degeneration within the family, occurs with fatal consequences every time that a breach is made in the sanctity and indissolubility of marriage, in the fidelity to conjugal fecundity, every time that paternal authority is set aside, either by the abdication of their rights on the part of parents or by insubordination on the part of the children.

The happiness of a family circle is indeed something great, noble and pure. But—and who will dare to deny it—this happiness is the reward of fidelity to austere duties, to victories over obstacles and attractions, over unruly passions and temptations of the flesh or of the heart. Courage is needed, a courage generous and—above all—

steadfastly abiding throughout the years, throughout life. Unless we strangely overlook the weakness of human nature or obstinately close our eyes in the face of evidence, we must admit that such courage cannot be aroused, still less maintained, only by the arguments of cold, plain reason.

Pure doctrine, sublime morality, the eternal hopes of Christian faith contribute greatly to producing this courage, but it is not mainly exterior action that gives the religion of Christ its salutary influence, its wonderful power to safeguard purity, the holiness of marriage and of the family in the midst of a false civilization, corrupted and corrupting. Christ acts in souls by the infusion of His grace more than by His teachings, His exhortations and His promises; it is above all in the Eucharist that He is "fountain of life and holiness." What a holy shrine that home becomes in which the father, the mother, the children live by eating and drinking the Body and Blood of God!

When a family so lives by Christ that, by its consecration to the Heart of Christ, it has ratified its union with Him who has overcome the world, has dedicated itself to the service and to the Kingdom of this Divine Heart, and has made of His reign the ideal by which it is inspired and towards which all its desires are drawn; when many families, moved by the same spirit, drawn towards the same ideal, are united in the close-knit integrity of the Mystical Body of the Man-God, when these families are numbered by thousands and hundreds of thousands, when a million fathers and mothers and millions and millions of children with passionate ardor consecrate all their energies to promoting the cause and the reign of Jesus, who shall measure the power of such an army under such a leader? . . .

Your consecration to the Heart of Jesus seals a pact between Him and your families. He has taken the initiative by His promise; "I will bless them," He said to Saint Margaret Mary. You, for your part, with all the solemnity that your means will allow, and with the blessing of the priest, have put His picture in the place of honor in your homes, proclaiming Him your sovereign and officially promising to consider and to treat Him as such. He will never fail to keep His word; He is the faithful God. Do not fail to keep your own. Make Him reign in you and around you.

Once consecrated, your dwelling place is thenceforth a sacred place, nothing must be there that could offend the eyes, the ears, the Heart of Jesus. He is its King; He must receive from your fidelity a permanent homage of respect, of devotion, of love. As a most loving Head of your home, He is intimately associated with every part of your life, and there could be no sorrow or joy, no anxiety or hope from which you could leave Him out. Your home is the Kingdom of Christ; it is sacred.[11]

What Pius XII desires for the families of each nation he desires for the human family as a whole: its entire consecration to God in the unity of faith. It is the primary desire of God the Father that the Mystical Body of His Son shall grow until it is coextensive with the human race, each man a member of the body whose soul is the Holy Spirit of Love. The apostles among those members (and who shall delimit them!) have the timeless mandate: "Go, teach all nations." At the time of the first twelve, the whole world was mission territory; it took one thousand years to achieve the total conversion of Europe. Then, after the sudden expansion of the world in the sixteenth century, missionary waves swept out into the new lands and tongues. Missions struck root and grew through the two following centuries, until in the twentieth the science of missiology developed, enabling the missionaries as never before to integrate racial heritages into the life of the Church.[12] The theology of the missions discovers love as the source of zeal: the passion of the Heart of the Son for the glory of the Father who prays "that all may be one as Thou in Me and I in Thee, . . . that the Love wherewith Thou hast loved Me may be in them."[13] It was natural that the Devotion to the Sacred Heart should spur on and keep pace with the mission movement until, as Our Lord said to Sister Josefa: "Today, Devotion to My Heart is the means of touching hearts used by the greater number of those who work to extend My kingdom." On the Feast of Pentecost, 1940, Pius XII beatified Mother Philippine Duchesne, Religious of the Sacred Heart and pioneer missionary of the Devotion in North America. In so doing he glorified a life of austere and burning zeal that spent itself under the hardest frontier conditions to bring the knowledge and love of the Divine Heart to the settlers and Indian tribes along the Missouri River. At an audience the Pope said:

Zeal is an ardent desire to make God reign everywhere, the active clinging of the creature to the will of God, that essential will of the Creator which can have no other end than Himself. The Lord has made all things for His own sake. The divine Word, in taking flesh like to ours, felt in His Heart, as does each of us in his own heart, together with the beatings of His physical life, the reactions of all those movements that stir the soul, those attractions and repulsions from which, only too often in the case of most men, spring unruly desires. But in His case these movements were always under the control of the soul and brought into harmony with the Divine Will, thus becoming the mainspring and the sustenance of His moral life: "My meat is to do the will of Him who sent Me."[14] From this interior movement there sprang like a flame this burning wish: "Father, Thy kingdom come, Thy will be done!" Thus, the Sacred Heart of Jesus is rightly called a fire of love: "Heart of Jesus, burning furnace of charity." Now he who draws near to a fire will be inflamed; he who plunges into it will be consumed, for "fire never saith: It is enough."[15] To enter into the Sacred Heart is to become a willing prey of the flames of love.

In fact, it is not too bold to see a link between the wonderful missionary impulse which marks the last two centuries and the spread of devotion to the Sacred Heart. While the century of Voltaire came to an end, while the Revolutionary storm was driving thousands of priests from France, some of the latter went to America to plow the furrows where many others after them, including religious like Mother Duchesne, would come to sow the Gospel. The doctrinal truth of the Devotion had been proclaimed only a few years before and it had spread abroad with irresistible strength. The zeal which it kindled carried legions of souls beyond the seas to work in the apostolate. It was then that beside the older religious Orders, beside the Society of Jesus which came to life again, beside the disciples of Saint John Eudes and the daughters of Saint Francis de Sales and Saint Jane Frances de Chantal, there came into being a number of young congregations, nearly all of which added to the old and rigorous practice of the evangelical counsels two new notes: Devotion to the Sacred Heart and missionary zeal.[16]

But in the twentieth century the apostolate is by no means limited to the foreign mission field. The faith must also be restored where it has been lost, and revitalized where it has atrophied; society as a whole is the true mission field of modern apostles. This problem is studied, together with the means of meeting it, in *The Sacred Heart and Modern Life*:

After twenty centuries of prayer and work, today more than a billion men are strangers to the true faith, separated from the one flock and the one shepherd. Undoubtedly the Mystical Body has increased numerically; Christianity has penetrated into many parts of the world, civilizing the natives and bringing life for their souls. But the picture of frightful misery in society, in families, in individuals, the spectacle of millions and millions of human beings enslaved by tyranny and vice—in a word by the devil—causes such grief that, to remedy it even a little, a man of heart would willingly sacrifice life itself. Think of Christ still in agony in the midst of those races corrupted by false worship—how few true apostles stay with Him, united with Him in prayer and pain. How few share His agony of blood.

Intolerable to the eyes of a Christian is the present condition of that world for which Christ offered His life in sacrifice. Does not a heavy burden of responsibility weigh on those who have received the gift of faith and with it many other graces, when they consider the lamentable state of Christianity and the myriads of pagan souls to whom similar divine gifts might have meant salvation and sanctity? . . .

The term "pagan" no longer applies exclusively to those countries in which Christianity has not yet become indigenous. In some old Christian countries many parishes are without priests; the de-Christianized people are in need of missionaries. It is not easy to be a home-missioner; it too often requires heroism without glamor and without adventure. But "to love Christ," says the author, "is a consuming experience. . . . It is to be gripped by the thought of the apostolate." And he continues:

This overwhelming grief is sharpened by a poignant anguish. The old religions long hostile to Christianity have coalesced into solid blocs. They confront the traditional preaching apostolate with a granite-like resistance. Today it would seem as if the forces of Islamism, Buddhism, paganism, and the mounting number of false or irreligious ideologies, have so penetrated the civilization of East and West, moulding the customs and modifying the national ethos of even the most densely populated areas, that apostolic weapons hallowed by long use are now blunted against a surface hardened by time.

How can the dynamic spirit be recaptured that once made these methods true channels of life for souls? The answer can be heard on all sides. All men, especially the élite, can be converted by charity alone. . . . The apostolate of love will be as effective today as it was in the early days of the Church. If Christians will show Christ's charity to the peoples who walk in darkness and in the shadow of death and who are ignorant of the true life, then the truths of faith will shine in enlightened hearts. But if this charity is to be pure, sincere and brilliant like the Magi's star, its strength must be drawn from the Heart of Christ—no other source will do.

Let the truth—God is love—shine in our lives. Let us show that the

God-man has loved us infinitely and that Christ loves in us. Then our Christianity will scale mighty ramparts of fear and diffidence, just as a ray of light pierces the darkness. Charity as powerful as this is a miracle of grace. Experience proves with amazing exactness that the Heart of Christ in communicating His love to those who are united to Him has also performed necessary and unexpected miracles. If, in our day, devotion to the Heart of Christ were to inflame the missionaries in France, in Europe, in the whole world, if their great concern were the rapid spread of the kingdom of God, then the hope and promise of many conversions would be confirmed by an immediate "Return to Christianity." . . .[17]

With regard to the separated churches: Catholics find in the devotion to the Sacred Heart the most direct and powerful means of closing these regrettable breaches, because this devotion is diametrically opposed to all causes of division, and at the same time fosters in our hearts the love of Christ, who is the principle of unity. . . . Who does not see that devotion to the Sacred Heart has this exact purpose: the perfect union of all men in Jesus Christ, and that it drives us, so to speak, into the paths of apostolic love, even to the total sacrifice of self in order that the Mystical Body may increase. To remain deaf to the repeated appeals of the one Priest and Shepherd, not to add our tribute of belief to the solemn promises of the graces that He has promised to those who would listen to His voice—this would be to surrender the most assured hope of bringing all the sheep into one fold. Is it possible that by our indifference we could allow the opportune hour of this apostolate to escape? . . .

During the twentieth century Our Lady and contemplative souls have repeated Christ's reproaches. Apostles alone can solve this appalling crisis. God's justice and love require reparation. He awaits it with a kind of impatience. Insistently He asks that apostles be willing to pray, to suffer, to devote themselves in reparation for men's misdeeds. So distressing is human wretchedness that the Heart of Christ untiringly repeats the *sitio* of Calvary in the hope that He will find the needed thousands and thousands of generous souls who, hearing His anguished cry, will sell all to follow the Savior and work for the salvation of souls. The form varies, but the urgency of His appeal is unmistakable: . . .

Let My consecrated souls beg confidently for the advent of their divine King: that is, for My universal sovereignty. Let them have no fear, let them hope in Me, let them trust in Me. Let them be burnt up with zeal and charity for sinners. . . . Let the world hear from their lips how great is My kindness, My love and My mercy. . . .[18]

Already in many places the Holy Spirit is inspiring undertakings like those described in the Acts of the Apostles. Although some long-established institutions seem in their old age to be losing ground, new organizations, daring and fervent, are astonishing the world. The language of these new apostles is the same as that of the chosen mystics. It is evident that both have received the same Spirit.[19]

Thus now, by the mid-century, it can be said of the Devotion to the Sacred Heart as of the Faith itself that "its sound has gone forth to the ends of the earth" as the work of the Spirit of Love who will "renew the face of the earth." With theory tested and practice approved, it has worked its way into every mode of life. There is, however, one form of its expression which is still in evolution, still being fashioned by trial and error. It is representation of the Sacred Heart in art. There is not in this case, as there is for Our Lady or for the Passion, an art-tradition centuries old, and a succession of masterpieces in painting or in sculpture to set standards and provoke high artistic achievement.

Yet the matter is vital, for a devotion of such wide practice will necessarily call for popular representation, and there is need here above all of a profound aesthetic insight and a disciplined power of execution to make visible to the eye a devotion which has of its very nature a strong appeal to sentiment and an overfacile symbol to portray. The history of its iconography so far may be traced through the following periods:[20] first, the early Middle Ages, in which the wounded side was portrayed in manuscript designs; second, the late Middle Ages and Renaissance, in which the Heart itself appeared in heraldic or symbolic design in stone, stained glass and metal work,[21] at first simply and then flamboyantly; third, the seventeenth and eighteenth centuries, in which the Heart with the symbols made familiar by Paray appeared with ever-fuller elaborations, first by itself and then in the breast of the Savior; fourth, full-length paintings of "Le Christ au Sacré Coeur," dominant in the nineteenth. The characteristic virtues and vices of each school of art have attended this development, until now in the twentieth century artistic effort moves back and forth between opposite poles: cheap popular production of the sentimental, and earnestly aesthetic creations of liturgical and modernistic art. Artists today grapple with this theme in which the realistic and the spiritual must be supremely combined. In perhaps no other subject of religious art is the challenge greater, failure more lamentable, and success more to be desired. For the need for worthy representation comes not only from the fact that the Church has always encouraged her children to see, hear and touch, that they may the more lovingly believe in the invisible, the silent and the intangible, but from the further fact that in this case a sacred promise is at stake: "I will bless every place where an image of My Heart shall be exposed and honored."

The same challenge is felt in the art of literature. Many of the extracts in this book, especially those of a meditative character written in earlier ages, show that a response to the beauty of Love is perhaps easier in rhythmic words than in paint or marble. Conversely, perhaps nowhere is bathos more fatally easy than in a poem on the same subject. But a high gift of words, matched to a corresponding intensity of faith charged with feeling, can produce poems like the three following. The "Hymn to the Sacred Heart" was written by Paul Claudel, one of a series of poems interpreting the liturgical cycle of Feasts entitled *Corona Benignitatis*. It is an expression of the return of art to faith in the Catholic Renaissance of modern France:

At the end of this third month since the Annunciation, which
    is June,
The woman with whom even God has set Himself in tune
Feels the first thrust of her Child, and near her heart another
    Heart beating.

In the womb of the sinless Virgin will this new era start;
The Child who is before time takes hold of time in His
    Mother's Heart.
The first Mover is moved by a human breath fleeting.
Mary, bearing the burden conceived by the Spirit's power,
Has withdrawn far from men's sight in her secret prayer-bower,
The dove in the Canticle from the rock-cracks, crying like a
    lute.

She stirs not, nor says one word; she adores.
She is within the depth of things; God for her is no longer
    out of doors.
He is His own work, her Son, her little one, her flesh's fruit.

The whole universe is at rest, Caesar has closed Janus' door,
The sceptre has been taken from David, the Prophets speak
    no word more.
It is here, this night deeper than night, this dawn with no
    morning star to tell.

Satan reigns; the whole world gives him gold and incense ris-
    ing as breath,
God creeps like a thief into this paradise of death.
It was a woman who was first cheated; now a woman cheats
    hell.

O God hidden in the woman, O Cause tight-caught,
Jerusalem knows nothing, Joseph himself has no thought;
The mother, all alone with her Child, knows His touch as a
    secret grace.

Now You are before us like a book spread open on the cross;
All is consummated, save that You have not yet suffered the
    last loss.
It is true that Your very mother would not know Your
    frightening face.

It is true that from the soles of Your feet to the crown of
    Your head
We see no place on Your body that, by man's will, has not
    bled.
But You still have a Heart not yet pierced through.

Son of God, for so many centuries by a rope round Your neck
    they have dragged You low;
The very prostitutes would shudder to see You so.
The resemblance that was Your face has been effaced from You.

And wise men, seeing You, shake their heads, and turn away
    a little to smile.
They know better than You do what You meant all the while!

Something quite usual and banal, nothing that is really Your
    own!

They have left nothing of You behind, nor face nor word;
They have cast lots on Your garments, and have cut them
    over to a style preferred.
There is not much left now for those good women, or those
    apostles to own.

You are dead, and the sun has gone dark;
On the outstanding cross a corpse is shown stark.
Friend, if You fail us, what have we besides You?

You did what You could; we give You no blame or rebuff.
But that mystery in the Father's heart—was it not already
    deep enough
But that You must take our nothingness and add death thereto?

Well, if we have not You living, we have You dead.
But the centurion who saw You die, he was not contented;
Throwing himself at You, he has stabbed and opened You
    wide.

The lance goes in the ribs and pierces through,
For the pagan struck at random—but Your faithful do
    better by You.
To us alone belongs the deep, the secret wound of the side.

"Love has disarmed Me, and My Father has no defence
    against you.
Know, at last, this Heart which you have pierced through,
From which gushes the blood on the altar which the chalice
    pours again."

Lord, You have had enough pain; we would do You no more
    harm.
Ah, by that wound which shall never close deliver us too
    from harm!
Did You have to be struck so hard that blood and water
    sprang after pain?

O wound truly royal, O sap of God oozing out!
O blow so proudly dealt straight through the side to the depths
Till it pierced to the very core of the Trinity above!

And it is You whom they call the strong, the inaccessible!
Heaven and earth astounded gaze on this debauch unutterable—
This scandal of a God wounded and drunk with love.

Ah, since You have willed it so, clothing Yourself in animal
    man,
Know now for Yourself the torment of love, for You can,
The state of a pierced Heart that like wax melts away.

Shall we ever close Your wound, when it is God who is
    opened thus?
What comfort can we give You when the Infinite suffers for us,
What love give back to You, O God, when the Infinite desires?

By this rose in its sixth month, which flowers with so sweet
    a smell;
By the whole world in its sixth month which opens under the
    pressing light so well,
Ah, I have guessed right that it was a sorrowing Heart!

No rose is worth anything to me without its thorn;
Little is love to me from which divine pain is shorn.
At the cost of Your Heart, what are all the heavens to me?

Ah, since they laugh at You, and since yonder lies hell,
Come, hide Yourself with me, O Word made flesh, and dwell
As when Margaret Mary in her poor convent once knew You
    nigh.

That I may hold You alone, as Mary once cloistered You,
    apart.
How shall I not hear Your voice, who feel Your beating Heart?
For, "I swear it by Myself" said the Lord God, "I live still, I."[22]

The following "Litany for the Feast of the most Sacred Heart"
is taken from a modern German interpretation of the liturgical
cycle, *Hymns to the Church*, by Gertrud von Le Fort. In it, the soul
speaks to the Church, who answers:

Your voice speaks:
Now I will pray the ardor of the soul as a great litany is prayed.
Now I will raise the song of praise that is not sung but loved.
Blood-red secret of all that is:
Holy Heart, divine Heart, almighty Heart,
Be loved, Love, eternal Love, be Thou eternally loved.

Heart in the dark of a frozen world,
Be loved, Love!
Flame-shadow over all the false brightness of the world,
Be loved, Love!
Burning sign in all the false rest of the world;
Lonely Heart, flaming Heart, unquenchable Heart:
Be loved, everlasting Love.

Heart deep as the nights that have no face:
Be loved!
Heart strong as the waves that have no shores:
Be loved!
Heart tender as little children that have no bitterness:
Be everlastingly loved!

Rose from the flower-beds of the invisible,
Rose from the chalice of the humble maiden,
Blossoming rose-bush, in which heaven and earth are entwined:
Be loved, everlasting Love!

Royal Heart in the flowing mantle of Thy blood,
Be loved!
Brother-Heart in the wild mockery of the thorny crown:
Be loved!
Breaking Heart in the stark ornament of Thy death wounds,
Heart dethroned, Heart betrayed, Heart cruelly martyred:
Be loved, everlasting Love, be everlastingly loved.

Heart before whom the mighty find their knees,
We ask Thee for Thy love.
Heart before whom the careless find their tears:
We ask Thee for Thy love.
Heart in whom thieves and murderers yet find forgiveness,
Great Heart, Heart of mercy, Heart of glory,
We ask Thee for Thy love!

Red-thorn of our gladness,
Sorrow-thorn of our repentance,
Fair evening glow of our own setting,
We ask Thee for Thy love.

Crimson cloth that turns sin pale as death:
We ask Thee for Thy love.
Ruby stream after which the sick souls thirst:
We ask Thee for Thy love.
Whispering nearness in which parted friends may meet;
We ask Thee for Thy love.

Comforting lamp of the distressed,
Lighthouse of the persecuted and disgraced,
Hidden chamber in which the gentle dead may yet breathe,
All-knowing Heart, all guiding Heart, ultimate Heart:
We ask Thee for Thy love.

Heart that takes us all to itself,
Heart that strikes the center of all our hearts,
Heart that breaks the proud hearts of us all;
We ask Thee for Thy love.

Heart that makes solitude into a great people:
We ask Thee for Thy love.
Heart that makes discord into a united people:
We ask Thee for Thy love.
Heart in which the whole world becomes Thy people:
We consecrate ourselves to Thy love.
Overflowing Heart, overflaming Heart, overstorming Heart:
Be loved Lord, Love, everlasting Love, be everlastingly loved.

That Thy dawn may break with kindling light,
We consecrate ourselves to Thy love.
That Thy day may bring fire to our hearts,
We consecrate ourselves to Thy love.
That Thy day may burn all our hearts into Thine,
We consecrate ourselves to Thy love.
Mighty Heart, ineluctable Heart, all-consuming Heart.

Fire! Fire! The angels' wings are burning, the swords of the
    seraphim are aflame!

The lights of heaven are burning, the depths of earth are
    burning, rocks and yesterdays are all aflame!
The expectation of all creatures burns—the spirit burns in
    the darkness of high thought.
All has been taken from love, all must become love; sing:
    "Holy, Holy, Holy!" rustling flames of the seraphim!
Heart from which the heavens draw their glory,
Heart from which suns and constellations draw their begin-
    ning and their end,
Heart from which the souls of the Blessed draw their blessedness,
World-ordering Heart, world-conquering Heart, Thou only
    Heart of hearts:
Amen. Amen. May the day of Thine infinite love come
    quickly.[23]

It was to the Heart of Christ on the cross that the thoughts of
Edith Sitwell turned when bombs were falling upon London in
1940. During "the Raids, Night and Dawn" she wrote her poem
"Still Falls the Rain":

Still falls the Rain—
Dark as the world of man, black as our loss—
Blind as the nineteen hundred and forty nails
Upon the Cross.

Still falls the Rain
With a sound like the pulse of the heart that is changed to
    the hammer-beat
In the Potter's Field, and the sound of the impious feet
On the Tomb:
        Still falls the Rain
In the Field of Blood where the small hopes breed and the
    human brain
Nurtures its greed, that worm with the brow of Cain.

Still falls the Rain
At the feet of the Starved Man hung upon the Cross.
Christ that each day, each night, nails there, have mercy on
    us—
On Dives and on Lazarus:
Under the Rain the sore and the gold are as one.

Still falls the Rain—
Still falls the Blood from the Starved Man's wounded side:
He bears in His Heart all wounds—those of the light that
    died,
The last faint spark
In the self-murdered heart, the wounds of the sad
    uncomprehending dark,
The wounds of the baited bear—
The blind and weeping bear whom the keepers beat
On his helpless flesh . . . the tears of the hunted hare.

Still falls the Rain—
Then—O Ile leape up to my God: who pulls me doune—
See, see where Christ's blood streames in the firmament:
It flows from the Brow we nailed upon the tree
Deep to the dying, to the thirsting heart
That holds the fires of the world—dark-smirched with pain
As Caesar's laurel crown.

Then sounds the voice of One who like the heart of man
Was once a child who among beasts has lain—
"Still do I love, still shed my innocent light, my Blood,
    for thee."[24]

Here it may be well to return to the image of the lens: the light-lines of tradition, moving nearer, from remote points in Scripture and history, had been drawn together by the Revelations to Saint Margaret Mary and had met in a focal point which we may localize in the year 1765, when the Devotion was officially accepted by the Magisterium of the Church. But they did not end where they met; they crossed and journeyed on with new intensity and with new color for having passed through the lens. New rays of the Devotion are becoming distinct as synthesis replaces analysis in its theological development. The earlier tendency of scholars to limit the Devotion to the forms made familiar by Paray was a step necessary for clarity and accuracy. Now, greater freedom of treatment and of expression can develop from within the Devotion and radiate out from it in new aspects, each authentically "Sacred Heart."

Such evolution is a natural and necessary result of the changes of thought, custom and speech which affect the Church. She is, as Cardinal Suhard has reminded us, transcendent,[25] but she may, like living people, be clothed in the modes of the age and speak its idiom, for she is also immanent in the world that she continuously redeems. The same is true of the Devotion by which she invigorates the life of grace that flows from the unchanging Sacraments. A certain timeliness in devotional practices is desirable if they are to be of vital importance to the young people who hold the future in their hands. External practices which do not appeal will be dropped as unessential or as an actual impediment. A living Devotion stays young; it moves abreast with the Church in her conquest of time.

Light is thrown on this matter by a challenging chapter in *Le Coeur*[26] entitled "Crisis and Evolution in the Devotion to the Sacred Heart," where a study, based on statistical research, is made of the appeal of the Devotion to young leaders of militant Catholic Action in France in 1945. A misunderstanding, amounting in some cases to positive dislike, was found in this group. The reasons for this, it is claimed, are to be found in "activism," and in a need for virility, simplicity and corporateness in the spiritual life. The students and militants of today are nourished on the Liturgy and on the Gospels; they are inspired by a sense of the Mystical Body, of the conquest of the world for Christ. They find the older forms of the Devotion inadequate; its practices together with "private revelations" are unpopular. The conclusion is drawn that to assure its force among the future leaders of the nation the Devotion must be presented in a form "more Scriptural, more liturgical, more theological."

The situation in one country in 1945 may not be present elsewhere to the same degree ten years later, but the suggested remedy is everywhere present. Devotion to the Sacred Heart is being presented in books, in preaching, in study, as precisely that which the youth of today are craving; a vital source of prayer and of apostolate, to be drawn from Scripture, Liturgy and theology. The passages in the rest of this chapter will illustrate these three points successively.

The following study of the fundamental relation of the visions of Saint Margaret Mary to the Epistles of Saint Paul will show not only how Scripture can illuminate the Devotion, but how the Devotion can illuminate Scripture. The two disciples on the road to Emmaus cried out: "Was not our heart burning within us while

He opened to us the Scripture?"[27] The author shows that the victory won by the Devotion to the Sacred Heart against so much opposition is due to the profound theology on which it is based, and that without that dogmatic foundation the Revelations at Paray could not have received such credit in the Universal Church:

The Pauline character of these works by Saint Margaret Mary is even more remarkable than is the height to which they soar. Anyone, however slightly acquainted with the doctrine of Saint Paul, with the history of the unfolding of that doctrine and the vicissitudes and troubles through which it has reached its actual development, cannot but be astonished at meeting so frequently, in the writings of Saint Margaret Mary, with expressions so nearly akin to those of Saint Paul. Indeed one may say that at times the humble religious, travelling in spirit along the way opened up for her by the Apostle, lets fall words and phrases more Pauline than those of Saint Paul himself.

Since, therefore, the theology underlying the devotion to the Sacred Heart of Jesus is almost identical with Saint Paul's characteristic teaching, it must be of supreme interest and profit to study this devotion in the light of the Apostle's writings. There are, indeed, so many points of contact between theology and devotion, that devotion must of necessity receive special light and strength from theology. Now, a singular phenomenon is observable in the Epistles of Saint Paul, namely, that just as without once pronouncing the holy name of Mary he nevertheless affords the firmest doctrinal foundation upon which to build her cultus; so in like manner, without using the words "Heart of Jesus," he gives us in reality a complete theology of the worship of that Divine Heart. . . .

The frequency with which Saint Paul insists upon the close affinity between love and the heart is worthy of consideration. More notable still is the variety of points of view and the diverse shades of meaning which he discovers in this connection. For Saint Paul the heart is, as it were, the receptacle of love. "The charity of God is poured forth in our hearts."[28] Love is also the object and end towards which the heart should tend: "May the Lord direct your hearts into the love of God."[29] From another point of view, the heart is the fount from which love proceeds: "The aim of admonition is charity out of a pure heart."[30]

Not alone love itself, but also the whole interior man as well as the entire affective life with its bearing upon love find their focus in the heart. . . .[31]

Let us now apply this teaching of the Apostle to our Lord Jesus Christ and to His divine Heart. To begin with the latter, if our persons, our bodies, our hearts are the habitations and temples of the Holy Spirit, with how much greater reason is this true of the Sacred Heart of our Lord Jesus Christ, so fittingly invoked by the Church as "the holy Temple of God," and "the Tabernacle of the most High," and this not only on account of the presence and ineffable union of the divine Person of the Word, but also because of the presence and indwelling of the Holy Spirit.

That the plenitude of the Holy Spirit and of grace resides in the Heart of Jesus, and that His plenitude overflows upon us, is easily proved from Saint Paul's writings. It is indeed one of the most fundamental truths of his theology that all grace and spiritual blessing come to us through Christ and in Christ. It is with profound emotion that he states, or rather hymns, this truth in the lyrical outburst with which he opens the Epistle to the Ephesians: "Blessed be the God and Father of our Lord Jesus Christ, who hath blessed us with every spiritual blessing on high in Christ: yea, in Him He singled us out before the foundation of the world, that we might be holy and blameless in His sight."[32] And to the Colossians he adds: "In Him dwelleth all the fulness of the Godhead corporally: and in Him ye attain your fulness. . . ."[33] Since then in the language of Saint Paul the word "grace" in all its variety of meanings signifies nothing less than the Holy Spirit with His gifts and activity, and since the Holy Spirit in His special function pours forth His gifts and exercises His activity in the heart, it follows that the plenitude of grace which comes to us from Christ is nothing else than the Holy Spirit which flows from out His Heart into ours . . .[34]

It must be said again that the foregoing doctrine of Saint Paul would of itself be sufficient, even had he given us no other, to transfigure and lift above all other devotions the devotion to the Heart of Jesus. Moreover, it alone can explain those repeated expressions of Saint Margaret Mary which at first sight appear enigmatical, wherein she affirms her desire to think no thought save with the mind of Christ, to feel no love save with His divine Heart. The following is one of those truly wondrous paragraphs which show incontestably how the same Christ who thought, felt and spoke in Paul and by Paul, likewise thinks, feels and speaks in Margaret Mary and by Margaret Mary. Writing to Sister de la Barge at the end of October, 1689, the saint says ". . . and after we have lost our heart of corruption in these divine flames of pure love, we must have a heart entirely new that shall make us live from henceforth a completely renovated life with a new heart that has new thoughts, new affections and new operations in purity and fervor in all our actions." This means that there must be nothing left of self, but that the divine Heart of Jesus must be substituted for ours in such a wise that He alone lives and works on us and for us; His will must so keep our will annihilated that it may be able to act without any resistance on our part; and, in fine, His affections, His thoughts, His desires should be substituted for ours, but especially His love, which shall love Himself in us and for us. And thus this lovable Heart being all in all for us, we shall be able to say with Saint Paul that "we no longer live but that it is He who lives in us." Years before the saint had written with wonderful succinctness to Mother de Saumaise: "Another time, Jesus Christ impressed Himself upon me in such a manner that it seems to me, since then, that there remains to me no other being, no other life but His. . . ."[35]

Saint Margaret Mary knew, of course, that the desire of Our Lord for the establishment of a new Feast was a matter that would affect the life of the whole Church. She may not have realized how admirably it would lead to a new understanding of the very nature of the Church as a body whose members live as one through love. The study of her writings in the light of Saint Paul makes this clearer to our day than it was to hers. The parallel continues:

The last texts make us pass over from one formula, *in Christo Jesu,* to another, *in corde Jesu.* The transition may be effected by the comparison of two profoundly moving passages from the writings of Saint Paul and Saint Margaret Mary. We have seen that the unity of the Mystical Body of Christ is the divine power which raises to the heights of mysticism the devotion to the Heart of Jesus. But whence is this close union? Saint Paul answers: "one body and one spirit; as also ye were called in one hope, that of your calling: One Lord, one faith, one Baptism: one God and Father of all."[36] It seems hardly possible to express more clearly or more forcefully this sevenfold unity. Nevertheless, we have to confess that this time the Apostle to the Gentiles is left behind by the lowly virgin of Paray-le-Monial. Her phrase has a power, a succinctness, a depth of meaning, a divine radiance, that belong only to the words of Jesus Christ Himself: "one single heart, one single God." This sentence seems to include the various elements dispersed throughout Saint Paul's Epistles, and to fuse and organize them into a complete theology of the Heart of Jesus. "One single Heart," the Heart of Jesus Christ; one single love, the love of the Holy Spirit; for one single God, our heavenly Father, the Father of all! All humanity glorifying the Father with the Heart of the Son, and with the love of the Holy Spirit.

Once only does Saint Paul speak directly of the Heart of Jesus, but this single text is so significant, so rich in meaning, that it alone would justify the conclusions arrived at by combining together passages which bear only indirectly upon the subject. To the Philippians Saint Paul says: "God is my witness how I yearn for you all in the heart of Christ Jesus."[37] A thorough exposition of the meaning of these words has been given elsewhere. Let it be enough to point out here, firstly, that Saint Paul can love with the very Heart of Jesus Christ because of his mystical identification with our Savior; secondly, that he appeals to this same Heart as an earnest or supreme proof of the unshakable love which he has for the Philippians. These facts being granted, two points stand out and give a unique and fundamental importance to the text, while they clear away any doubts against the validity of our argument.

Paul loves with the Heart of Jesus Christ, simply because He who lives in him is Jesus Christ, and because to live is to love and one loves with the heart. So it will be seen that the double connection established between life and love and the heart in general, and between the unity and life of the Mystical Body of Christ and Christ's Heart in particular, is thoroughly well founded and is in conformity with the mind of Saint Paul. It is quite legitimate to apply first and chiefly to the Heart of Jesus those passages which treat of His Mystical Body and include a mention of charity and of the heart; especially so when, far from being mere dispassionate or theoretical explanations, they are passages truly overflowing with love.[38]

The riches of Scripture in connection with the Devotion are best revealed by the texts which have been accommodated to the Liturgy of the Sacred Heart. Both Office and Mass were reshaped by the Sacred Congregation of Rites in 1928 when Pius XI issued the *Miserentissimus Redemptor,* giving to the Feast, already a double of the First Class, a privileged Octave. The sign of the Church's deepening awareness of the validity of the Devotion for all times and all places, and of its integral place in her own life, is found in the Introit to the new Mass which replaced the official *Miserebitur* and all local and votive Masses: "Cogitationes Cordis ejus a generatione in generationem."[39] Penetrating studies of the new Mass and Office soon appeared; it was recognized that:

For the Church, even more than for individuals, or for any other society, grace may consist in time and circumstance, and the Church is careful not to let such an opportunity pass. The Holy Ghost, soul of the Church, cannot be found wanting. He breathes, regardless of any obstacle, at the hour of His divine wisdom and knowledge, which is always the hour of His love. The Church's compositions in the nineteenth century are as much inspired by the Holy Ghost and worthy of our acceptance as those of the first, the fifth and the twelfth. They are the true nourishment of the soul, its infallible manual of guidance and direction. The mere fact, therefore, of the composition of a new Office for an existent feast is a lesson from which we should profit. The liturgical composition of such an Office is likewise a new source of life offered to our zeal.[40]

The public prayer of the *Ecclesia Orans* has thus become not only the definitive but the most perfect expression of the Devotion, as it echoes "the fundamental piety of the *Corpus Mysticum,* voicing in public the private piety of all her children, no longer groups of 'devotees' but 'members of member,'" as is revealed by Jürgensmeier:

The piercing of the side (or heart) of Jesus is strongly emphasized in the liturgy of the Feast of the Sacred Heart. In the hymn of the first Vespers in this Office, the Church prays: "Ex corde scisso Ecclesia Christo jugata nascitur," the piercing of the heart of Christ upon the cross heralds the birth of His Mystical Bride, the Church. Nearly all the Breviary Homilies of the Church Fathers are concerned with the same idea: the Church was formed out of the blood and water (redemption and Baptism) flowing from the pierced side of Jesus. Laurentius Justinianus presents the following parallel: as Eve, formed out of the side of the sleeping Adam, became the mother of all mankind, so the Church, the glorious Bride of Christ, the "spiritual Adam," was formed from the side, emitting blood and water, of the sleeping Saviour upon the cross. The open side of Jesus is the "fountain of all grace." The Preface expresses this with all solemnity: "It was Thy will that the heart of Thy only begotten Son upon the Cross should be pierced by the lance of the soldier, in order that the divine munificence, compassion and grace should flow forth from the sanctuary of His open heart upon us."

In this passage, liturgy manifests the relation between the piercing of the Heart of Jesus and the mystical body of Christ. Through it the Sacred Heart is shown to have a deep, mystical connection with the *Corpus mysticum Christi,* at least in the most essential points dealing with salvation. Through the mystical body, the Devotion to the Sacred Heart is imbued with a deep and sublime significance surpassing the usual tenor of its contents.

Disregarding the piercing of the Sacred Side in its significance for salvation, and considering the prayers on this subject from a purely moral standpoint, it is clear that its delineation would not correspond either with liturgy or with the Breviary. But if liturgy and the Breviary are properly understood, then every First Friday would be a particular feast day in honor of the mystical body of Christ, the faithful manifesting of the sublime, mystical union with the Head by a greater participation in the Holy Eucharist. A reverent and solemn celebration of the Feast of the Sacred Heart would be the greatest feast day in the life of the Mystical Body.

This is an indication of the deep, inner union between the heart of Jesus and the *Corpus mysticum Christi,* both of which are based upon the same fundamental principle of piety. The form of devotion distinguishing the veneration of the Sacred Heart, which manifests love, repentance and the desire to imitate Christ, also characterizes the piety of the mystical union with Him. The mystical member gains a deeper comprehension of the Sacred Heart devotion from the truth of the *Corpus mysticum.* Furthermore, the veneration of the Sacred Heart indicates a simple and obvious way to attain to the Head of the Mystical Body through the "Heart of Jesus."

The veneration of the Sacred Heart, being a part of the piety of the *Corpus mysticum Christi,* is dedicated to Christ in deed and intention, and is an expression of oneness with Him: "Thine we are, Thine we will be, and in order to grow still closer to Thee, we freely dedicate ourselves today to Thy most Sacred Heart." In intention and in deed, this devotion strives after conformity with the heart of Jesus, imitating His principles and His virtues, the love for and unity with Him leading to atonement. This is its most profound meaning, for love is the language which makes the deepest impression and which is most easily understood; it brings the love of the man Jesus Christ to the member, helping him, through the most Sacred Heart, to grow up in Him Who is the Head.[41]

These studies of Scripture and Liturgy lead to the theological studies of the present day, and here we find, as always in the life of the Church, that gain does not mean loss; the new does not supplant the old, but grows from it. For now, as in the beginning, we must still enter the Heart of Christ in His Passion (for it was then that it was pierced), but only to find ourselves awakened to glory in that same Heart, not dead but living. It is still true that "matters relating to Christ's humanity are the chief incentive to devotion," but also that "devotion itself has for its object matters concerning the god-head."[42] We find that the radiant thought-lines antecedent to Saint Margaret Mary are in our day asserting themselves with a new force for having passed through the lens of Paray; prayer and thought are rediscovering the *principalis cordis* of Origen, the "inner heart of God's secret places" of Gilbert of Hoyland, the "dwelling-place of the elect . . . where all mysteries are first wrought" of Monsieur Olier, the "spaces of eternity filled with love before and after" of Saint John Eudes. The dogmatic searchings of the eighteenth century, the refinements and distinctions of the nineteenth and early twentieth, have done their work. The colors revealed by the theological spectrum are now merging into the white light of divinity. For now that it is recognized beyond controversy that the immediate object of the Devotion is the Heart of Christ considered as the symbol of His love, and primarily of His human love, so it is realized with greater urgency that the Heart, together with the whole human nature of Christ, is *instrumentum conjunctum divinitatis*. Devotion to the Sacred Heart at the present time is steadily leading into the depths of the Triune God. We read:

It is for us to meditate on the most beautiful texts of Saint John the Evangelist concerning the Word, the Father, and the Spirit of Love, to make our own in some measure "all the treasures of wisdom and knowledge" which are held in the Heart of Jesus, "burning furnace of charity."

"He who believes in Me, from his breast shall flow rivers of living water." It is not a later commentator, it is Saint John himself who adds: "And this He said of the Spirit which those who believe in Him should receive."[43] The Heart of Jesus wills to give us to quench our thirst at the "river of living water, clear as crystal, coming from the throne of God and of the Lamb,"[44] according to the image of the same inspired author.

Verbum spirans amorem, writes Saint Thomas, in his dense, precise style. The Word of God is the source of Love. From Him proceeds the Spirit of Love. Such is the Key to the cult of the Sacred Heart. It is a theological cult, it is a Trinitarian cult. It seems that this point has not been brought sufficiently into relief, even in Thomistic theology.

The human intelligence of Jesus Christ was gifted with the beatific vision from the first instant of the conception of the Word in the womb of the Blessed Virgin Mary. From then on the Word, in as much as He was man, rejoiced in Himself as Word, and in the Father of whom He is the mirror and the splendor; thus rejoiced in and through the faculty of intellectual knowledge belonging by right and by fact to the human nature which He had assumed. This satisfying and pacifying illumination has to do with the greatest psychological mystery of the human intelligence assumed by the Word. That which the elect enjoy only after death, the Incarnate Word enjoyed from the first moment of His becoming human, in a measure which surpasses our possibilities of appreciation.

But the elect are not called only to the Beatific Vision, intellectual participation in the first procession of the Trinity, participation realized through luminous contact with the Word. The elect, declares Saint John of the Cross, are called to participate, over and above, in a correlative manner, on the plane of the procession of love, in the spiration which has for its end and its reason for being, the very Person of Love, the Holy Spirit, worthy love of the Word and of the Father. He writes:

> The Holy Spirit lifts the soul on high, and informs it, so that she breathes towards God the same breath of love which the Father breathes to the Son and the Son to the Father, which is the Holy Spirit Himself whom They breathe in her, in the said transformation . . . The soul united and transformed in God, breathes in God, to God, the same divine Spiration which God, being in her, breathes in Himself towards her.
>
> The soul exercises its work of understanding, of knowledge and of love, conjointly with the Trinity, like the Trinity itself, always in a participated manner, God operating that in her.
>
> "Father, I will that where I am they also whom Thou hast given Me may be with Me, that they may see the glory which Thou hast given Me," that is to say, doing in us by participation, the same work which I myself do by nature, which is to spirate the Holy Spirit.
>
> For the soul, that means to participate in God by exercising with Him and in His company the Work of the Holy Trinity, in the way which we have said, because of the substantial union between the soul and God.[45]

If only the highest mystical experience allows Saint John of the Cross to analyze and to express on the plane of lived dogma these values both transcendent and immanent, he himself affirms none the less that the possession of them is a thing willed by God for each of His children of adoption in the measure fixed by Himself in His infinite wisdom. Our supernatural adoption is Trinitarian; that is its originality, that is its richness. Supernatural psychology finds its completion, its plenitude in the beatific vision and in the spiration of the Holy Spirit.

Now, among all created natures there is one that dominates over all the others, that of Christ, first-born among many brothers. If there is one soul of which it is true to affirm an equality of love, it is indeed that of Jesus. It would be an anomaly to affirm for the human intelligence of Christ the sublime unfolding of the beatific vision and to deny to His human will a parallel effective participation in the spiration of the Spirit. More than any other created spirit the soul of Christ enjoyed, in His spiritual faculties, the processions of Wisdom and of Love of the Holy Trinity.

At this point in his article, Father Philip of the Trinity quotes briefly from the monumental work *The Theology of the Mystical Body,* by Father Emile Mersch, S.J. That quotation has been here expanded somewhat to include other passages from that great book, where the human love of Christ is studied in the section on the Holy Spirit which rises to a triumphal climax in the words "Sacred Heart":

Although the assumed humanity is not the divinity nor spiration, it subsists in Him who is the Spirator of the Holy Spirit and is truly and intrinsically the humanity of Him from whom the Holy Spirit proceeds. . . . Christ's humanity possesses this relationship to the Holy Spirit in the most intrinsic way possible, that is, by the personality that is its own. . . . Even in spirating the Holy Spirit the Word is He who has become man and who makes the sacred humanity His own; consequently He spirates in union and communion with His human nature. . . . But what is special to spiration and makes the Son the Spirator is Love, the Love that unites Him to the Father and constitutes Him principle of the Spirit, for the spiration of the Holy Spirit is accomplished by way of love. Consequently love must also adapt the assumed humanity to be the humanity of the Spirator. This is a human love, for it belongs to a human nature; yet it is a love that surpasses the resources of a human nature left to itself, since it is called forth by union with divine love. This love is theological charity, such as it existed in Christ. Love such as this had to be found in Christ's human nature. Human nature necessarily admits of spiritual love, for it is a spiritual nature. In Christ this love has to be love of God and the Spirator. Therefore it has to be a divinized love, so as to be worthy of God, who is the Spirator. . . .

However we may envisage Christ's charity, it always has the appearance of being a way of loving that is proper to a man who is the Spirator. This is the mystery of His love: the love of the Sacred Heart.[46]

Here we return to the original article into which this expanded quotation from Father Mersch has been woven. Together they form a thought-unit: the divineness of Christian love.

In the very name of the unicity of the metaphysical personality of the Incarnate Word, there here shines forth the highest and most mysterious dimension of His human psychology on the supernatural and mystical plane, that of created participation in the Trinitarian life: vision and spiration. Scripture and Liturgy often bring together the Heart and the Spirit. It is above all of Jesus that it is true to affirm: charity has been poured forth in His Heart by the Holy Spirit which has been given to Him. The wounded Heart of Jesus is truly the symbolic revelation of the suffering Love of the Incarnate Word, and this Love is inseparable from the Holy Spirit.

Jesus loves us as the divine Word with that impulse with which He spirates love in union with the Father; He also loves us as the Incarnate Word by His human will drawn into the Spiration of the Spirit of Love. Of this inseparable double love—the latter being explained only by the former—His wounded Heart is the most precious symbol, worthy of adoration, of the adoration of love. "Greater love than this no man has, than to give his life for his friend," and Jesus died for love of us upon the Cross. It is merciful love and not justice that is the decisive and determining reason for the bloody sacrifice of Calvary. The Heart victim of merciful love is at once the masterpiece and the highest expression of the Spirit of Love. . . .

The cultus of the Sacred Heart englobes the fundamental mysteries of the Trinity and of the redemptive Incarnation, that is the mystery of Love in its infinite plenitude as in the expression of its mercy. Thus, and only thus, all is summed up in the Heart of Jesus, which is truly "the synthesis of all religion," according to the strong expression of Pope Pius XI in the Encyclical *Miserentissimus Redemptor*.

This Heart is the revelation of the love of charity which includes the love of God and of the neighbor, the plenitude of the law. This wounded Heart is the revelation of the love that worked our redemption under the sign of suffering through the superabundance of mercy.

But the Redemption is, in fact, for the Trinity as a means to an end. Under the sign of the cross, this Heart is the sensible revelation of our vocation as children of God called to communicate in the Trinitarian life at the touch of the Spirit of Love who transforms us into brothers and co-heirs of the Word in filial abandonment to the

Father. "Because you are sons, God has put into your hearts the Spirit of His Son by which you cry Abba, Father."[47] It is the way of spiritual childhood.

Our minds must be able to link spontaneously the blood of that Heart to the impulse of love that inflames the human will of Christ, and this impulse itself to the Respiration of Love which rhythms the movements of the Trinitarian life. Conceived by the Holy Spirit in the womb of the Virgin Mary of spotless heart, His wounded Heart remains the living symbol of the bonds of merciful love which in the Mystical Body link the Head to the members in the unity of the Holy Spirit. The Heart of Christ the Redeemer cannot be thought of without the Holy Spirit.[48]

This grasp of the Devotion to the Sacred Heart in its Trinitarian aspect reveals that its work in the life of the Church on earth is pre-eminently the work of the Spirit of Love. The author of *The Sacred Heart and Modern Life* carries his thought still further in the following:

The Holy Spirit dwells in the Heart of Christ in a unique way which we will try to describe and contemplate. There is nothing more wonderful in the spiritual world nor in all the visions of the contemplatives. . . .

The Holy Spirit, the substantial Love of the Father and the Son, is not only given to the Heart of Christ but belongs to Him personally as our human love belongs to us. The Spirit of Christ is what is best, most precious, most intimate, most personal to Him. All the other attributes of His human nature, however closely bound to His Person, are far from being united to Him as is His Spirit. His Spirit is the breath of His Life, His one Love, His only beatitude, the one personal bond between the Father and the Son, His one inspiration, His one power, His only will, His Law. His Spirit is Himself in the sense that the Spirit expresses in an infinite way the total gift of the Son to the Father. The Spirit is equal to the Son. The Spirit belongs to the Son.

When we try to realize what the Holy Spirit is to Christ we must first picture a man in whom is concentrated all the power of love that has ever animated a human heart or ever could animate it in any order of creation, whether actual or imaginary. That is not a dream. That Man is Christ; or rather, Christ is infinitely more because the Holy Spirit, Who is His Spirit, belongs to Him as His own. He is not only from Him and in Him, but of Him. He gives Him to Himself when He wills, as He wills, in the measure in which He wills, because the Spirit proceeds from Him. We can never fathom the infinite

depths of this twofold power of Christ: the procession of the Spirit from His Divine Nature as Son, and the overflowing as of an ocean of love upon His human nature, according to the measure which He Himself has freely determined.

The Heart of Christ possesses the fulness of the Holy Spirit. The Holy Spirit is wholly in Christ, because He gives the Spirit to Himself. All Love is in Him. Is it possible to imagine a creature more filled with the Spirit? No. Just as God is "infinitely greater than any conceivable being"—"quo major cogitari nequit"—so also is the Heart of Christ. The ocean has only a relative fulness; the sun only a relative heat. Beauty and truth are only abstract concepts. There is no true plenitude on earth except in Christ.

Because Christ possesses the fulness of the Spirit, His Heart is the one source of every outpouring of the Spirit. If we consider all the countless manifestations of love that have ever taken place in the history of mankind or that ever may take place on earth or in heaven, and if we trace them to their source, we find that source in the Heart of Christ, for the Holy Spirit is freely poured into that Heart by Christ Himself. Saint Paul, dazzled by this revelation, cries out in words that seem emphatic but which fall far short of the truth: "That you may be able to comprehend with all the saints what is the breadth and length and height and depth, to know also the charity of Christ which surpasseth all knowledge." If therefore we want to receive the Holy Spirit, we must ask it of the Heart of Christ.[49]

Long ago, in the thirteenth century, the beginning of that "tempus modernum" in which divine love must continually manifest itself anew to inflame a world grown cold, Our Lord let Saint Gertrude listen to His "double heart-beat," reflecting His love for His Father and for men. Today theology studies this "double law." The vision of a mystic has become the way of life for modern men who seek to be co-redeemers with Christ of the world around them; there is "a double law of love in the Heart of Christ":

First, in His relation to the Father: The Son of God, in becoming man, did not cease to be wholly Son. He renounced nothing of His personal relation to the Father. The life of the Trinity continued without variation. But He raised His human nature to the Triune Life. Christ no less than the Word is wholly turned to the Father. He loves the Father with the same strength; He offers the same filial obedience. Undoubtedly, human nature cannot equal the power of the Divine Nature. Christ's Human nature, nevertheless, was so penetrated, transfigured and animated by the Holy Spirit, Who is Christ's own Spirit, that it was radically impossible that it should not be attuned, harmonized, unified with the divine nature in the Love of the Father. The law of Christ's love is His filial dependence on the Father.

Through the Holy Spirit, there was found upon our earth this incomparable mystery: a Man like ourselves began to love God as only God can love, and He did it by means of a creature. Up to that time there had been on earth no adoration of God by God, or praise and obedience given to God by God, and in order that the Redemption be accomplished there was needed a sacrifice offered to God by God.

Another mystery has been given to the world by the action of the Holy Spirit: a man like ourselves, Christ, participated in the beatitude of God's love, not through passing consolations but by the personal possession of the Spirit Who is the beatitude of the Trinity. For the infinite beatitude of the Trinity, the inexhaustible source of all beatitude is Love,—the Spirit Who is the mutual embrace of the Father and the Son. Christ is He Who is embraced by the Father with infinite tenderness in a Divine beatitude which no human ecstasy of joy can even suggest.

Secondly, in His relation to the world: Through the Holy Spirit, Christ enters into a new relation with the world. He is not only its Divine Architect and Workman "by Whom all things are made," He is not only the First-born, the King, the Crown, the Beginning and the End, but the bond in Whom the Holy Spirit in infinite love binds all creatures to their Creator. If creatures exist, if they are richly endowed, if their sins are blotted out by Divine Mercy, if they are called to eternal happiness, it is not because of their merit or their charm or because God has need of them; it is solely because of the Holy Spirit Who is the Love of the Heart of Christ. . . .

But while the Holy Spirit is the bond uniting Christ with the world, He is the gift of God to the world. The Holy Spirit is the supreme Gift, the infinite Gift, the unique Gift. Because He proceeds from Christ, He shows how profoundly Christ desires to give Himself. The Holy Spirit unites the two natures of Christ in a total and uninterrupted giving, parallel and equivalent aspects of a twofold gift. The Son, in His Divine Nature, gives Himself to the Father in infinite gratitude and obedience. The same Son, in His human nature, gives Himself wholly to the world in the Incarnation, in the Passion, in the Eucharist, in the Mystical Body. As God He has nothing that does not belong to the Father. As Man, He has nothing that is not given to the world. His law is total giving. Through the Spirit, Christ is wholly gift.

We must be careful not to think of the Heart of Christ apart from His Spirit, or of the Spirit apart from the Heart of Christ. Without the Holy Spirit, Christ is no longer Himself. And the Holy Spirit has no place in the world without the Heart of Christ. The devotion to the Sacred Heart unites the two inseparably.[50]

Perhaps it is by a law of divine compensation, of divine paradox, that a predominantly heaven-seeking line of Devotion to the Sacred Heart is pointing upward so clearly from a world in crisis between global war and the atomic chain-reaction—destructive or constructive—of the future. Perhaps it is again Saint John whose thought is directing the movement. He who drew from his rest upon the Heart of the Master who loved him singularly the strength to witness and to bear witness to the piercing of that Heart, he whose writing taught Saint Augustine that the Church was born from the piercing, he who showed Saint Gertrude that the Devotion to that Heart was for "later times," is a fitting guide from the crises of time into eternity, where all is "as it was in the beginning." Theologians, in unfolding the discourse after the Last Supper which he recorded, are following his eagle flight to the home of the Word, who is God, whose Heart of flesh is now at the right hand of the Father, praying for His members on earth that "the love wherewith Thou hast loved Me may be in them, and I in them." That love is the Holy Spirit, and the Devotion to the Heart that so loves leads straight into the Trinity. Mother Church, like His Mother Mary, will think these thoughts of Christ's Heart from generation to generation, till all her children have been called home into the Vision of Love.

NOTES

1. *Mystici Corporis* (America Press, 1943), p. 6.
2. *Ibid.,* p. 25.
3. In *Sertum Laetitiae,* addressed to the United States.
4. The Sacred Heart radio program is under the direction of Jesuits, in St. Louis, with regional centers in other cities. It was founded by Eugene P. Murphy, S.J., and by 1945 was offering 569 programs on 140 stations.
5. First Friday Clubs are now established in many cities, notably Detroit and Boston. Members receive Communion in their parish churches, then meet for lunch at a hotel or restaurant, with a priest moderator, who addresses them, after prayer in common.

6. This work was begun by Father Mateo Crawley-Boevey of the Picpus Fathers, at the request of a little girl to whom Our Lord spoke after Holy Communion, asking her for "golden pennies" of prayer and sacrifice with which to redeem souls. Members of Tarcisian groups have bank books and checks for their spiritual pennies.

7. This work of the Holy Hour at home is also promoted by the Picpus Fathers, an extension of the movement for the Enthronement of the Sacred Heart in families.

8. *Jésus, Roi d'Amour* (Chambly-canton, Canada, Centre National Canadien de l'Intronization, 1945), p. 21. The English version is *Jesus, King of Love* (National Center of the Enthronement, Fairhaven).

9. *Ibid.*, p. 23.

10. *Ibid.*, p. 30.

11. *Acta Apostolicae Sedis* XXXVII, July 25, 1945, p. 189.

12. For example, Rev. C. C. Martindale, S.J., claimed the theology of the Gospel of Saint John could not be fully explored until India had been converted, and had placed the true elements of her philosophy at the service of the Church. Devotion to the Sacred Heart would fulfill certain inherent racial instincts in Eastern peoples; see Section II in *Le Coeur* (Desclée, 1950). For a fuller study of missionary accommodation, see Jean Daniélou, *The Salvation of the Nations,* trans. by A. Bouchard (Sheed, 1949).

13. John 17, 22.

14. John 4, 34.

15. Prov. 30, 16.

16. From notes taken at the Papal audience given to alumnae of the Sacred Heart at the time of the beatification of Blessed Philippine Duchesne, Pentecost, 1940.

17. François Charmot, S.J., *The Sacred Heart and Modern Life,* p. 147.

18. *Ibid.*, pp. 157 ff. In this passage the author is quoting Sister Josefa Menendez.

19. *Ibid.*, p. 177.

20. See: Grimouart de Saint Laurent, "Les Images du Sacré Coeur au point de vue de l'histoire et de l'art," in *Revue de l'Art Chrétien,* XXVII, XXVIII, XXIX.

21. See: Gilbert Dolan, "Devotion to the Sacred Heart in Mediaeval England, in *Dublin Review,* CXX, 373.

22. Paul Claudel, *Corona Benignitatis* (Paris, 1915), p. 64. The English version is *Coronal,* trans. by Sister Mary David (New York, Pantheon, 1945).

23. Gertrud von Le Fort, *Hymns to the Church,* trans. by Margaret Chanler (Sheed, 1938), p. 53.

24. *The Complete Poems of Edith Sitwell* (New York, Vanguard, 1954), p. 265.

25. See: *Growth or Decline?* (Fides, 1948).

26. This compilation of *Etudes Carmelitaines* (Desclée, 1950) studies "the heart" from every point of view, natural and supernatural, the heart of man and the heart of Christ. It is illustrated by art reproductions from many lands and many periods, ranging from primitive drawings to surrealism.

27. Luke 24, 32.

28. Rom. 5, 5.

29. II Thess. 3, 5.

30. I Tim. 1, 5.

31. J. M. Bover, S.J., *Three Studies from St. Paul,* trans. by M. O'Leary (London, Burns, 1931), p. 1.

32. Eph. 1, 3–4.

33. Col. 2, 9–10.

34. Bover, *op. cit.,* p. 11.

35. *Ibid.,* p. 28.

36. Eph. 4, 4–5.

37. Phil. 1, 8.

38. Bover, *op. cit.,* p. 37.

39. The Encyclical *Haurietis Aquas* specifically includes the Liturgy among the sources of the Devotion to the Sacred Heart.

40. "The Eternal Chalice," in *Orate Fratres* (now *Worship*), V, 318.

41. Friedrich Jürgensmeier, *The Mystical Body of Christ,* trans. by H. Strauss (Sheed, 1954), p. 350.

42. *Supra,* Chapters II through VIII.

43. John 7, 38–39.

44. Apoc. 22, 1.

45. *Spiritual Canticle,* stanza 39.

46. Emile Mersch, S.J., *Theology of the Mystical Body* (Herder, 1951), Ch. XIV, pp. 425 ff.

47. Gal. 4, 6.

48. Philippe de la Trinité, O.C.D., "Du Coeur du Christ à l'Esprit de l'Amour," in *Le Coeur,* p. 385.

49. F. Charmot, from an unpublished sermon given on Pentecost, 1940.

50. *Ibid.*

CHAPTER XV

WATERS OF JOY
1956–On

In this final chapter it is the Vicar of Christ who will himself speak in the name of Christ to the present and to the future, in the fullest authoritative statement yet made on the Devotion to the Sacred Heart, the Encyclical *Haurietis Aquas*. Comment is here irrelevant; only a concise summary of omitted passages will accompany the text.

The present book has tried to tell something of the life-story of the Devotion in the words of those who, under the impulse of the Spirit of Love, have made it what it is. The story has proved to be inseparable from the larger life-story of the Church. And, "as Christ loved the Church with that triple love of which we have spoken, He still loves her most deeply." The "thoughts of His Heart from generation to generation"—from those past into our own generation, and into those to come—are here found:[1]

"You shall draw waters with joy out of the Savior's fountains."[2] These words, in which the Prophet Isaias symbolically foretold the manifold and rich gifts of God that Christianity was to reap, spontaneously come to Our mind as We recall the centenary of the proclamation in which Our predecessor of immortal memory, Pius IX, gladly granting the petition of the Catholic world, ordered the celebration of the feast of the Sacred Heart throughout the whole Church. . . . . We rightly see in this devotion, which everywhere grows more fervent, the inestimable gift which the Incarnate Word, our Divine Saviour, as the sole Mediator of grace and truth between the Heavenly Father and the human race, gave in recent times to the Church, His mystical bride, so that she could endure great trials and surmount difficulties. In virtue of this inestimable gift the Church is able to manifest her ardent love for her Divine Founder and in a fuller measure carry out the injunction given by Jesus Christ Himself, which St. John the Evangelist records: "Now on the last, the great day of the feast, Jesus stood and cried out, saying, 'If anyone thirst, let him come to Me and drink; he who believes in Me, as the Scripture says, from within him there shall flow rivers of living water.' He said this, however, of the Spirit whom they who believed in Him were to receive"[3]. . . .

Divine love has its origin in the Holy Ghost, who is the Personified Love both of the Father and the Son in the bosom of the August Trinity. Most aptly, then, does the Apostle of the Gentiles, echoing the words of Jesus Christ, attribute the infusion of charity in the souls of the faithful to this Spirit of Love. "The charity of God is poured forth in our hearts by the Holy Spirit who has been given to us."[4]

This intimate bond which, according to Sacred Scripture, exists between the divine charity that must burn in the souls of the faithful and the Holy Ghost, clearly shows to all, Venerable Brothers, the real nature of devotion to the Sacred Heart of Jesus. For it is perfectly clear that this devotion, if we examine its proper nature, is the highest act of religion.

It demands the full and absolute determination of surrendering and consecrating oneself to the love of the Divine Redeemer. The wounded Heart of the Saviour is the living sign and symbol of that love. It is likewise clear, even to a greater degree, that this devotion especially declares that we must repay divine love with our own love.

Indeed it flows from the very essence of love that the souls of men fully and completely submit to the rule of the Supreme Being, because the act of our love so depends upon the divine will that it forms, as it were, a certain oneness according to the words of Scripture, "He who cleaves to the Lord is one in spirit with Him."[5]. . .

The Holy Father here cites current erroneous views concerning the Devotion: that it is less suited than other devotions to the needs of the Church and the human race in our times; that it is on an equal footing with other forms of piety which the Church approves but does not command, an "additive" which each one is free to use or not; that it springs from emotion and is more fitted for women than for men, of little use to those fighting for the kingdom of God; that it encourages only "passive virtues."

Venerable Brothers, who does not see that such opinions are completely contrary to the teachings which Our predecessors publicly proclaimed from this chair of truth when they approved the devotion to the Sacred Heart of Jesus? . . .

But after We have duly thanked the Eternal God, We wish through this encyclical to urge you, and all Our dearly beloved children of the Church, to study diligently the teachings of Scripture, the Fathers and theologians—the solid foundations on which devotion to the Sacred Heart of Jesus rests.

For We are firmly convinced that we can rightly and fully appreciate the incomparable excellence and inexhaustible store of heavenly gifts of this devotion only when we study its nature in the light of divinely revealed truth. Only after piously meditating on the countless blessings flowing from this devotion can we worthily celebrate the first centenary of the feast of the most Sacred Heart of Jesus.

To give to the minds of the faithful a salutary teaching by virtue of which they can more easily and fully understand the true nature of this devotion and reap its abundant fruits, We shall explain those passages of the Old and New Testaments in which God's infinite love for mankind is revealed and set before us. We can, of course, never really study that love sufficiently. We shall then touch upon the chief points of the teaching of the Fathers and Doctors of the Church.

Finally We shall show in its true light the close connection that exists between the kind of devotion to be shown to the Heart of the Divine Redeemer and the veneration due to His love and the love of the August Trinity for all men. For We think that if the principal reasons for this noblest form of piety and the foundations on which it rests are set forth in the light of Scripture and the teaching handed down in the Church, the faithful can more easily "draw waters with joy out of the Saviour's fountains"[6]. . . .

The Holy Father here recalls the teaching of the early Councils concerning the hypostatic union, and the fact that the heart is the natural sign and symbol of love, the twofold reason why the Church adores the Heart of Christ. Then:

There is no doubt that Scripture never makes express mention of special veneration paid to the physical Heart of the Incarnate Word as the symbol of His most ardent love. If we must openly admit this, it cannot surprise us nor in any way lead us to doubt the divine love for us which is the principal reason for this devotion. This love is proclaimed and inculcated both in the Old and New Testaments in such vivid images as to greatly stir our souls. At times these images were presented in the Scripture which announced the coming of the Son of God made man. They can therefore be considered as the beginning of the sign and symbol of that divine love, that is of the most Sacred and Adorable Heart of the Divine Redeemer.

The Holy Father here gives many manifestations of God's love for man in the Old Testament, which lead to its full revelation in the New Testament: the Word Incarnate. Then:

Since then we are led to the very mystery of the infinite love of the Incarnate Word by the statement of that disciple "whom Jesus loved, the one who, at the supper, had leaned back upon His breast,"[7] it seems meet and just, right and availing unto salvation, Venerable Brothers, to linger awhile in the sweetest contemplation of that mystery. . . .

The mystery of the divine Redemption is first and foremost a mystery of love, that is, of the true love of Christ for His Heavenly Father, to whom the sacrifice offered on the Cross in loving obedience renders most abundant and infinite satisfactions for the sins of mankind. "By suffering out of love and obedience, Christ gave more to God than was required to compensate for the offense of the whole human race"[8]. . . .

However, that we may be able so far as it is possible for mortal man "to comprehend with all the saints what is the breadth and length and height and depth"[9] of the fathomless love of the Incarnate Word for His Heavenly Father and for men defiled by sin, we must understand that His love was spiritual, as becomes God, because "God is Spirit."[10] But it was not only spiritual. To be sure, the love with which God loved our first parents and the Hebrew people was of a spiritual nature. The expressions of love, so human, intimate and paternal which we read in the Psalms, in the writings of the prophets and in the Canticle of Canticles, are indications and manifestations of the truest but entirely spiritual love with which God loved the human race. On the contrary, the love spoken of in the Gospel, the letters of the apostles and the pages of the Apocalypse—all of which describe the love of the Heart of Jesus Christ—express not only divine love but also human sentiments of love.

The point is quite clear to all who are Catholics. For the Word of God assumed not a fictitious and empty body, as some heretics already maintained in the first century of the Christian era; they were condemned by St. John the Apostle in the most severe terms: "For many deceivers have gone forth into the world, who do not confess Jesus as the Christ coming in the flesh. This is the deceiver and the Antichrist."[11] But the Word actually united to His divine person an individual, integral and perfect human nature which was conceived by the power of the Holy Ghost in the most pure womb of the Virgin Mary. Nothing, therefore, was lacking in the human nature which the Word of God joined to Himself. Indeed He assumed a human nature in no way diminished or changed in its spiritual and bodily capacities, that is, a nature endowed with intelligence and free will and the rest of the internal and external faculties of perception, sense appetites and all natural impulses. . . .

Therefore, there can be no doubt that Jesus Christ took a human body having all the affections which are proper to it, among which love holds the first place. There can likewise be no doubt that He had a physical Heart like ours, since without this most excellent organ human life, even as regards affections, is impossible. Wherefore, the Heart of Jesus Christ, hypostatically united to the Divine Person of the Word, beyond doubt throbbed with love and the rest of the impulses of the affections which, however, were in perfect accord and harmony with His human will filled with divine love and with the infinite love itself which the Son shares with the Father and the Holy Ghost. There never was anything contrary or conflicting in these three kinds of love.[12]

Nevertheless, We say that the Word of God took upon Himself a "real" and perfect human nature and formed and fashioned for Himself a heart of flesh, which like ours could suffer and be pierced. We repeat that unless this teaching be considered not only in the light which is shed by the hypostatic and substantial union, but also in that of the redemption of mankind—its complement, as it were—this doctrine can be a stumbling block and foolishness to some, as Christ nailed to the Cross actually was to the Jews and Gentiles. . . .

Many references to Scripture and to the Fathers, showing that the only-begotten Son assumed a true human nature, are here given. Then:

We must, however, bear in mind that these quotations from Scripture and the Fathers and not a few similar ones which We did not cite, although they clearly attest that there were in Jesus Christ movements of the senses and affections and that He assumed human nature to accomplish our eternal salvation, never refer to His physical heart in such a manner as to clearly indicate it as the symbol of His infinite love.

But if the evangelists and the rest of the sacred writers do not clearly describe the heart of our Redeemer as responding to feelings and emotions no less than ours and as throbbing and palpitating on account of the various movements and affections of His soul and of the most ardent love of His human and divine wills, they do frequently, however, clearly record His divine love and those movements of the emotions connected with them, namely desire, joy, sadness, fear and anger as they are reflected in His countenance, words and manner of acting.

The countenance of our adorable Saviour was an indication and perfect mirror of those affections which, in various ways, moved His soul, and of the reactions which reached and touched His Most Sacred Heart. The observation based on common experience which the Angelic Doctor made concerning human psychology and what follows from it is pertinent to this matter: "The disturbance of anger reaches to the outward members and chiefly to those members which reflect more distinctly the emotions of the heart, such as the eyes, face and tongue."[13]

Wherefore the heart of the Incarnate Word is rightly considered the chief index and symbol of the threefold love with which the Divine Redeemer continuously loves the Eternal Father and the whole human race. It is the symbol of that divine love which He shares with the Father and the Holy Ghost, but which in Him alone, in the Word namely that was made flesh, is manifested to us through His mortal human body, since "in Him dwells the fullness of the Godhead bodily."[14]

It is moreover the symbol of that most ardent love which, infused into His soul, sanctifies the human will of Christ and whose action is enlightened and directed by a twofold most perfect knowledge, namely the beatific and infused.[15]

Finally, in a more direct and natural manner, it is a symbol also of sensible love, since the body of Jesus Christ, formed through the operations of the Holy Ghost in the womb of the Virgin Mary, has a most perfect capacity for feeling and perception, much more than the bodies of all other men.[16]

Since Scripture and the teachings of the Catholic Faith affirm that there is the highest possible harmony and agreement in the Most Holy Soul of Jesus Christ, and that He clearly directed His threefold love to accomplish our redemption, it is therefore obvious that we can most correctly consider and venerate the heart of the Divine Redeemer as signifying the image of His love, the proof of our redemption and the mystical ladder by which we climb to the embrace of "God our Saviour."[17]

Wherefore His words, actions, teachings, miracles, and in particular those deeds which more clearly testify this love for us—the institution of the Holy Eucharist, His most bitter passion and death, His Most Holy Mother whom He lovingly gave to us, the founding of the

Church and sending of the Holy Ghost upon the apostles and upon us—all these we must regard as proofs of His threefold love.

In like manner we must lovingly meditate on the pulsations of His most Sacred Heart by which, so to say, He Himself kept on measuring the time of His sojourn on earth up to the last moment when, as the evangelists testify "crying out in a loud voice 'It is consummated,' and, bowing His head, He gave up His spirit."[18]

Then the beating of His heart stopped, and His sensible love was interrupted until He arose from the tomb in triumph over death.

But after His glorified body was again united to the soul of the Divine Redeemer, the Conqueror of death, His Most Sacred Heart never ceased, and never will cease, to beat with imperturbable and calm pulsation. It will likewise never cease to signify His threefold love by which the Son of God is bound to His heavenly Father and the whole human race, of which He is by perfect right the mystical Head. . . .

Many beautiful pictures of the love of Our Lord as manifested in the Gospels are here given. Then:

Who in truth could describe in a worthy manner those beatings of the Divine Heart, the indications of His infinite love, when He bestowed His greatest gifts on man, that is, Himself in the sacrament of the Eucharist, His Most Holy Mother and the priestly office communicated to us? . . .

Rightly, therefore, one may affirm that the Divine Eucharist, both as a sacrament and as a sacrifice—the one He bestowed on men, the other He Himself continually offers "from the rising of the sun even to the going down"[19]—and the priesthood are all really the gifts of the Most Sacred Heart of Jesus.

Indeed another most precious gift of His Most Sacred Heart is, as We have said, Mary, the sweet Mother of God and the most loving Mother of us all. For she was the Mother of Our Redeemer according to the flesh and His associate in recalling the children of Eve to the life of divine grace. And so she is rightly hailed as the spiritual Mother of Mankind. Wherefore St. Augustine, in writing of her says: "Indeed she is the Mother of the members of the Saviour, which we are, because she co-operated by love so that the faithful who are members of that head might be born in the Church."[20]

And to the unbloody gift of Himself, under the appearance of bread and wine, Our Saviour, Jesus Christ, wished, as a special proof of His intimate and infinite love, to add the bloody sacrifice of the Cross. Indeed, in His way of acting, He gave an example of that

sublime charity which He set before His disciples as the highest measure
of love: "Greater love than this no one has, that one lay down his life
for his friends."[21] . . .

Therefore, there can be no doubt that the Most Sacred Heart of
Jesus, since it is most intimately the sharer of the life of the Incarnate
Word, and since it was assumed as an instrument of the Divinity, no
less than the other members of His human nature in accomplishing the works of divine grace and omnipotence,[22] is the true
symbol of the boundless love by which Our Saviour, through the
shedding of His blood, contracted a mystical marriage with the Church.
"Through charity He suffered for the Church who was to be united to
Him as His spouse."[23]

Therefore, from the wounded Heart of Our Redeemer, the Church,
the dispenser of the blood of the Redeemer, was born. From this
wounded Heart the grace of the sacraments, from which the children
of the Church draw supernatural life, flowed most profusely, as we
read in the sacred liturgy: "From the pierced Heart, the Church,
joined to Christ, is born. . . . Who pourest forth grace from Thy
Heart"[24] . . . .

The Holy Father then shows the glorified Heart of Christ, triumphant in heaven after the Ascension, still pouring its love upon
the Church, and continues:

The gift of the Holy Spirit to His disciples is the first clear sign of
His munificent charity after His triumphal ascent to the right hand of
the Father. Indeed after ten days the Spirit, the Paraclete, given by
the Heavenly Father, descended upon them gathered in the Cena-
culum, as He had promised them at the Last Supper: "I will ask the
Father and He will give you another Advocate to dwell with you
forever."[25]

This Spirit, the Paraclete, since He is the personified mutual love of
the Father for the Son and of the Son for the Father, is sent indeed
by both. Assuming the appearance of tongues of fire, He poured the
abundance of divine love and other heavenly gifts into their souls.
The infusion of this divine love also sprang from the Heart of our
Saviour "in whom are hidden all the treasures of wisdom and knowledge."[26]

Indeed, this love is the gift of the Heart of Jesus and His Spirit,
who is indeed the Spirit of the Father and the Son and from whom both
the rise of the Church and its remarkable spread are unfolded for all
the pagan nations which the worship of idols, hatred of brothers,
and corruption of morals as well as violence had befouled.

This divine love is the most precious gift of the Heart of Christ and of His Spirit. This love gave the apostles and martyrs that fortitude with which they were strengthened to fight even to the point of death, which they met with heroic spirit, to preach the truth of the gospel and to testify to it with their blood. This love gave to the Doctors of the Church a most ardent desire to teach and defend the Catholic Faith. . . .

There is nothing, then, which forbids us to adore the Most Sacred Heart of Jesus, since it participates in and is the natural and most expressive symbol of that inexhaustible love with which Our Divine Redeemer still loves mankind. That Heart indeed, even if it is no longer liable to the disturbances of this mortal life, still lives and beats. It is now inseparably joined with the Person of the Divine Word, and in it and through it with His divine will.

Wherefore, since the Heart of Christ overflows with divine and human love, and since it is abundantly rich with treasures of all graces which Our Redeemer acquired by His life and His sufferings, it is truly the unfailing fountain of that love which His Spirit pours forth into all the members of His Mystical Body.

Therefore the Heart of Our Saviour certainly expresses the image of the Divine Person of the Word and His twofold nature, human and divine. In it we can contemplate not only the symbol, but also, as it were, the sum of the whole mystery of our redemption.

When we adore the Most Sacred Heart of Jesus Christ, we adore in it and through it both the uncreated love of the Divine Word and His human love and all His other affections and virtues. This is so because both loves moved Our Redeemer to sacrifice Himself for us and for the whole Church, His Spouse. As the Apostle says: "Christ also loved the Church and delivered Himself up for her, that He might sanctify her, cleansing in the bath of water by means of the Word, in order that He might present to Himself the Church in all her glory, not having spot or wrinkle or any such thing, but that she might be holy and without blemish."[27]

As Christ loved the Church with that triple love of which We have spoken, He still loves her most deeply. This love moves Him as our Advocate to gain grace and mercy for us from the Father, "since He lives always to make intercession for them"[28]. . . .

We think that Our statements, confirmed by the teaching of the Gospel, have made it clear that essentially this devotion is nothing else than devotion to the human and divine love of the Incarnate Word and to the love which the Heavenly Father and the Holy Ghost have for sinful men.

For, as the Angelic Doctor teaches, the first cause of man's redemption is the love of the August Trinity. This love pouring forth
abundantly into the human will of Jesus Christ and His Adorable
Heart, moved Him to shed His blood to redeem us from the captivity
of sin.[29] "I have a baptism to be baptized with; and how distressed
I am until it is accomplished!"[30]

We know, therefore, that the devotion whereby we pay homage to
Jesus Christ's love for men through the august sign of the wounded
Heart of the Redeemer nailed to the Cross has never been entirely
unknown to Christian piety. In more recent times, however, this
devotion has become better known and wondrously spread throughout
the Church, particularly after the Lord Himself privately revealed
this divine mystery to some of His children, richly endowed with an
abundance of heavenly graces, and chose them as the messengers and
heralds of this devotion. . . .

The Holy Father here emphasizes that private revelations such
as those given to Saint Margaret Mary add nothing new to Catholic
doctrine, but do call men's minds "in an extraordinary and special
way" to the contemplation of the mystery of love. Then:

From the explanations which We have given, Venerable Brothers,
it is perfectly clear that the faithful must trace devotion to the Most
Sacred Heart of Jesus back to Sacred Scripture, tradition and the
liturgy, if they wish to understand its real meaning and, through
pious meditation, receive food to nourish and increase their religious
fervor. . . .

The Holy Father here enumerates and condemns still more objections to the Devotion: that it involves materialism and super-
stition; that it is a hindrance to mystical prayer; that it involves
false veneration of an image. The opposite is the truth on all these
points. Then:

Therefore, devotion to the Most Sacred Heart is so important that
it may be considered, so far as practice is concerned, the perfect
profession of the Christian religion. . . . There is, then, no doubt that
the faithful, in honoring the Most Sacred Heart of the Redeemer,
fulfill a most serious obligation by which they are bound to serve God
and dedicate themselves, and all they have, including their most
secret thoughts and actions, to their Creator and Redeemer, and in this
way obey the divine commandment: "Thou shalt love the Lord thy
God with thy whole heart, and with thy whole soul, and with thy

whole mind, and with thy whole strength."[31] The faithful know with certainty that they are primarily led to worship God not for their own spiritual or physical, temporal or eternal advantage, but on account of the goodness of God, whom they seek to serve by loving Him in return, by adoring Him and thanking Him. . . .

The reason for this devotion is not primarily to be sought in the blessings which Christ the Lord promised in private revelations. Rather it is that men should fulfill more fervently the principal duties of the Catholic faith, namely the obligations of love and expiation, and so also contribute greatly to their own spiritual advancement. . . .

The Holy Father here describes many evils, within and without the Church, current in the world today, and concludes:

Faced with so many evils which today more than ever deeply disturb individuals, homes, nations and the whole world, where, Venerable Brothers, is a remedy to be found?

Is there a devotion more excellent than that to the Most Sacred Heart of Jesus, one which is more in accord with the real nature of the Catholic faith or which better meets the needs of the Church and the human race today? What act of religion is nobler, more suitable, sweeter and more conducive to salvation, since this devotion is wholly directed to the love of God Himself?

Finally, what is more powerful than the love of Christ, which devotion to the Most Sacred Heart daily increases and fosters? This love can truly bring the faithful to live the law of the Gospel. If this law is rejected, is it possible to have genuine peace among men? For as the words of the Holy Ghost clearly teach, "The work of justice shall be peace"[32] . . . .

Greatly impelled by the desire to set up a firm defence against the wicked machinations of the enemies of God and His Church, and at the same time to lead back domestic and civil society to the love of God and neighbor, We do not hesitate to state emphatically that devotion to the Sacred Heart of Jesus is the most effective school of divine charity, on which the kingdom of God to be established in the souls of individuals, in families and in nations must rest. . . .

That graces for the Christian family and for the whole human race may flow more abundantly from devotion to the Sacred Heart, let the faithful strive to join it closely with devotion to the Immaculate Heart of the Mother of God. By the will of God, the Most Blessed Virgin Mary was inseparably joined with Christ in accomplishing the work of man's redemption, so that our salvation flows from the love of Jesus Christ and His sufferings, intimately united with the love and sorrows of His mother. It is, then, highly fitting that after due homage has been paid to the Most Sacred Heart of Jesus, Christian people who have obtained divine life from Christ through Mary, manifest similar piety and the love of their grateful souls for the most loving heart of our heavenly Mother. . . .

Given at Rome from St. Peter's, May 15, 1956, in the eighteenth year of Our pontificate.

Pius PP. XII

NOTES

1. The text of the present translation is that printed in the *Catholic Mind* for August, 1956, and published separately in pamphlet form by the America Press.

2. Is. 12, 3.

3. John 7, 37–39.

4. Rom. 5, 5.

5. I Cor. 6, 17.

6. Is. 12, 3.

7. John 21, 20.

8. *Summa Theologica,* III, q. 48, a. 2; ed. Leon., tom. 11 (1903), p. 464.

9. Eph. 3, 18.

10. John 4, 24.

11. 2 John 7.

12. Cfr. St. Thomas, *Summa Theologica,* III, q. 15, a. 4; q. 18, a. 6; ed. Leon., tom. 11 (1903), pp. 189 and 237.

13. *Summa Theologica,* I–II, q. 48, a. 4; ed. Leon., tom. 6 (1891), p. 306.

14. Col. 2, 9.

15. Cfr. *Summa Theologica,* III, q. 9, a. 1–3; ed. Leon., tom. 11 (1903), p. 142.

16. Cfr. *Ibid.,* III, q. 33, a. 2, ad 3m; q. 46, a. 6: ed. Leon., tom. 11 (1903), pp. 342, 433.

17. Tit. 3, 4.

18. Matt. 27, 50; John 19, 30.

19. Mal. 1, 11.

20. *De Sancta Virginitate,* VI, P.L. XL, 399.

21. John 15, 13.

22. Cfr. S. Thom. *Summa Theologica,* III, q. 19, a. 1: ed. Leon., tom. 11 (1903), p. 329.

23. *Summa Theologica,* Suppl., q. 42, a. 1, ad 3m: ed. Leon., tom. 12 (1906), p. 81.

24. *Hymn. ad Vesp. Festi. SSmi Cordis Iesu.*
25. John 14, 16.
26. Col. 2, 3.
27. Eph. 5, 25–27.
28. Heb. 7, 25.
29. Cfr. *Summa Theologica,* III, q. 48, a. 5: ed. Leon., tom. 11 (1903), p. 467.
30. Luke 12, 50.
31. Mark 12, 30; Matt. 22, 37.
32. Is. 32, 17.

EPILOGUE

THE HEART OF MARY

When the controversy concerning the authentic establishment of the Devotion to the Sacred Heart was at its height, those who opposed its approval by Rome raised an objection: if the request for such a Feast were granted, a request for a Feast in honor of the Immaculate Heart of Mary would inevitably follow! The objection was valid, though hardly in the sense intended. It was indeed according to the divine plan that the Heart of the Mother should follow the Heart of the Son in the public cultus of the Church. Although mentioned but sparingly in the pages of this book, Our Lady has been present throughout; she who first "pondered these things in her heart" has alone practiced perfectly Devotion to the Sacred Heart, for she alone can give to her Son the fulness of love that His Heart desires.

The two devotions run parallel along many lines. Both spring from the same root dogma of Christianity, the Incarnation; at the Council of Ephesus it was declared that Mary was rightly to be called the Mother of God because she is the mother of the Man who is God in virtue of the hypostatic union, and all honor paid to her follows from this prerogative. Both have their roots deep in Scripture, where the heart of the mother in the Gospels responds to the call of the Lover as only a heart conceived without sin could do. Both have been an integral part of the life of the Church from the beginning, latent and implicit at first, developing specific roles and forms as the centuries passed. And in our own times the Vicar of Christ has united the two inseparably in *Haurietis Aquas*.

But this very development reveals also the fundamental difference between the two devotions, a difference which follows from the theological relations between them, and enhances the glory of each. It is the same difference which exists between the Creator and His perfect creature: the one is adored for His own sake, the other is honored for the sake of the only Adorable. To the theandric Heart of Jesus is given the worship of latria; to the purely human heart of His Mother that of hyperdulia. The Mother reflects all glory and love back to her Son. The proper object of the devotion to the Immaculate Heart is, then, the physical heart of Mary considered as a symbol of her love for God and for men; it refers to the person of Mary as revealed in her interior life and her apostolic love for souls; and that person is the Mother of the God-man and of His Mystical Body, the Church.

The Immaculate Heart appears in flashes of lyric beauty in mediaeval treatises like that of Saint Bernardine of Siena, who saw the seven recorded words of Our Lady as "seven flames from her heart." It became widely recognized when Saint John Eudes told the world how "Jesus, who is the heart of His Father, and the Holy Ghost, who is the heart of the Father and of the Son, were given to Mary to be the soul of her soul and the heart of her heart." Later, a petition to the Sacred Congregation of Rites implored: "Let us go to the eternal Father through the Heart of Jesus, and to the Heart of Jesus through the Heart of Mary." Pius IX sanctioned a votive mass of the Immaculate Heart, and in 1946 Pius XII extended the Feast to the universal Church. Since then the observance of the First Saturday has begun to spread, while Confraternities and Guards of Honor offer perpetual prayer and reparation to the heart of the Mother of God who became the Mother of men on Calvary. From Our Lady herself, at Fatima, has come the needed call to prayer and penance. In response, at the darkest hour of global warfare, our Holy Father consecrated the whole world to her, saying:

As the Church and the entire human race were consecrated to the Sacred Heart of Jesus, so that, reposing all hope in Him, He might become for them the sign and pledge of victory and salvation, so we in like measure consecrate ourselves forever to thee and to thy Immaculate Heart, our Mother and Queen, that thy loving patronage may hasten the triumph of the Kingdom of God; and may all peoples proclaim thee blessed and with thee raise their voices to resound from pole to pole in the chant of the everlasting Magnificat of glory, love and gratitude to the Heart of Jesus, where alone they can find truth, light and peace.

APPENDIX

SCRIPTURAL SOURCES OF THE LITANY OF THE SACRED HEART

1. Heart of Jesus, Son of the Eternal Father.
    "Simon Peter answered and said: Thou art Christ the Son of the living God." Matt. 16, 16.
2. Heart of Jesus formed by the Holy Ghost in the womb of the Virgin Mother.
    "But while he thought on these things behold the angel of the Lord appeared to him in his sleep, saying: Joseph, son of David, fear not to take unto thee Mary thy wife, for that which is conceived in her is of the Holy Ghost." Matt. 1, 20.
3. Heart of Jesus substantially united to the word of God.
    "And the Word was made flesh and dwelt amongst us (and we saw his glory the glory as it were of the only begotten of the Father) full of grace and truth." John 1, 14.
4. Heart of Jesus of infinite majesty.
    "And when the Son of Man shall come in his majesty, and all the angels with him, then shall he sit upon the seat of his majesty." Matt. 25, 31.
5. Heart of Jesus, sacred temple of God.
    "Jesus answered, and said to them . . . Destroy this temple and in three days I will raise it up."
    "But he spoke of the temple of his body." John 2, 19, 21.
6. Heart of Jesus, tabernacle of the Most High.
    "Neither by the blood of goats, or of calves, but by his own blood, entered once into the holies, having obtained eternal redemption." Heb. 9, 12.
7. Heart of Jesus, house of God and gate of heaven.
    "and trembling he said: How terrible is this place! this is no other but the house of God; and the gate of heaven." Gen. 28, 17.
8. Heart of Jesus, burning furnace of charity.
    "To know also the charity of Christ, which surpasseth all knowledge, that you may be filled unto all the fullness of God." Eph. 3, 19.

9. Heart of Jesus, abode of justice and love.

> "Thou hast loved justice and hated iniquity."   Heb. 1, 9.

10. Heart of Jesus, full of goodness and love.

> "Who said to him: why askest thou me concerning good? One is good, God."   Matt. 19, 17.

11. Heart of Jesus, abyss of all virtues.

> "Thou hast loved justice and hated iniquity; therefore God, thy God, hath anointed thee with the oil of gladness above thy fellows."   Heb. 1, 9.

12. Heart of Jesus, most worthy of all praise.

> "And again, when he bringeth in the first begotten into the world, he saith: and let all the angels of God adore him."
>
>   Heb. 1, 6.
>
> "And they sung a new canticle saying: Thou art worthy, O Lord, to take the book, and to open the seals thereof; because thou wast slain, and hast redeemed us to God, in thy blood, out of every tribe, and tongue, and people and nation."   Apoc. 5, 9.

13. Heart of Jesus, king and center of all hearts.

> "Thou hast subjected all things under his feet. For in that he hath subjected all things to him, he left nothing not subject to him. But now we see not as yet all things subject to him." Heb. 2, 8.

14. Heart of Jesus, in whom are all the treasures of wisdom and knowledge.

> "In whom are hid all the treasures of wisdom and knowledge."
>
>   Col. 2, 3.

15. Heart of Jesus, in whom, dwells the fullness of divinity.

> "For in him dwelleth all the fullness of the Godhead corporeally."
>
>   Col. 2, 9.

16. Heart of Jesus, in whom the Father was well-pleased.

> "And as he was yet speaking, behold a bright cloud overshadowed them. And lo, a voice out of the cloud saying: this is my beloved Son, in whom I am well pleased: hear ye him."
>
>   Matt. 17, 5.

17. Heart of Jesus, of whose fullness we have all received.

> "And of his fullness we all have received, and grace for grace."
>
>   John 1, 16.

18. Heart of Jesus, desire of the everlasting hills.

> "The blessings of thy father are strengthened with the blessings of his fathers; until the desire of the everlasting hills should come; may they be upon the head of Joseph, and upon the crown of the Nazarite among his brethren."   Gen. 49, 26.

19. Heart of Jesus, patient and most merciful.

"And the Lord direct your hearts in the charity of God and the
   the patience of Christ."   II Thess. 3, 5.
20. Heart of Jesus, enriching all who invoke Thee.
   "The same is Lord over all, rich unto all that call upon Him."
                                                     Rom. 10, 12.
21. Heart of Jesus, fountain of life and holiness.
   "You shall draw water with joy out of the Savior's fountains."
                                                     Is. 12, 3.
22. Heart of Jesus, propitiation for our sins.
   "And He is the propitiation for our sins."   I John 2, 2.
23. Heart of Jesus, loaded down with opprobrium.
   "He shall be filled with reproaches."   Jer., Lam. 3, 30.
24. Heart of Jesus, bruised for our offences.
   "He was wounded for our iniquities, He was bruised for our
   sins . . . and by His bruises we are healed."   Is. 53, 5.
25. Heart of Jesus, obedient unto death.
   "He humbled Himself, becoming obedient unto death."
                                                     Phil. 2, 8.
26. Heart of Jesus, pierced with a lance.
   "One of the soldiers with a spear opened His side."
                                                     John 19, 34.
27. Heart of Jesus, source of all consolation.
   "Come to me, all you that labor and are burdened, and I will
   refresh you."   Matt. 11, 28.
28. Heart of Jesus, our life and resurrection.
   "We declare unto you the life eternal which was with the Father
   and hath appeared to us."   I John 1, 2.
29. Heart of Jesus, our peace and reconciliation.
   "Through Him to reconcile all things unto Himself, making
   peace through the blood of His cross."   Col. 1, 20.
30. Heart of Jesus, victim for sin.
   "The wicked have wrought upon my back."   Ps. 128, 3.
31. Heart of Jesus, salvation of those who trust in Thee.
   "Whosoever shall call upon the name of the Lord shall be
   saved."   Rom. 10, 13.
32. Heart of Jesus, hope of those who die in Thee.
   "The Lord Himself shall come down from heaven with commandment . . . and the dead who are in Christ shall rise first."
                                                     I Thess. 4, 13.
33. Heart of Jesus, delight of all the saints.
   "The city hath no need of the sun nor of the moon to shine in it,
   for the glory of God hath enlightened it and the Lamb is the
   lamp thereof."   Apoc. 21, 23.

BIBLIOGRAPHY

Bainvel, Jean, *Devotion to the Sacred Heart, Its Doctrine and Its History*, trans. by E. Leahy. London, Burns, 1924.

Battista, Varani, Blessed, *True Devotion to the Passion*. New York, Kenedy, 1925.

Benson, R. H., *A Book of the Love of Jesus*. St. Louis, Herder, 1913.

Bernard, Saint, *Sermons on the Canticle of Canticles*, Vol. II. Dublin, 1920.

Biskupek, A., *Litany of the Sacred Heart*. Milwaukee, Bruce, 1956.

Blunt, Hugh Francis, *The Heart Aflame*. Milwaukee, Bruce, 1947.

The Book of the Sacred Heart of Jesus. London, Burns, 1935.

Bougaud, Louis Victor, *Life of Saint Margaret Mary*. New York, Benziger, 1890.

Bover, J. M., *Three Studies from St. Paul*, trans. by M. O'Leary. London, Burns, 1931.

Bremond, Henri, *Histoire Littéraire du Sentiment Religieux en France*, Vol. III. Paris, 1929.

Camm, Dom Bede, *Foundress of Tyburn Convent*. London, Burns, 1934.

Century of the Sacred Heart (anon.). New York, Benziger, 1924.

Chandlery, P. J., *Friends and Apostles of the Sacred Heart*. London, Burns, 1915.

Charmot, F., *In Retreat with the Sacred Heart*. Westminster, Newman, 1956.

————*The Sacred Heart and Modern Life*, trans. by Kathryn Sullivan. New York, Kenedy, 1952.

Claude la Colombière, Blessed, *Meditations on the Passion*, trans. by Mother Mary Philip. London, Burns, 1933.

————*The Servant of the Sacred Heart*, G. O'Neill, ed. St. Louis, Herder, 1933.

————*Spiritual Direction*, trans. by Mother Mary Philip. London, Burns, 1934.

Claudel, Paul, *Corona Benignitatis Anni Dei*. Paris, 1915.

————*Coronal*, trans. by Sister Mary David (English-language version of *Corona Benignitatis Anni Dei*). New York, Pantheon, 1945.

Crawley-Boevey, Mateo, *Holy Hours*. Fairhaven, Conn., National Center of the Enthronement, 1943.

———*Jesus, the King of Love*. Fairhaven, Conn., National Center of the Enthronement, 1943.

———*Six Discourses on the Enthronement of the Sacred Heart in the Home*. Clyde, Mo., Benedictine Convent, 1942.

Croiset, Jean, *Devotion to the Sacred Heart of Our Lord Jesus Christ*. Westminster, Newman, 1949.

Dalgairns, J., *Devotion to the Sacred Heart of Jesus*. New York, Benziger, 1910.

Donnelly, F. P., *The Heart of the Church; the Sacred Heart in the Liturgy*. New York, Kenedy, 1938.

Fastes de la Dévotion au Sacré Coeur de Jesus du XII Siècle à nos Jours. Evreux, 1901.

Francoisi, Xavier de, *Dévotion au Sacré Coeur de Jésus et au Saint Coeur de Marie; Notions Doctrinales et Pratiques*. Paris, 1876.

———*Le Sacré Coeur de Jésus et la Tradition*. Tournai, 1908.

Froment, François, *La Véritable Dévotion au Sacré Coeur de Jésus Christ*. Brussels, 1891 (1st. ed. 1699).

Gallifet, Joseph, *The Adorable Heart of Jesus* (English-language version of *De Cultu Sacrosancti Cordis*). Philadelphia, 1890.

Galot, Jean, S.J., *The Heart of Christ*, trans. by John Chapin. Westminster, Newman, 1955.

Gertrude the Great, Benedictines, ed. London, Sands, 1913.

Gertrude, Saint, *True Prayers of Saints Gertrude and Mechtilde*, trans. by J. Gay. London and New York, Sheed, 1936.

Ghéon, Henri, *The Secret of Saint Margaret Mary*. London and New York, Sheed, 1937.

———"The Secret of Saint Margaret Mary" in *Secrets of the Saints*. New York, Sheed, 1944, 1954.

Graham, A., *The Christ of Catholicism*. New York, Longmans, 1947.

Guitton, G., S.J., *Perfect Friend*. St. Louis, Herder, 1956.

Hamon, A., *Histoire de la Dévotion au Sacré Coeur*, 5 vols. Paris, 1923–39.

John Eudes, Saint, *The Admirable Heart of Mary*. New York, Kenedy, 1948.

Josefa Menendez, Sister, *Un Appel à l'Amour*. Toulouse, 1944.

———*The Way of Divine Love*. Westminster, Newman, 1949.

Juliana of Norwich, *Revelations of Divine Love*. Westminster, Newman, 1952.

Konz, F., *The Sacred Heart of Christ*. New York, Benziger, 1936.

Larkin, Francis, *Enthronement of the Sacred Heart of Jesus*. Catechetical Guild Educational Society, 1956.

Le Fort, Gertrude von, "Litany for the Feast of the Sacred Heart," *Hymns to the Church*, trans. by Margaret Chanler. New York, Sheed, 1937.

Lebrun, C., *Spiritual Teaching of Saint John Eudes*. London, 1934.

Leo XIII, *Annum Sacrum*. English version in *Great Encyclical Letters*. New York, Benziger, 1903.

———*Divinum Illud*. New York, America Press, 1944.

Lepicier, A. M., *Jesus Christ the King of Our Hearts*. New York, Benziger, 1921.

Love of the Sacred Heart, Illustrated by Saint Gertrude. London, Burns, 1921.

Love of the Sacred Heart, Illustrated by Saint Mechtilde. London, Burns, 1922.

McGratty, Arthur R., *The Sacred Heart, Yesterday and Today*. New York, Benziger, 1951.

Madeleine Sophie, Saint, *Esprit et Vertus*. Paris.

———*Vie d'Oraison*. Paris, Brou, 1925.

Manning, Henry Edward, Cardinal, *The Glories of the Sacred Heart*. London, 1876.

Margaret Mary, Saint, *Letters*, trans. by C. Herbst. Chicago, Regnery, 1954.

———*Vie et Oeuvres*, 3 vols. Paris, 1915.

Mary of the Divine Heart, by L. Chasle. New York, Benziger, 1906.

Mary Philip, Sister, *A Jesuit at the English Court*. London, Burns, 1922.

———*Life of Blessed Margaret Mary Alacoque*. St. Louis, Herder, 1919.

Matulich, S., *The Heart of the King*. Milwaukee, Bruce, 1935.

Mercier, Desiré Joseph, Cardinal, *Pastoral Letters*. Malines, 1915.

Monahan, M., *Saint Madeleine Sophie*. New York, Longmans, 1925.

Moore, T., *The Heart of the King*. America Press Pamphlet, 1944.

———*The Heart of the Queen*. Apostleship of Prayer Pamphlet, 1949.

Nilles, Nikolaus, *De Rationibus Festorum Sacratissimi Cordis Jesu*, 2 vols. Oeniponte, 1875.

————*Cor Jesu, Divini Redemptoris Nostri Caritatis Symbolum.* Innsbruck, 1872.

Nix, H. J., *Cultus SS. Cordis Jesu et Purissimi Cordis B. V. Mariae.* Freibourg, 1905.

————*Sanctissimo Cordis Jesu, Cur Sint Addicti et Consecrati Societatis Jesu Filii.* Syandrade, 1875.

Noldin, H., *Die Andacht Heiligesten Herzen Jesu.* Innsbruck, 1903. English version, *Devotion to the Sacred Heart.* New York, Benziger, 1905.

Petrovits, J., *Devotion to the Sacred Heart.* St. Louis, Herder, 1925.

Pinamonti, J. P., *The Immaculate Heart of Mary.* Philadelphia, 1890.

Pius XI, *Caritati Compulsi.* Washington, D. C., National Catholic Welfare Conference, 1932.

————*Miserentissimus Redemptor.* America Press Pamphlet Series, No. 12.

Pius XII, *Haurietis Aquas.* New York, America Press, 1956.

Price, G. E., *England and the Sacred Heart.* London, Burns, 1913.

Richstaetter, Karl, *Die Hertz-Jesu Verehrung des Mitteralters.* Pustet, 1923.

————*Illustrious Friends of the Sacred Heart,* trans. by H. Merriam. St. Louis, Herder, 1930.

————*Mediaeval Devotions to the Sacred Heart.* London, Burns, 1925.

Ryan, F., *Our Lady of Fatima.* Dublin, 1943.

Stuart, Janet Erskine, *Prayer in Faith,* Vol. II. New York, Longmans, 1936.

————*The Society of the Sacred Heart.* Roehampton, 1915.

Tauler, John, *Meditations on the Life and Passion of Our Lord.* New York, Benziger, 1925.

Thomas à Kempis, *Prayers and Meditations on the Life of Christ,* Vol. I of *Works.* St. Louis, Herder, 1904.

Vermeersch, A., *Practical Devotion to the Sacred Heart.* New York, Benziger, 1909.

Walsh, W. T., *Our Lady of Fatima.* New York, Macmillan, 1947.

Watkin, Dom Aelred, *The Heart of the World.* London, Burns, 1954.

Yeo, M., *These Three Hearts.* Milwaukee, Bruce, 1940.

INDEX